T0236487

Communications in Computer and Information Science 570

Commenced Publication in 2007
Founding and Former Series Editors:
Alfredo Cuzzocrea, Dominik Ślęzak, and Xiaokang Yang

More information about this series at http://www.springer.com/series/7899

Sokratis K. Katsikas · Alexander B. Sideridis (Eds.)

E-Democracy – Citizen Rights in the World of the New Computing Paradigms

6th International Conference, E-Democracy 2015
Athens, Greece, December 10–11, 2015
Proceedings

 Springer

Editors
Sokratis K. Katsikas
Gjøvik University College
Gjøvik
Norway

Alexander B. Sideridis
Agricultural University of Athens
Athens
Greece

ISSN 1865-0929 ISSN 1865-0937 (electronic)
Communications in Computer and Information Science
ISBN 978-3-319-27163-7 ISBN 978-3-319-27164-4 (eBook)
DOI 10.1007/978-3-319-27164-4

Library of Congress Control Number: 2015957118

Printed on acid-free paper

This Springer imprint is published by SpringerNature
The registered company is Springer International Publishing AG Switzerland

Preface

This book contains the proceedings of the 6th International Conference on e-Democracy (e-Democracy 2015), held in Athens, Greece, December 10–11, 2015. The conference continued from previous events that have always been held in Athens, the cradle of democracy, every two years, starting in 2005.

Information and communication technologies move fast; faster than society, faster than governments, faster than the law. Connectivity is already impressive, but the near future brings about the interconnection of everything, via the Internet of Things. It also brings fundamental changes to our computing paradigm, with cloud computing gaining momentum and being expected to become the prevalent computing paradigm in the years to come. Increasingly more data are being collected, about almost everything one can imagine; and they remain there, in cyberspace, forever, sometimes even resisting efforts to delete them. These data are so attractive that a new field, going by the name of "big data" has already emerged. All these developments constitute in most cases an improvement in our everyday lives, but sometimes infringe on our rights as citizens. The challenge, therefore, is to safeguard citizen rights in the face of a new era, land-marked by new computing paradigms.

This was the theme of the sixth occasion of the International Conference on e-Democracy. The conference was organized by the Scientific Council for the Information Society, in co-operation with the Hellenic Data Protection Authority and a number of European and Greek universities and academia. It was intended, similarly to previous occasions, to provide a forum for presenting and debating the latest developments in the field, from a technical, political, and legal point of view. e-Democracy 2015 brought together academic researchers, industry developers, and policy makers. We thank the attendees for coming to Athens to participate and debate the new emerging advances in the area of e-democracy.

The conference program included five technical papers sessions that covered a broad range of topics, from privacy in e-voting, e-polls, and e-surveys to legal issues of e-democracy, to e-government and e-participation. Furthermore, the program included three sessions of invited short papers briefly describing progress within European research and development projects. The relevant topics ranged from security and privacy in the cloud to secure architectures and applications to enabling citizen-to-government communication. The conference attracted many high-quality submissions, each of which was assigned to four referees for review, and the final acceptance rate was 39 %.

We would like to express our thanks to all those who assisted us in organizing the event and formulating the program. We are very grateful to the Program Committee members for their timely and rigorous reviews of the papers. Thanks are also due to the Organizing Committee for the event. Last but by no means least, we would like to thank all the authors who submitted their work to the conference and contributed to an interesting set of conference proceedings.

December 2015

Sokratis K. Katsikas
Alexander B. Sideridis

Organization

Conference Honorary Chair

Alexander B. Sideridis   Agricultural University of Athens, Greece

Steering Committee

Chair

Sokratis K. Katsikas   Gjøvik University College, Norway

Vice-chair

Vasilis Zorkadis   Vice-President of SCIS, Greece

Secretary

Philippos Mitletton   Secretary General of SCIS, Greece

Members

Charalampos Patrikakis	Technological Educational Institute of Piraeus, Greece
Constantina Costopoulou	Agricultural University of Athens, Greece
Constantine Yialouris	Agricultural University of Athens, Greece
Elias Pimenidis	University of the West of England, UK
Irene Vassilaki	Board Member of SCIS, Greece
Lazaros Iliadis	Democritus University of Thrace, Greece
Spyros Voulgaris	Vrije Universiteit, The Netherlands

Technical Program Committee

Chair

Sokratis K. Katsikas   Gjøvik University College, Norway

Members

Isaac Agudo	University of Malaga, Spain
Evgenia Alexandropoulou	University of Macedonia, Greece
Zacharoula Andreopoulou	Aristotle University of Thessaloniki, Greece
Maria Bottis	Ionian University, Greece
Christos Bouras	University of Patras, Greece
Athena Bourka	ENISA, Greece
David Chadwick	University of Kent, UK
Vassilios Chryssikopoulos	Ionian University, Greece

Nathan Clarke	Plymouth University, UK
Tina Costopoulou	Agricultural University of Athens, Greece
Ernesto Damiani	Università degli Studi di Milano, Italy
Sabrina De Capitani Di Vimercati	Università degli Studi di Milano, Italy
Christos Douligeris	University of Piraeus, Greece
Prokopios Drogkaris	University of the Aegean, Greece
Carmen Fernández-Gago	University of Malaga, Spain
Simone Fischer-Hübner	Karlstad University, Sweden
Sara Foresti	Università degli Studi di Milano, Italy
Steven Furnell	Plymouth University, UK
Jürgen Fuß	University of Applied Sciences Upper Austria, Austria
Dimitris Geneiatakis	Aristotle University of Thessaloniki, Greece
Christos Georgiadis	University of Macedonia, Greece
Dimitris Gouscos	University of Athens, Greece
Stefanos Gritzalis	University of the Aegean, Greece
M.P. Gupta	Indian Institute of Technology Delhi, India
Marit Hansen	Unabhängiges Landeszentrum für Datenschutz Schleswig-Holstein, Germany
Lazaros Iliadis	Democritus University of Thrace, Greece
Dimitra Kaklamani	National Technical University of Athens, Greece
Christos Kalloniatis	University of the Aegean, Greece
Ioanna Kantzavelou	Technological Educational Institute of Athens, Greece
Zoe Kardasiadou	European Union Agency for Fundamental Rights, Austria
Sotiris Karetsos	Agricultural University of Athens, Greece
Maria Karyda	University of the Aegean, Greece
Spyros Kokolakis	University of the Aegean, Greece
Nicholas Kolokotronis	University of the Peloponnese, Greece
Panayiotis Kotzanikolaou	University of Piraeus, Greece
Costas Lambrinoudakis	University of Piraeus, Greece
Maria Lambrou	University of the Aegean, Greece
Konstantinos Limniotis	University of Athens, Greece
Antonio Lioy	Politecnico di Torino, Italy
Javier Lopez	University of Malaga, Spain
Nikos Lorentzos	Agricultural University of Athens, Greece
Euripidis Loukis	University of the Aegean, Greece
Emmanouil Magkos	Ionian University, Greece
Vicky Manthou	University of Macedonia, Greece
Nikolaos Marianos	University of the Aegean, Greece
Giannis Marias	Athens University of Economics and Business, Greece
Olivier Markowitch	Université Libre de Bruxelles, Belgium
Vashek Matyas	Masaryk University, Hungary
Vojtech Merunka	Czech University of Life Sciences in Prague, Czech Republic
Lilian Mitrou	University of the Aegean, Greece

Contents

Legal Issues

Security and Privacy in the Cloud

Secure Architectures and Applications

Enabling Citizen-to-Government Communication

Privacy in E-Voting, E-Polls and E-Surveys

On the Necessity of Auditing for Election Privacy in e-Voting Systems

Aggelos Kiayias[1], Thomas Zacharias[1]($\boxtimes$), and Bingsheng Zhang[2]

[1] Department of Informatics and Telecommunications,
University of Athens, Athens, Greece
{aggelos,thzacharias}@di.uoa.gr
[2] Security Lancaster Research Centre, Lancaster University, Lancaster, UK
b.zhang2009@gmail.com

Abstract. The importance of voter auditing in order to ensure election integrity has been extensively studied in the e-voting literature. On the other hand, the necessity of auditing to protect voter privacy in an e-voting system has been mostly overlooked. In this work, we investigate election privacy issues that appear in the state-of-the-art implementations of e-voting systems that apply *threshold public key encryption* (TPKE) in the client like Helios and use a bulletin board (BB). More specifically, we show that without PKI support or -more generally- authenticated BB "append" operations, such systems are vulnerable to attacks where the malicious election server can act as a man-in-the-middle between the election trustees and the voters, hence it can learn how the voters have voted. We suggest compulsory trustee auditing as countermeasure for this type of man-in-the-middle attacks. Furthermore, we propose a list of guidelines to avoid some common, subtle, yet important problems that may appear during the implementation of any TPKE-based e-voting system.

1 Introduction

E-voting systems have emerged as a powerful technology to improve the election process by reducing election cost, making election preparation and tally computation faster and increase voter participation for various underrepresented social groups including voters that face considerable physical barriers and overseas voters. In addition, several e-voting systems [2,5,12–14,19,32,36,42] are *end-to-end verifiable*, i.e., voters and auditors can directly verify the entire election process

A. Kiayias—Research supported by ERC project CODAMODA and project FINER of the Greek Secretariat of Research and Technology.

T. Zacharias—Research supported by project FINER of the Greek Secretariat of Research and Technology.

B. Zhang—Work completed while at the National and Kapodistrian University of Athens. Research supported by project FINER of the Greek Secretariat of Research and Technology.

© Springer International Publishing Switzerland 2015
S.K. Katsikas and A.B. Sideridis (Eds.): E-Democracy 2015, CCIS 570, pp. 3–17, 2015.
DOI: 10.1007/978-3-319-27164-4_1

and be assured that no entities, even the election authorities, have manipulated the election result.

A major class of e-voting systems [1, 2, 5, 16, 19, 23, 30, 31, 41] necessitate *client-side cryptography* (CSC); we call those CSC e-voting systems. In a CSC e-voting system, the voter makes use of a *voter supporting device* (VSD), which functionality is to generate an encrypted vote and submit it to the system on behalf of the voter. In addition, the VSD provides the voter with some additional information so that the voter can audit the execution of the election procedure either on her own or with the help of an *auditing supporting device* (ASD). Many CSC e-voting systems have been used in real-world binding procedures such as in the elections of scientific organizations [2], academic institutions [41], or even local government [23] and national elections [1]. As a consequence, analyzing and challenging the security of CSC e-voting systems has been a prominent theme in e-voting literature [9, 10, 22, 33, 35, 39, 40].

In their seminal work [7], Benaloh and Yung argue for distributing the administration of an election into multiple authorities in order to enhance its privacy. In our work, we shed light on the design and implementation details that are necessary for the security of *multi-authority* CSC e-voting systems. In particular, we study the election privacy of an important category of multi-authority CSC e-voting systems that include [2, 5, 16, 19, 31, 41] which construction utilizes a *threshold public key encryption (TPKE) scheme* (like threshold El Gamal [38] encryption) as follows: there is a set of *trustees* so that each trustee generates a pair of partial decryption and public keys and provide their keys into an *election authority* (EA), along with *zero-knowledge (ZK) proofs* [24] of correct key pair generation. The EA is responsible for posting the partial public keys and the corresponding ZK proofs on a publicly accessible *bulletin board* (BB). Then, the voters, using their VSD can encrypt their votes using the election public key that derives from the partial public keys and submit them to the EA. After the voting period ends, the EA processes the encrypted votes (either using the *additive homomorphic*[1] property of the TPKE scheme or via mixnets [11]) to provide anonymity. Then, it sends the product of this process to every trustee which responds with their share of partial decryption of the tally and ZK proofs of correct decryption. Finally, the EA posts the information it receives from the trustees on the BB, so that the voters or any auditor can verify the election result.

The most widely used representative of TPKE-based e-voting systems is Helios [2]. In our work, we bring to surface a flaw in the current implementation of Helios that sounds the alarm for the preservation of voter privacy. Specifically, we observe that as yet, no precaution has been taken against the potential for the EA to replace the trustees' public keys with ones of its choice without becoming detected. Namely, since it is not required from the trustees to verify the integrity of the election public key that is posted on the BB before

---

[1] The additive homomorphic property of an encryption scheme suggests that multiplying the encryptions of two messages m_1 and m_2 under some public key, results in an encryption of $m_1 + m_2$ under the same public key.

election starts, there is nothing that prevents a malicious EA from launching this *man-in-the-middle* replacement attack. It is obvious that if this attack happens, then all the cast votes of the honest voters are directly exposed to the EA since they have been encrypted under the adversarial public key.

In detail, our contributions are:

1. We present the design and implementation defects that make any TPKE-based e-voting system susceptible to man-in-the-middle attacks where an adversary that controls the EA can break voter privacy simply by posting public keys of its choice on the BB.
2. We propose simple countermeasures to deal with this type of attacks against TPKE-based e-voting systems without PKI support [2,31,41]. Namely, each trustee should audit the e-voting process by verifying the correct record of its partial public key on the BB. We argue that given a robust BB, the proposed enhancement eliminates the possibility of such man-in-the-middle attacks. Moreover, in case of an adversarially controlled BB, our countermeasure makes the system private against an election authority that acts as a *covert adversary* [3], i.e. an adversary that may deviate arbitrarily from the protocol specification, but does not wish to be detected cheating.
3. We provide a list of guidelines to avoid some common, subtle, yet important problems that may appear during the implementation of any TPKE-based e-voting system.

Related Work. *Formal definitions of election privacy.* Benaloh and Fischer [17] provided a computational definition of voter privacy while the notion of *receipt-freeness* has been first studied by Benaloh and Tuinstra [6]. Chevallier-Mames et al. [15] introduced definitions for unconditional privacy and receipt-freeness. Formal definitions for voter privacy and receipt-freeness have been proposed in the context of applied pi calculus [20] and the universal composability model [25, 37]. In [34], the level of privacy of an e-voting system is measured w.r.t. to the observation power the adversary has in a protocol run. In [9], Bernhard et al. proposed a game-based notion of ballot privacy. Their definition was extended by Bernhard, Pereira and Warinschi [10] by allowing the adversary to statically corrupt election authorities. Very recently, a game-based definition of voter privacy that also captures receipt-freeness has been presented in [32]. An extensive study of game-based definitions of voter privacy can be found in [8].

Security analysis and attacks against e-voting systems with client-side cryptography. In [33], Kremer, Ryan and Smyth proved verifiability of Helios 2.0 in a symbolic framework. Similarly, Smyth et al. [39], introduce a computational framework for defining verifiability as a set of properties and perform an analysis of Helios and the JCJ [30] e-voting system in this framework. The ballot privacy of Helios is studied in [9,10]. The security of the Estonian and the Norwegian e-voting system has been analyzed in [22,40] respectively. In [29], Jefferson et al., study the impact of man-in-the-middle attacks on e-voting security, expecially by spoofing the voting server.

Helios is among the most widely used e-voting systems. As a result, several works studied and challenged the security of Helios. Estehghari and Desmedt [21] described an attack based on vulnerabilities of the voter's browser that compromised the integrity of Helios 2.0. A fix to prevent launching this attack was considered in Helios's upgrade to version 3.0. In [26], Heiderich *et al.* presented an XSS attack against Helios and exposed serious security threats (these vulnerabilities were fixed by the developers of Helios). Cortier and Smyth [18] discovered an important attack on Helios 2.0 and 3.0, where the adversary can break the ballot secrecy of an honest voter by replaying his encrypted vote for a corrupted user that he controls. The attack can be generalized by exploiting the malleability of the Helios ciphertexts. They proposed a solution to this attack and proved the privacy that their solution achieves using applied pi calculus.

Küsters, Truderung and Vogt [35] introduced a new type of attacks that they name clash attacks, which compromise the integrity of Helios, for variants where the ballots are not linked with the identities of the voters. Bernhard, Pereira and Warinschi [10] showed that the Fiat-Shamir (FS) transformation where only the first move of the sigma protocol is hashed (weak FS), makes Helios susceptible to integrity attacks. They claimed that if the statement is also hashed (strong-FS), then Helios may withstand their attacks.

2   Preliminaries

2.1   Notation

Throughout this paper, we use λ as the security parameter. A shorthand $x \xleftarrow{\$} \mathcal{X}$ denotes that x is drawn uniformly at random from a set $\mathcal{X}$. For algorithms and distributions, the notation $x \leftarrow \mathsf{Alg}(I)$ means that the element x is sampled according to the output distribution of Alg on input I. If Alg is a probabilistic algorithm, then we write $x \in \mathsf{Alg}(I)$ to denote that x is a possible output of Alg on input I. By $\langle x \rangle$, we denote the encoding of x as an element of some message space $\mathcal{M}$. The length of string x is denoted as $|x|$. By $\mathsf{negl}(\cdot)$, we denote that some function is *negligible*, i.e. it is asymptotically smaller than the inverse of any polynomial.

2.2   Threshold Public Key Encryption Schemes

Let $\mathsf{Ser}_1, \ldots \mathsf{Ser}_k$ be a set of k decryption servers. A (t, k)-*threshold public key encryption (TPKE) scheme* TPKE is a quintuple of algorithms (TPKE.Gen, TPKE.Combine, TPKE.Enc, TPKE.Dec, TPKE.Recon) defined as follows:

- The *partial key generation* algorithm TPKE.Gen that on input 1^λ outputs the partial public key and secret key pair $(\mathsf{pk}_i, \mathsf{sk}_i)$ for Ser_i.
- The *public key construction* algorithm TPKE.Combine that on input $\mathsf{pk}_1, \ldots,$ pk_k computes the public key pk.
- The *encryption* algorithm TPKE.Enc that on input pk and a message M in some message space $\mathcal{M}$ outputs a ciphertext C.
- The *partial decryption* algorithm TPKE.Dec that on input sk_i and a ciphertext C either outputs a message share M_i or aborts.

– The *plaintext reconstruction algorithm* TPKE.Recon that on input a set of t message shares $M_{i_1}, \ldots, M_{i_t}$ outputs the message M or aborts.

The most common instantiation of a TPKE (employed in [2,5,16,19,31,41]) is the (t, k)-*threshold El Gamal cryptosystem* [38] that is *IND-CPA secure* under the *Decisional Diffie-Hellman* (DDH) assumption.

2.3   Zero-Knowledge Proofs

Let $\mathcal{L}$ be an **NP** language. A *zero-knowledge (ZK) proof system* $\Gamma = (\mathcal{P}, \mathcal{V})$ for $\mathcal{L}$ [24] is a pair of an (potentially unbounded) interactive *prover* algorithm $\mathcal{P}$ and an interactive *verifier* PPT algorithm $\mathcal{V}$ that satisfies the following properties (informally stated):

- **Completeness:** for every statement $x \in \mathcal{L}$, $\mathcal{P}$ makes $\mathcal{V}$ accept with at least $1 - \mathsf{negl}(|x|)$ probability.
- **Soundness:** for every statement $x \notin \mathcal{L}$, any malicious prover $\mathcal{P}^*$ cannot make $\mathcal{V}$ to accept with more than $\mathsf{negl}(|x|)$ probability.
- **(Computational) Zero-Knowledge:** for every statement $x \in \mathcal{L}$, any PPT verifier $\mathcal{V}^*$ cannot learn anything other than the fact that $x \in \mathcal{L}$ by interacting with $\mathcal{P}$, with probability more than $\mathsf{negl}(|x|)$.

3   A General TPKE-based e-Voting System

Let E be an e-voting system. We consider four parameters: a security parameter λ that determines the security level of the underlying cryptographic primitives, the number of voters n, the number of candidates m and the number of trustees k, which comprise the election committee that guarantees the privacy of the election. We use the notation $\mathcal{V} = \{V_1, ..., V_n\}$ for the set of voters, $\mathcal{P} = \{P_1, ..., P_m\}$ for the set of candidates and $\mathcal{T} = \{T_1, \ldots, T_k\}$ for the set of trustees. For simplicity, we consider the case of *1-out-of-m elections*, where the set of allowed selections is the collection of singletons, $\{\{P_1\}, \ldots, \{P_m\}\}$, from the set of candidates $\mathcal{P}$.

3.1   Entities of an e-Voting System

In detail, the entities involved in an e-voting system E are:

– The *Election Authority (EA)* that sets up the election and communicates initialization data to all other components. Additionally, the EA is responsible for posting the election results and possibly some election audit information on the BB.
– The *Credential Distributor (CD)*.
– The *Bulletin Board (BB)*, where the election result and all necessary audit information is posted. The BB allows only an "append" operation and recognizes at minimum one entity (the EA).

- The *Voters* who are equipped with a *voter supporting device (VSD)* (that can be a tablet, PC or other network enabled equipment) as well as an *auditing supporting device (ASD)* that can be the same as the VSD or a different network enabled device.
- The *Trustees* that constitute a subsystem responsible for the election tally. Each trustee is equipped with its own pair of *trustee supporting device (TSD)* and ASD.

3.2   Description

Let TPKE = (TPKE.Gen, TPKE.Combine, TPKE.Enc, TPKE.Dec, TPKE.Recon) be an IND-CPA TPKE scheme as described in Sect. 2.2. For every security parameter λ, partial key pair $(\mathsf{pk}_i, \mathsf{sk}_i) \leftarrow \mathsf{TPKE.Gen}(1^\lambda)$, $i = 1, \ldots, k$ and public key $\mathsf{pk} \leftarrow \mathsf{TPKE.Combine}(\mathsf{pk}_1, \ldots, \mathsf{pk}_k)$ we define the following **NP** languages:

$$\mathcal{L}_\lambda = \left\{ \mathsf{pk}_i \mid \text{there is an } \mathsf{sk}_i^* : (\mathsf{pk}_i, \mathsf{sk}_i^*) \in \mathsf{TPKE.Gen}(1^\lambda) \right\},$$

$$\mathcal{L}_{\lambda,\mathsf{pk}} = \{ C \mid \text{there is a } P \in \mathcal{P} : C \in \mathsf{TPKE.Enc}(\mathsf{pk}, \langle P \rangle) \} \quad \text{and}$$

$$\mathcal{L}_{\lambda,\mathsf{pk},sk_i} = \{ (C, M_i) \mid M_i \leftarrow \mathsf{TPKE.Dec}(\mathsf{sk}_i, C) \}.$$

Informally, $\mathcal{L}_\lambda$ is the language of valid partial public keys, $\mathcal{L}_{\lambda,\mathsf{pk}}$ is the language of the well-formed encrypted votes under pk and $\mathcal{L}_{\lambda,\mathsf{pk},sk_i}$ is the language of valid pairs of encryptions under pk and partial decryptions for trustee T_i.

A TPKE-based e-voting system E consists of a quintuple of algorithms and protocols $\langle$**Setup, Cast, Tally, Result, Verify**$\rangle$ as follows:

• *The protocol* **Setup**$(1^\lambda, \mathcal{P}, \mathcal{V}, \mathcal{T})$: each T_i uses its TSD to run $\mathsf{TPKE.Gen}(1^\lambda)$ and receive the partial key pair $(\mathsf{pk}_i, \mathsf{sk}_i)$. It sends pk_i to the EA along with a ZK proof of $\mathsf{pk}_i \in \mathcal{L}_\lambda$ by *proving knowledge of* sk_i. If there is a proof that EA does not verify, then EA aborts the protocol. Upon receiving all $\mathsf{pk}_1, \ldots, \mathsf{pk}_k$, EA computes the election public key $\mathsf{pk} \leftarrow \mathsf{TPKE.Combine}(\mathsf{pk}_1, \ldots, \mathsf{pk}_k)$. Then, it posts the public parameters, Pub, which include the election information Info, pk, the partial public keys $\mathsf{pk}_1, \ldots, \mathsf{pk}_k$ as well as the ZK proofs of knowledge of $\mathsf{sk}_1, \ldots, \mathsf{sk}_k$ in the BB. Namely, the election transcript τ of the BB is initialized as Pub. Finally, EA generates the voter credentials $s_1, \ldots, s_n$, where s_ℓ contains a voter identifier ID_ℓ and sends $s_1, \ldots, s_n$ to the CD. In turn, CD checks the uniqueness of each ID_ℓ, $\ell = 1, \ldots, n$ and issues the credentials $s_1, \ldots, s_n$ to the voters $V_1, \ldots, V_n$ respectively.

• *The protocol* **Cast**: each voter V_ℓ chooses a candidate selection $\{P_{j_\ell}\}$ and sends $(\mathsf{ID}_\ell, \{P_{j_\ell}\})$ to her VSD. The VSD reads pk from the BB and creates a ciphertext $C_\ell \leftarrow \mathsf{TPKE.Enc}(pk, \langle P_{j_\ell} \rangle)$, where $\langle P_{j_\ell} \rangle$ is the encoding of candidate P_{j_ℓ}. In addition, it attaches a ZK proof of *ballot correctness* π_ℓ showing that $C_\ell \in \mathcal{L}_{\lambda,\mathsf{pk}}$. The *encrypted ballot* generated is $\mathbf{B}_\ell = (C_\ell, \pi_\ell)$. Upon the generation of $\mathbf{B}_\ell$, the VSD provides V_ℓ with a *ballot tracker* (e.g. a hash of $\mathbf{B}_\ell$), Tr_ℓ, so that V_ℓ can locate $\mathbf{B}_\ell$ in the BB after election ends. Next, V_ℓ must choose either one of the following options (see Sect. 5.2 for the importance of this step):

(i) *Cast* her vote. In this case, V_ℓ provides VSD with her credential s_ℓ. Subsequently, VSD submits $\mathbf{B}_\ell$ to the EA using s_ℓ.

(ii) *Audit* the ballot $\mathbf{B}_\ell$ via its ASD, by requiring the VSD to provide all the randomness used to generate $\mathbf{B}_\ell$. In this case, the ballot $\mathbf{B}_\ell$ is spoiled and when the audit is finished, V_ℓ requests a new ballot $\mathbf{B}'_\ell$, possibly under a different candidate selection $\{P'_{j_\ell}\}$. After V_ℓ has received the new ballot tracker T'_ℓ, she will be prompted to audit-or-cast $\mathbf{B}'_\ell$.

When EA receives a submitted ballot vote $\mathbf{B}_\ell = (C_\ell, \pi_\ell)$, it checks that it is well-formed by verifying the ZK proof π_ℓ. If the check fails, then EA aborts the protocol. After voting ends, EA updates its state with the pairs $\{(\mathrm{ID}_\ell, \mathbf{B}_\ell)\}_{V_\ell \in \mathcal{V}_{\mathsf{succ}}}$ of cast votes and the associated identifiers, where $\mathcal{V}_{\mathsf{succ}}$ is the set of voters that voted successfully.

• **The protocol** *Tally:* the EA processes $\{(\mathrm{ID}_\ell, \mathbf{B}_\ell)\}_{V_\ell \in \mathcal{V}_{\mathsf{succ}}}$ (either using the additive homomorphic property of the TPKE scheme or via mixnets [11])[2] to provide anonymity. Then, the EA sends the processed votes to all trustees. Every trustee T_i, $i = 1, \ldots, k$, uses their TSD to perform the following computation: it uses sk_i and all ciphertexts $\{C_\ell\}_{V_\ell \in \mathcal{V}_{\mathsf{succ}}}$ to compute T_i's partial decryption of the tally denoted by R_i. Then, it sends R_i to the EA along with a ZK proof of *correct partial decryption*. If there is a proof that EA does not verify, then it aborts the protocol. After all trustees finish their computation, EA updates the BB's transcript τ with $\{(\mathrm{ID}_\ell, \mathbf{B}_\ell)\}_{V_\ell \in \mathcal{V}_{\mathsf{succ}}}$ along with all the partial decryptions and the respective ZK proofs sent by the trustees.

• **The algorithm** *Result:* computes the election result R as the output of $\mathsf{TPKE.Recon}(R_{i_1}, \ldots, R_{i_t})$, where $R_{i_1}, \ldots, R_{i_t}$ is any subset of t out-of-the k partial decryptions $R_1, \ldots, R_k$.

• **The algorithm** *Verify* (τ, Tr_ℓ): outputs 1 if and only if the following conditions hold:

1. The structure of the information posted on the BB and all election information is correct (using Info).
2. There exists a ballot in the BB that matches the ballot tracker Tr_ℓ.
3. The ZK proofs for the correctness of all ballots on the BB verify.
4. The ZK proofs for the correctness of all trustees' partial decryptions verify.

4   A Man-in-the-middle Attack Against Voter Privacy

In Sect. 3, we described a general TPKE-based e-voting system. Notice that in our description there is no way for the BB to authenticate the trustees' data (this typically requires a user-side PKI which is hard to deploy in practice) and the trustees are not required to audit the information posted in the BB e.g., as in Helios [2].

---

[2] For instance [5,19,27,31] apply the homomorphic operation on the encrypted votes while [16,41] use mixnets in order to provide anonymity.

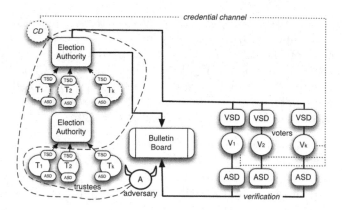

Fig. 1. The man-in-the-middle against a TPKE-based e-voting system.

Unfortunately, this oversight might cause subtle privacy problems when the EA is malicious. In order to achieve voter privacy, it is necessary to ensure that at least one of the trustees participates in the election audit. For instance, this is consistent with claims made in the Helios web server material where it is argued that voter privacy is guaranteed unless all the trustees are corrupted, see [28]. Nevertheless, the trustee auditing step is optional and there are no proper instructions regarding the necessity of the trustee verification process. Moreover, the current Helios implementation (Helios v4 [27]) makes it very difficult for someone without technical knowledge and understanding of the code to do so.

In Sect. 4.1, we introduce a generic man-in-the-middle (MitM) attack against the voter privacy of a TPKE-based e-voting system when the trustee auditing step is not performed. Next, in Sect. 4.2, we demonstrate our attack against Helios as a specific instance of the attack methodology. In Sect. 4.3, we propose simple countermeasures that deal with this type of attacks.

4.1 The System Vulnerability and Our MitM Attacks

Recall that a typical TPKE-based e-voting system mainly consists of EA, BB, and VSD, and it forms a star network as depicted in Fig. 1. Namely, the BB, all the trustees and all the VSDs are connected through the central node, the EA[3]. Such a network topology is sensible and is followed by systems used in practice (including Helios) since it avoids additional pairwise communication between the entities participating in the election; this has a number of advantages. First of all, it significantly reduces the development and deployment complexity, as

---

[3] One may think of the EA being part of the BB; we separate the two entities in our work in order to enable the BB to be completely passive; having a passive BB is important in practice since a robust implementation for the BB will distribute the responsibility of maintaining the election transcript to a set of servers which will be required to execute an agreement protocol for each append operation that should be readable by honest parties.

the entire e-voting system can be realized by a single server. Secondly, it is consistent with a reasonable level of usability, as the administrators only need to keep the election server online and all the other election parties are able to participate in the election asynchronously without any coordination. On the other hand, as expected, the star network topology makes the system vulnerable to a MitM class of attacks when the central node (i.e. the election server) is compromised. Furthermore, the lack of PKI support makes it impossible for a third-party auditor to identify the actual sources of messages that appear in the BB. This problem is recognized in terms of election integrity, and the concept of *individual verifiability* is widely adopted to mitigate this problem by preventing the malicious election server from tampering the submitted ballots. Nevertheless, little attention is given to the contributions of the election trustees even though it is equally important to ensure the integrity of trustees' messages (i.e. the election parameters) in the BB.

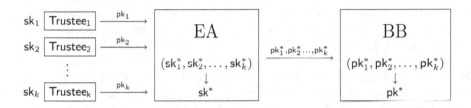

Fig. 2. A MitM attack against the voter privacy of a TPKE-based e-voting system.

Our attack assumes that only the EA is controlled by the adversary, whereas the rest of the TPKE-based e-voting system entities and all the supporting devices remain honest. In a nutshell, the MitM attack works as depicted in Fig. 2. During the election setup phase, the malicious EA follows the **Setup** protocol description and interacts with the real trustees $T_1, \ldots, T_k$ to jointly generate the real election public parameters Pub and the real voters' credentials $s_1, \ldots, s_n$. Meanwhile, the malicious EA (conceptually) creates another set of fake trustees, $T_1^*, \ldots, T_k^*$ and generates the fake election public parameters Pub* and the fake voters' credentials $s_1^*, \ldots, s_n^*$ by running the **Setup** protocol with the fake trustees "in its mind", obtaining $sk_1^*, \ldots, sk_k^*$. The malicious EA then publishes Pub* on the BB and thus all the voters will use the fake election parameters during the **Cast** protocol. Obviously, the malicious EA is able to learn every voter's choice from the public transcript on the BB. In the tally phase, the malicious EA can provide presumably fake bulletin board information to the real trustees and invoke the **Tally** protocol with them. The purpose of this step is to make the real trustees believe that the election tally result is produced by themselves, whereas the adversary can simply perform the actual election tally itself and publish the corresponding election result in the BB. It is easy to see that all the information posted on the BB is consistent in the sense that it is publicly verifiable by all the voters and the election result is correct.

4.2   Instantiation of Our MitM Attack Against Helios

For concreteness, we demonstrate our MitM attack against Helios. There are many variants of Helios in the literature — some use aliases, some use homomorphic tally while others use mix-net tally, etc. However, our attack can apply to all the variants with respect to their latest implementations. Our attack does not tamper the javascript code, therefore it is impossible to detect our attack by checking the integrity of the source code as observed at the client side.

Recall that the latest version of Helios v4 uses k out of k threshold (lifted) ElGamal encryption. During the election setup phase, each trustee T_i, $i = 1, \ldots, k$ locally generates a pair of ElGamal partial keys $(\mathsf{pk}_i, \mathsf{sk}_i)$ and sends pk_i to the EA. At this step, a fingerprint (SHA256 hash digest) of the partial public key pk_i is computed and provided to the trustee. It is suggested that the trustees keep the fingerprints of their partial public key and confirm that they are properly stored on the election server. However, there is no further instruction to indicate to the trustees where and how to verify the consistency of this information. Notice that there is no interface for the trustees to verify whether their partial public keys are correctly used to produce the (combined) election public key during the **Setup** protocol.[4] In fact, only the (combined) election public key is used to generate the election fingerprint (i.e. a SHA256 hash digest of the JSON format of the election definition) after an election is fixed (or "frozen" in Helios terminology). Moreover, the voters are only given the (combined) election public key at the *voting booth* page in the **Cast** protocol, so it is impossible to check the validity of the partial public keys even if the trustee is also an eligible voter. During the tally phase, the trustees are given their partial public key fingerprints to prevent them from using incorrect partial secret keys. The information displayed on the tally page can never be used for auditing purposes, because every trustee should first identify himself by submitting a unique token to the EA before receiving the content. Hence, the malicious EA can specifically tailor a (inconsistent) view of the tally page for each trustee. Finally, the partial public key information is not even displayed on the bulletin board, which only contains the submitted voters' ciphertexts.

In our MitM attack, the malicious EA receives pk_i from the trustee T_i, $i = 1, \ldots, k$ during the election setup phase. Then, it generates another set of fake partial ElGamal key pairs $(\mathsf{pk}_i^*, \mathsf{sk}_i^*)$ and computes the fake election public key $\mathsf{pk}^* = \prod_{i=1}^{k} \mathsf{pk}_i^*$. When the election is frozen, the malicious EA switches the real election public key with pk^*, so pk^* is used to generate the election fingerprint. In the voting booth, the voters are given pk^* to encrypt their choices, and thus it is consistent with the election fingerprint. In the tally phase, the malicious EA sends the real trustee T_i his partial public key pk_i; therefore, the hash of pk_i matches the fingerprint stored by T_i and the trustee should perform tallying as usual. Once T_i submits the decryption values, the malicious EA mimics the same process with T_i^* (in its "head") and posts the fake decryption factors instead. Clearly, all the information on the BB is publicly verifiable.

---

[4] Note that each trustee does not know the other trustees' actual partial public keys.

Remark. If a trustee carefully checks the public verification page, it is possible to find out that its partial public key is missing. However, the user is never instructed to perform such a step; besides this, the highlighted Verified indication hints to the user that everything is okay. We stress that the voters' privacy is violated already even in the case where the trustees check the public verification page *after* voting phase ends (as the voters will have already encrypted the votes under the adversarial public key).

Our MitM attack can be launched against any TPKE-based e-voting system which, like Helios, (i) does not urge that the trustees directly verify that their partial public keys were correctly published and (ii) does not allow for any third party to verify the source of the partial public keys (as in [31,41]). Note that having the EA sign BB data like in [5] does not prevent the attack, since BB consistency is not violated from the EA's point of view (the adversarial public key is posted on the BB by the EA itself). On the contrary, our MitM attack can be prevented when the trustees collaboratively verify their partial public keys either via a verifiable secret sharing scheme [19] or with PKI support [16].

4.3   Countermeasures

In this section, we propose two countermeasures for the MitM attack described in Sect. 4.1 and for TPKE-based e-voting systems without PKI support [2,31,41]. Each countermeasure suits a specific threat model for the BB.

First of all, as shown in Fig. 1 and commonly used in the e-voting literature [2, 5,16,19,31,41], the BB is considered to be passive and robust in the sense that posting on the BB is done in an append-only way. In this model, the trustee auditing step should be performed *immediately after* the election setup phase and *before* the voting phase starts. Since the adversary cannot modify the election public key in the BB, it cannot decrypt the encrypted votes without knowing all the partial secret keys. Hence, the voters' privacy is preserved, if at least one of the trustees remains honest.

In an alternative threat model, we consider a *covert* adversary [3] (i.e. an adversary that may deviate arbitrarily from the protocol specification, but does not wish to be detected cheating) that may also fully corrupt the BB but cannot link the identity of the auditing party (including both voters and trustees) with the ASD that is used. In this model, the trustee auditing step should be performed *after* the end voting phase and the interaction between the BB and a trustee's ASD should be indistinguishable from an interaction between the BB and any voter's ASD. Observe that the election public key that has been used for vote encryption is determined w.r.t. a specific voter's ballot tracker. This is because the said public key can be deducted from the statement of any ZK proof of ballot correctness. In order to pass the trustee auditing, the adversary has to post the real public key on the BB whereas in order to pass the voter auditing, it has to post the fake public key. Since the adversary cannot tell whether an auditing party is a trustee or a voter, it will either (i) be discouraged from launching the MitM attack or (ii) eventually be detected.

5 Implementation and Deployment Guidelines

In this section, we present guidelines to avoid some common, subtle, yet important problems one may encounter during the implementation and deployment of a TPKE-based e-voting system. Those oversights may affect the integrity and privacy of an election in practice.

5.1 Supporting Trustee Auditing

In a typical TPKE-based e-voting system, trustees are introduced to prevent the EA from learning the voters' choices. However, as we illustrated in Sect. 4, trustee auditing has not been properly highlighted in the deployment of e-voting systems. Specifically, we demonstrated how a TPKE-based e-voting system is vulnerable to a MitM type of attack if a trustee auditing mechanism is not included in the procedure. Therefore, the trustees should be enforced to take the responsibility of guaranteeing the validity of the election parameters on the BB by following the auditing process and registering a complaint to stop the election in case the process fails, so that the misbehavior of a malicious EA can be caught without breaching voter privacy (assuming an honest and passive BB), or at least be detected (in case of BB corruption).

5.2 Providing Proper Instructions for the Audit-or-cast Step

The audit-or-cast step described in Sect. 3.2 (also known as the "Benaloh-challenge" [4]) is a mechanism that prevents a malicious local computer from casting votes that do not reflect the voter intent. When it is performed correctly, the voter is able to catch a cheating VSD with some probability β. However, implementations that include the Benaloh challenge as part of their code (including Helios and Zeus [41]) do not provide sufficient instructions to the voters about the correct application of the procedure. As a result, most voters do not know how to audit the ballot in a proper way. For instance, humans are usually weak randomness sources and therefore it is better to avoid relying on the voters free will to audit if they feel they like to do it. Instead of leaving to the voters the option to audit if they prefer, the alternative is to present a specific instruction as a template that will implement the Benaloh-challenge. For example, for $\beta = 1/2$, the voters, each time they (re)visit the audit-or-cast step, should be asked to flip a coin in order to choose whether they will audit or cast the encrypted ballot. It can be argued that many voters may find the above procedure out of the ordinary and will not follow it or will follow it incorrectly. Still, the objective is to get at least a small number of voters to follow it properly so that some level of verifiability may be achieved. Alternatively, it is better to enforce a ballot auditing step to all voters as, e.g., done in [32].

5.3 Maintaining the Uniqueness of Ballot Trackers

An important consideration for the integrity of elections is that there is no PKI support among all the election participants in a typical TPKE-based e-voting system. Hence, it is impossible for a third-party auditor to link the recorded ballots on the BB to their actual sources. To address this issue, a TPKE-based e-voting system needs to require from the voters to check whether their cast ballots are properly recorded using their ballot trackers. This is widely adopted in practice to achieve individual verifiability. As noticed by Küsters *et al.* [34], if the malicious EA and VSD are able to furnish the same ballot tracker to multiple voters a *clash attack* can be mounted. Therefore, it is mandatory to guarantee ballot tracker uniqueness even when the entire e-voting system is compromised. A way to achieve that, as we suggest to implement here, is to include a unique voter identifier that is not generated/assigned by the e-voting system in the receipt. This number is unique to the voter and cannot be controlled by the malicious EA and VSD.

5.4   Implementing ZK Proofs Properly

ZK proofs are powerful tools that enable one to show that a given statement is true without conveying extra information; ZK protocols are extensively employed in TPKE-based e-voting systems. Those protocols are quite delicate and often their incorrect implementation is leading to security problems. As an example, the Fiat-Shamir heuristic is widely employed in e-voting systems in order to efficiently transform an interactive ZK proof to a non-interactive one in the random oracle model. A Fiat-Shamir transformation has been called "weak" if the challenge is produced by only hashing the first move of a sigma protocol, and has been called "strong" if the statement is also hashed to produce the challenge. Helios is susceptible to an attack against integrity when the weak Fiat-Shamir transformation is used, as shown in [10]. Currently, the latest version of Helios V4 code [?7] still uses the weak Fiat-Shamir transformation, and thus the implementation of Helios fails to provide verifiability.

References

1. https://www.valimised.ee/eng/
2. Adida, B.: Helios: web-based open-audit voting. In: USENIX Security Symposium (2008)
3. Aumann, Y., Lindell, Y.: Security against covert adversaries: efficient protocols for realistic adversaries. J. Cryptology **23**(2), 281–343 (2010)
4. Benaloh, J.: Simple verifiable elections. In: Wallach, D.S., Rivest, R.L. (eds.) EVT. USENIX Association (2006)
5. Benaloh, J., Byrne, M.D., Eakin, B., Kortum, P.T., McBurnett, N., Pereira, O., Stark, P.B., Wallach, D.S., Fisher, G., Montoya, J., Parker, M., Winn, M.: STAR-vote: a secure, transparent, auditable, and reliable voting system. In: EVT/WOTE 2013, August 2013
6. Benaloh, J.C., Tuinstra, D.: Receipt-free secret-ballot elections (extended abstract). In: STOC (1994)
7. Benaloh, J.C., Yung, M.: Distributing the power of a government to enhance the privacy of voters (extended abstract). In: PODC (1986)

8. Bernhard, D., Cortier, V., Galindo, D., Pereira, O., Warinschi, B.: A comprehensive analysis of game-based ballot privacy definitions. Cryptology ePrint Archive, Report 2015/255 (2015). http://eprint.iacr.org/

9. Bernhard, D., Cortier, V., Pereira, O., Smyth, B., Warinschi, B.: Adapting helios for provable ballot privacy. In: Atluri, V., Diaz, C. (eds.) ESORICS 2011. LNCS, vol. 6879, pp. 335–354. Springer, Heidelberg (2011)

10. Bernhard, D., Pereira, O., Warinschi, B.: How not to prove yourself: pitfalls of the fiat-shamir heuristic and applications to helios. In: Wang, X., Sako, K. (eds.) ASIACRYPT 2012. LNCS, vol. 7658, pp. 626–643. Springer, Heidelberg (2012)

11. Chaum, D.: Untraceable electronic mail, return addresses, and digital pseudonyms. Commun. ACM **24**(2), 84–88 (1981)

12. Chaum, D.: Surevote: technical overview. In: Proceedings of the Workshop on Trustworthy Elections, WOTE, August 2001

13. Chaum, D., Essex, A., Carback, R., Clark, J., Popoveniuc, S., Sherman, A., Vora, P.: Scantegrity: end-to-end voter-verifiable optical-scan voting. IEEE Secur. Priv. **6**(3), 40–46 (2008)

14. Chaum, D., Ryan, P.Y.A., Schneider, S.: A practical voter-verifiable election scheme. In: di Vimercati, S.C., Syverson, P.F., Gollmann, D. (eds.) ESORICS 2005. LNCS, vol. 3679, pp. 118–139. Springer, Heidelberg (2005)

15. Chevallier-Mames, B., Fouque, P.-A., Pointcheval, D., Stern, J., Traoré, J.: On some incompatible properties of voting schemes. In: Chaum, D., Jakobsson, M., Rivest, R.L., Ryan, P.Y.A., Benaloh, J., Kutylowski, M., Adida, B. (eds.) Towards Trustworthy Elections. LNCS, vol. 6000, pp. 191–199. Springer, Heidelberg (2010)

16. Clarkson, M.R., Chong, S., Myers, A.C.: Civitas: toward a secure voting system. In: 2008 IEEE Symposium on Security and Privacy (S&P 2008), pp. 354–368, May 2008

17. Cohen, J.D., Fischer, M.J.: A robust and verifiable cryptographically secure election scheme (extended abstract). In: FOCS (1985)

18. Cortier, V., Smyth, B.: Attacking and fixing Helios: An analysis of ballot secrecy. ePrint Archive, 2010:625 (2010)

19. Cramer, R., Gennaro, R., Schoenmakers, B.: A secure and optimally efficient multi-authority election scheme. In: Fumy, W. (ed.) EUROCRYPT 1997. LNCS, vol. 1233, pp. 103–118. Springer, Heidelberg (1997)

20. Delaune, S., Kremer, S., Ryan, M.: Verifying privacy-type properties of electronic voting protocols. J. Comput. Secur. **17**(4), 435–487 (2009)

21. Estehghari, S., Desmedt, Y.: Exploiting the client vulnerabilities in internet e-voting systems: hacking helios 2.0 as an example. In: EVT/WOTE (2010)

22. Gjøsteen, K.: Analysis of an internet voting protocol. IACR Cryptology ePrint Archive, 2010:380 (2010)

23. Gjøsteen, K.: The Norwegian internet voting protocol. IACR Cryptology ePrint Archive, 2013:473 (2013)

24. Goldwasser, S., Micali, S., Rackoff, C.: The knowledge complexity of interactive proof-systems (extended abstract). In: STOC (1985)

25. Groth, J.: Evaluating security of voting schemes in the universal composability framework. In: Jakobsson, M., Yung, M., Zhou, J. (eds.) ACNS 2004. LNCS, vol. 3089, pp. 46–60. Springer, Heidelberg (2004)

26. Heiderich, M., Frosch, T., Niemietz, M., Schwenk, J.: The bug that made me president a browser- and web-security case study on helios voting. In: Kiayias, A., Lipmaa, H. (eds.) VoteID 2011. LNCS, vol. 7187, pp. 89–103. Springer, Heidelberg (2012)

27. Helios. Helios github repository. https://github.com/benadida/helios-server. Accessed 31 July 2014
28. Helios. Helios privacy claims. https://vote.heliosvoting.org/privacy. Accessed 31 July 2014
29. Jefferson, D.R., Rubin, A.D., Simons, B., Wagner, D.: Analyzing internet voting security. Commun. ACM **47**(10), 59–64 (2004)
30. Juels, A., Catalano, D., Jakobsson, M.: Coercion-resistant electronic elections. IACR Cryptology ePrint Archive 2002:165 (2002)
31. Kiayias, A., Korman, M., Walluck, D.: An internet voting system supporting user privacy. In: ACSAC (2006)
32. Kiayias, A., Zacharias, T., Zhang, B.: End-to-end verifiable elections in the standard model. In: Oswald, E., Fischlin, M. (eds.) EUROCRYPT 2015. LNCS, vol. 9057, pp. 468–498. Springer, Heidelberg (2015)
33. Kremer, S., Ryan, M., Smyth, B.: Election verifiability in electronic voting protocols. In: Gritzalis, D., Preneel, B., Theoharidou, M. (eds.) ESORICS 2010. LNCS, vol. 6345, pp. 389–404. Springer, Heidelberg (2010)
34. Küsters, R., Truderung, T., Vogt, A.: Verifiability, privacy, and coercion-resistance: new insights from a case study. In: IEEE Symposium on Security and Privacy, pp. 538–553. IEEE Computer Society (2011)
35. Küsters, R., Truderung, T., Vogt, A.: Clash attacks on the verifiability of e-voting systems. In: IEEE Symposium on Security and Privacy, pp. 395–409. IEEE Computer Society (2012)
36. Kutylowski, M., Zagórski, F.: Scratch, click & vote: E2E voting over the internet. In: Chaum, D., Jakobsson, M., Rivest, R.L., Ryan, P.Y.A., Benaloh, J., Kutylowski, M., Adida, B. (eds.) Towards Trustworthy Elections. LNCS, vol. 6000, pp. 343–356. Springer, Heidelberg (2010)
37. Moran, T., Naor, M.: Receipt-free universally-verifiable voting with everlasting privacy. In: Dwork, C. (ed.) CRYPTO 2006. LNCS, vol. 4117, pp. 373–392. Springer, Heidelberg (2006)
38. Pedersen, T.P.: A threshold cryptosystem without a trusted party. In: Davies, D.W. (ed.) EUROCRYPT 1991. LNCS, vol. 547, pp. 522–526. Springer, Heidelberg (1991)
39. Smyth, B., Frink, S., Clarkson, M.R.: Computational election verifiability: Definitions and an analysis of Helios and JCJ. Technical report
40. Springall, D., Finkenauer, T., Durumeric, Z., Kitcat, J., Hursti, H., MacAlpine, M., Alex Halderman, J.: Security analysis of the Estonian internet voting system. In: SIGSAC (2014)
41. Tsoukalas, G., Papadimitriou, K., Louridas, P., Tsanakas, P.: From helios to zeus. In: EVT/WOTE. USENIX Association (2013)
42. Zagórski, F., Carback, R.T., Chaum, D., Clark, J., Essex, A., Vora, P.L.: Remotegrity: design and use of an end-to-end verifiable remote voting system. In: Jacobson, M., Locasto, M., Mohassel, P., Safavi-Naini, R. (eds.) ACNS 2013. LNCS, vol. 7954, pp. 441–457. Springer, Heidelberg (2013)

A Comparison of the Effects of Face-to-Face and Online Deliberation on Young Students' Attitudes About Public Opinion Polls

Amalia Triantafillidou[1(✉)], Prodromos Yannas[2], Georgios Lappas[1],
and Alexandros Kleftodimos[1]

[1] Digital Media and Communication,
Technological Education Institute of Western Macedonia, Kastoria, Greece
{a.triantafylidou, lappas,
kleftodimos}@kastoria.teikoz.gr
[2] Business Administration,
Piraeus University of Applied Sciences, Aigaleo, Greece
prodyannas@teipir.gr

Abstract. This study compared the effects between face-to-face and online deliberation on young citizens' attitudes about opinion polls. Two parallel experiments were conducted to test the outcomes of the two modes of deliberation in terms of (a) significance, (b) direction, and (c) valence of changes. Results suggest that online deliberation affected more respondents' attitudes compared to its face-to-face counterpart. Both modes of deliberation induced more opinion shifts towards the opposite direction of the initial attitudes instead of opinion reinforcements. Interestingly, the effect of the online deliberation was considered as more positive compared to the face-to-face deliberation, as online participants became more in favor of polls, pollsters and their relationships with politicians and the media. On the contrary, face-to-face participants became less in favor of the mediatization of polls and their impact on citizens-government communication and voting behavior. Hence, findings of this research highlight the potential role of online settings in facilitating effective deliberations.

Keywords: Face-to-face deliberation · Online deliberation · Opinion polls · Attitudes' change

1 Introduction

Public deliberation is regarded an integral part of democracy [1, 2]. According to [1], democratic decisions should be based on "informed, enlightened, and authentic" opinions of citizens which can be achieved through political deliberation. However, several theorists posit that it is almost impossible to manage large-scale deliberations due to the size and unruliness of the public [e.g., 3] as well as the cost of organizing such events. These impracticalities of an "ideal public deliberation" turned researchers' attention to other more innovative solutions for deliberative democracy such as "mini-publics" (e.g., consensus conferences, citizen juries, planning cells, deliberative polls) [4]. These mini-publics are comprised of ordinary citizens who are characterized

© Springer International Publishing Switzerland 2015
S.K. Katsikas and A.B. Sideridis (Eds.): E-Democracy 2015, CCIS 570, pp. 18–32, 2015.
DOI: 10.1007/978-3-319-27164-4_2

by some kind of representativeness [4] and engage participants in "symmetrical, face-to-face, and equal deliberation" [3, p. 17]. Besides the face-to-face forms of mini-publics, online deliberative events have been proposed by a number of researchers as another solution to the deficiencies of mass-public deliberation [5]. Indeed, a new stream of research suggests that the Internet is a viable channel through which large-scale deliberations can be made practical [6].

There exist conflicting viewpoints regarding the impact of new technologies on democracy. On the one hand are the "cyberoptimistics" who argue that the Internet is an effective platform for deliberation [7] that encourages different points of views [8] to be heard even from people who were not likely in the past to participate in political discussions and were marginalized [9] or indifferent to politics. Moreover, the anonymity on the Internet along with the absence of physical presence improves the quality of discussion since participants feel free to express their sincere opinions on an equal basis with other online discussants [10]. Hence, a more "enlightened exchange of ideas" is encouraged [11, p. 267]. It is also argued that new technologies can foster debates which are based on rational argumentation [12]. This argumentative aspect of online discussions could be partly attributed to their asynchronous and written format [10].

On the other side, the "cyberskeptics" highlight a number of obstacles regarding the deliberative potential and maturity of online discussions. For example, several scholars point out that the Internet tends to increase inequalities in representation [13]. The digital divide threatens the quality of online deliberations since most of the times these discussions are dominated by like-minded individuals [14]. This compatibility between online discussants leads to a polarization of views [10] that sabotage the basic requirement of deliberation which is the exchange of different viewpoints [12]. In addition, the sincerity of participants is not strongly secured as people on the Internet have the choice to conceal their identities using nicknames [10]. Another important caveat in online discussions is the predominance of "flaming" and the use of offensive and hostile language [13].

However, as Wright [15] notes researchers should not worry whether the Internet has a "revolutionary" or a "normalization" impact on deliberative democracy but rather concentrate on the effects of the Internet. He further points out that experimental designs can provide fruitful insights regarding the impact of online deliberations.

Until now, most of the studies on online deliberation have focused on analyzing the content and quality of deliberations that take place among usenet newsgroups and discussion forums [11, 14, 16] whereas few studies have examined the impact of online deliberation on participants using experimental designs. Moreover, there is a lack of studies that attempt to compare the effects between face-to-face and online deliberation on citizens' attitudes using real experiments. Hence, the purpose of the present study is to test whether a deliberation conducted in a computer-mediated environment produces similar or different changes in citizens' attitudes compared to a face-to-face deliberation. Towards this end, an online as well as an offline deliberative experiment was conducted. Note that, in the online experiment participants used their real names to deliberate with other discussants. Thus, participation in the online deliberation was not anonymous. This was done to (a) ensure that participants in the online mode responded sincerely to the deliberation, and (b) avoid the phenomenon of flaming.

2 Effects of Face-to-Face and Online Deliberation

The effects of offline deliberation are well established in the literature. According to [18], offline deliberation helps citizens become more informed about the issue of discussion. Moreover, it is argued that deliberation has a positive impact on citizens' attitudes [2] since citizens often "revise preferences in light of discussion, new information, and claims made by fellow participants" [18, p. 309]. The deliberation's effect on attitude change is particularly evident in experimental designs such as deliberative polls [19].

Similar positive effects on citizens' attitudes have been reported by researchers in the context of online deliberations [20]. For example, the study of [21] reports the results of an online deliberation experiment which examined the effects of computer-mediated deliberation on citizens' views about energy issues in Finland. The experiment was a live-event based on small-group discussions that took place through webcams. Findings indicate that online participants changed attitudes in six out of nine statements on energy issues. For example, participants became less supportive about the creation of another nuclear plant and the use of coal and peat in energy production in Finland. On the other hand, after the online deliberation, discussants held more positive attitudes regarding the need for improved energy saving and policy. Reference [22] investigated the effects of deliberation that takes place in computer-mediated environments. Toward this end a random sample of American citizens was surveyed prior to and after real-time electronic discussions. Discussion topics focused around the 2000 US presidential elections and health care reform issues. Although, in most of the issues discussed, participants did not change significantly their attitudes, on the issues where significant changes were observed citizens moved toward more rational views and agreed with the opinions promoted by policy elites.

While there is a critical number of studies which examine the effects of each mode of deliberation (i.e., face-to-face, and online) in isolation, few studies have compared the impact of the two modes on citizens' attitudes. Reference [23] conducted a face-to-face and an online deliberative poll to test whether the two experimental designs can yield the same changes in attitudes of citizens in regards to a number of United States policy issues (i.e., military intervention, trade and economic relations with other countries, and global environment). Although the two designs differ not only in the mode of delivery but also in the recruitment of samples, the panel experts, and the length of small group discussions, results indicated that the effects of face-to-face deliberation were almost identical with those of online deliberation.

The study of [24] also compared the outcome of a face-to-face deliberation with an online deliberation experiment around gun-related issues. Findings indicate that both experiments produced similar positive changes on citizens' issue knowledge, and political efficacy. However, offline deliberation proved to be more effective in influencing citizens' willingness to participate in politics than online deliberation. Reference [25] reported the differences in the effects between face-to-face and online deliberation settings in regards to citizens' opinion about global warming. Interestingly, online deliberation induced the expression of different opinions and led to higher levels of disagreement compared to the face-to-face mode. On the other hand, face-to-face deliberation proved to be of higher quality compared to the online deliberation.

Reference [26] testing the effects of offline as well as online deliberation on issues regarding public school consolidation and quality found that both online as well as face-to-face deliberation did not produce significant changes in policy attitudes whereas the reading material was an important factor for the changes found in the opinions of participants. Moreover, the comparison of the two settings indicates that face-to-face deliberation had stronger effects to policy attitudes than its online counterpart.

The aforementioned inconsistent findings call for further exploitation of the effects of the two types of settings (i.e., online versus offline) on the deliberative outcome.

3 Research Objectives

We expect that face-to-face as well as computer-mediated deliberation have an impact on citizens' attitudes. Specifically, the study's objectives are the following:

1. To describe the effects of face-to-face deliberation in terms of (a) number, (b) direction (i.e., opposite shift or reinforcement), and (c) valence (i.e., positive or negative) of significant changes on citizens' attitudes.
2. To describe the effects of online deliberation in terms of (a) number, (b) direction (i.e., opposite shift or reinforcement), and (c) valence (i.e., positive or negative) of significant changes on citizens' attitudes.
3. To compare the effects of face-to-face deliberation with its computer-mediated counterpart.

4 Method

In order to achieve the objectives of the present study two parallel deliberations, one face-to-face and one online, were conducted to reveal whether online deliberation has similar effects compared to traditional face-to-face deliberative events.

4.1 Procedures

The face-to-face deliberative poll was conducted on October 17, 2014 at a conference room of a Technological Education Institute in a Northwestern city in Greece. The face-to-face discussants were 93 students who volunteered to participate in the deliberation. The sample of the face-to-face deliberation consisted of 69.9 % females and 30.1 % males while the majority of the students were seniors (78.5 %). In addition, 86.2 % of the respondents spend less than one hour a day reading newspaper or internet articles about politics and watching political television programs.

Upon arrival, students completed an initial questionnaire. Then, the sample was given a written material that consisted of 19 pages and contained information about the issues under deliberation organized around pro and con arguments. Then each of three experts (a politician, an election expert and pollster, and a journalist) presented his opinions, engaged in dialogue with the other panelists and responded to the questions made by participants. Discussion was supervised by a moderator whose responsibility was to (a) make sure that the discussion proceeds in an orderly fashion, (b) address and guide the panelists (c) encourage audience participation, and (d) keep the discussion focused on the topic and within the allotted time. After the discussion, the sample was asked to complete the same initial questionnaire.

The online deliberation took place from December 30, 2014 to February 11, 2015. Participants of the experiment were again students of a Technological Education Institute in a Northwestern city of Greece. A total of 149 students, registered for the Public Opinion Polls course, agreed to participate in the project. It should be noted that participants were told in advance that they would be rewarded with extra credit for the course. Regarding the online sample, 81.9 % of the online discussants were females and 84.6 % were seniors. Furthermore, the majority of the online sample exhibited low involvement with politics since 62.4 % of the respondents spend less than one hour a day reading newspaper or internet articles about politics and watching political television programs.

In order to test whether the online sample was similar with the face-to-face, chi-square tests of independence were conducted and coefficient phi was calculated. Based on the results the online sample was significantly (p < 0.05) different compare to the offline in terms of gender ($\chi^2 = 4.685$, sig = 0.030, phi = 0.139), semester of attendance ($\chi^2 = 15.206$, sig = 0.030, phi = 0.251), and level of political involvement ($\chi^2 = 15.250$, sig = 0.030, phi = 0.254). However, based on the values of the phi coefficient the differences in the characteristics of the two samples appeared to be negligent.

The online experiment was conducted via the Wordpress software. Using the Wordpress tool a website was created specifically for the needs of the online deliberative project. Participants were required to create an account determining a username and a password. Students were instructed to set usernames using their real names and surnames. Moreover, students were asked to authenticate before accessing the deliberation materials and every time they accessed the platform.

At the beginning of the project students received an email that informed them to create an account on the website and answer a pre-deliberation questionnaire that was embedded in the platform. Afterwards participants were instructed to read the written material and watch a video that were posted on the website. The written material was the same as the one used in the face-to-face deliberation. Moreover, the online video included the recorded speeches delivered by the three experts of the face-to-face deliberative panel. The use of video helps "improving deliberative quality and making online mode more comparable with the face-to-face" [27, p. 192–193].

Then participants began to deliberate online with other participants by posting text messages about their views and comments. Note, that students could join the discussion from their home computers anytime at their own convenience. Thus, the online discussion was asynchronous in nature. Discussions were supervised by a moderator whose responsibility was to erase duplicate messages and respond to technical questions of participants. As in the face-to-face deliberation we wanted to minimize the influence of the moderator on the outcome of deliberation.

Students were also given the opportunity to formulate questions they would like to be answered by the three experts. These questions were relayed to the experts and their answers were posted on the deliberation website. Then students received an email which instructed them to read the answers of experts before completing the post-deliberation questionnaire.

4.2 Deliberation Topic and Experts

The subject of the face-to-face deliberative poll was "Political Public Opinion Polls". The subject matter for discussion included five main areas (1) reliability-accuracy of opinion polls, (2) data manipulation in public opinion polls by media organizations, pollsters and politicians, (3) use of public opinion polls by politicians in decision making process, (4) impact of polls on political participation, and (5) impact of polls on voting behavior. The deliberation topic was chosen bearing in mind that the participants were students.

The three experts were also carefully chosen and were comprised of a well known politician, a well reputed expert and pollster, and renowned journalist.

4.3 Questionnaire and Measurement of Opinions

The pre as well as the post deliberation questionnaire included 31 questions that measure the attitudes of participants around the five main issues about polls. Specifically, to measure participants' attitudes regarding the reliability-accuracy the first seven items (see Table 1) were used (e.g., polls always produce reliable results; a sample of 1000–1500 people can accurately represent the universe of potential voters). Opinions of respondents regarding the extent to which data in public opinion polls are manipulated by media organizations, pollsters and politicians were measured using seven items. Example of items are: Media organizations manipulate and publish selectively the results of opinion polls in order to exert influence on public opinion and when the clients of opinion polls are either parties or politicians then the chances of reporting results which favor them are increased. Participants' attitudes regarding the use of public opinion polls by politicians in policy making process were measured through seven items such as: politicians need surveys to pursue the right policies and politicians use polls to specify the top issues of concern to the electorate and set their political agendas. Perceived impact of polls on political participation was measured using five items (e.g., through polls citizens can make their voices heard and participate in the policy making process and polls create a more democratic society). Finally, perceived impact of polls on voting behavior of citizens were assessed through five items such as: polls affect undecided voters and help them vote and polls may lead people to abstain from voting since they believe that their vote wouldn't make a difference to the election outcome. Responses to all questions were elicited through five-item likert scales ranging from 1: Strongly Disagree to 5: Strongly Agree.

4.4 Results

In order to examine the effects of face-to-face as well as online deliberation on citizens' opinions regarding polls we checked the differences between pre to post deliberation attitudes of students using independent t-tests. Results of the tests are presented in Table 1 (Appendix A).

As Fig. 1 shows both modes of deliberation significantly affected a number of attitudes. Overall, in the face-to-face condition, 7 out of 31 attitude statements

Table 1. Direction of attitudes' shift and valence of impact across the five deliberation topics

Participants' attitudes about (number of statements)	Face-to-Face		Online	
	Direction of shifts (number of shifts)	Valence of impact	Direction of shifts (number of shifts)	Valence of impact
Reliability-accuracy of opinion polls (7)	Reinforce (1)	Positive	Reinforce (1)	Positive
Data manipulation in public opinion polls by media organizations, pollsters and politicians (7)	Opposite shift (1) –	Negative –	Reinforce (1) Opposite shift (5)	Positive Positive
Use of public opinion polls by politicians in decision making process (7)	Opposite shift (2) –	Positive –	Opposite shift (1) Reinforce (1)	Negative Positive
Impact of polls on political participation (5)	Opposite shift (2)	Negative	Reinforce (1)	Positive
Impact of polls on voting behavior (5)	Reinforce (1)	Negative	–	–

exhibited statistical significant changes (items A3, B1, C2, C3, D2, D3, E4) whereas in the online condition the corresponding number was 10 out of 31 (items A3, B1, B2, B3, B4, B5, B6, C1, C7, D2).

The discussion of the results is organized as follows. For each one of the five main issues, the exact attitude statements that exhibited significant changes are described, first for the face-to-face treatment and then for the online. Then, the direction of the significant changes is discussed. Direction refers to whether the deliberation reinforced respondents' opinions (higher mean values after the deliberation) or shifted opinions towards the opposite direction (lower mean values after the deliberation. Moreover, the changes are interpreted in terms of valence. In particular, valence refers to the qualitative outcomes of deliberation. A positive change means that respondents become more in favor about the reliability of polls and their impact on voters as well as exhibit higher levels of trust regarding the use of polls by politicians and media organizations. On the other hand a negative change suggests that respondents after the deliberation become skeptical and less in favor about the accuracy of polls and their use by politicians and media.

In regards to participants' opinions about the accuracy and reliability of opinion polls both modes produced quite similar results. Specifically, in both conditions after the deliberation, respondents were significantly more likely to agree than before (higher mean value after the deliberation) that "a sample of 1000–1500 people could accurately represent the universe of potential voters". Hence, the face-to-face mode of deliberation as well as the online reinforced participants' opinion regarding the representativeness of opinion polls.

As far as, participants' attitudes about data manipulation in public opinion polls by media organizations, pollsters and politicians' results suggest that online deliberation induced changes in more opinion statements (6 out of 7) than its face-to-face counterpart (1 out of 7). In the face-to-face condition, after the deliberation, respondents were significantly more likely to disagree than before (lower mean values) that "media

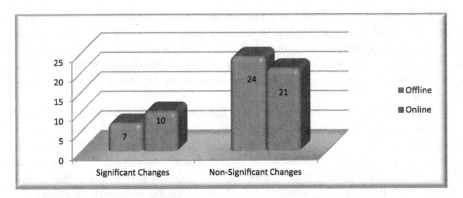

Fig. 1. Number of significant changes across the two modes of deliberation (offline versus online)

organizations most of the times fairly present and publish the results of opinion polls". Hence, in regards to citizens' attitudes about media presentation of polls, the offline mode shifted citizens' attitudes in the opposite direction from their initial attitudes causing more negative views about the mediatization of polls.

On the contrary, online deliberation produced contradictory results compared to the face-to-face mode. After the online deliberation, respondents were significantly more likely to agree than before (higher mean value after the deliberation) that "media organizations most of the times fairly present and publish the results of opinion polls". Hence, the online mode reinforced their opinions. In addition, after the online delib-eration, respondents were significantly more likely to disagree than before (lower mean values) that (1) "media organizations manipulate and publish selectively the results of opinion polls in order to satisfy the interests of their (sponsors)", (2) "media organi-zations manipulate and publish selectively the results of opinion polls in order to exert influence on public opinion", (3) "many polling organizations selectively report opinion polls results in order to influence public opinion in a certain direction", (4) "when the clients of opinion polls are either parties or politicians then the chances of reporting results which favor them are increased", (5) "results of opinion polls are manipulated by the political offices of parties or candidates in order to influence public opinion". In all of the above cases online deliberation changed citizens' attitudes towards the opposite direction from their initial opinion. No significant changes were found in citizens' attitudes on the above mentioned 5 attitude statements after the face-to-face deliberation. It can be argued that online deliberation changed participants' attitudes by suppressing their negative views about the misuse of polls by media, polling organizations and politicians. As a consequence, after the online deliberation, students became less skeptical to the general idea that polls were deliberatively manipulated by pollsters, media, and politicians in order to influence the public opinion. Thus, participants decreased their mistrust towards the use of polls by media and politicians after the online deliberation. The question still lingers why a shift in the opposite direction was observed in the online deliberation mode that was not observed in the offline mode. Without having all the information at our disposal, we could posit that online participants either didn't look at all the posted material or engaged in selective exposure in processing information and were persuaded by the most easily accessible information at hand (known by what social psychologists refer as availability bias).

Regarding the attitude statements about the use of public opinion polls by politicians in decision making process, the different modes of deliberation changed 2 out of 7 statements. However, they did not change the same attitude statements. After the face-to-face deliberation, respondents were significantly more likely to disagree than before (lower mean values) that "politicians and political parties use public opinion polls to assist them in the development of their election campaign strategies" and "election campaigns are dominated by public opinion polls". As a result the offline condition shifted participants' opinions in the opposite direction from their initial attitudes.

In a similar vein, participants in the online mode were significantly more likely to disagree than before (lower mean values) that "politicians need surveys to pursue the right policies". Hence, the online condition changed respondents' attitudes in the opposite direction from their initial opinions about the use of polls by politicians and made them less in favor about the need of politicians to use of surveys as an input in the policy making process. Furthermore, after the online deliberation, respondents were significantly more likely to agree than before (higher mean value after the deliberation) that "politicians use polls as a source of accurate information about the expectations and preferences of the electorate". This finding suggests that the online mode reinforced students' attitudes about the proper use of opinion polls by politicians and political parties.

The deliberative effect of the two experimental conditions was found to be different in the number (offline: 2 out of 5 statements, online: 1 out of 5 statements) and pattern of changes in regards to citizens' attitudes about the impact of polls on political participation. In the face-to-face mode, after the deliberation, participants were significantly more likely to disagree than before (lower mean values) that "opinion polls facilitate a better communication between citizens and politicians" and "opinion polls serve as a communication channel between citizens and government and an indirect form of public participation". Thus, face-to-face deliberation changed respondents' attitudes in the opposite direction compared to their pre-deliberation attitudes and made them hold more negative views about the impact of polls on citizens-government communication. On the contrary, the online setting reinforced participants' attitudes about the positive role of polls on citizens' participation, since students were significantly more likely to agree than before (higher mean value after the deliberation) that "opinion polls facilitate a better communication between citizens and politicians". This difference found in the outcome of the two deliberations could be attributed to the asynchronous nature of the online condition. Specifically, it can be argued that online discussants might be more vulnerable to distractions by external cues which limit their attention span and their time spent on in-depth reading of the online arguments. As a consequence, online discussants might use heuristics (mental shortcuts) during their decision making by examining fewer cues and alternatives or integrating less information. This phenomenon might not be elicited in the offline condition where participants are more involved in the process due the live and synchronous nature of the setting. Thus, they might process in greater extent counterarguments and opposite views before making their post-deliberation judgments.

Lastly, only the face-to-face mode of deliberation caused changes in students' attitudes about the impact of polls on voting behavior (1 out of 5 statements). Specifically, after the offline deliberation, respondents were significantly more likely to agree than before (higher mean value after the deliberation) that "polls may lead people to abstain from voting out of certainty that their candidate or party would win". Again, the face-to-face setting reinforced students' negative views about the de-motivating effect of polls during elections.

5 Conclusion

The purpose of the present study was to test whether there are differences in the effects between face-to-face and computer-mediated deliberation on respondents' attitudes about opinion polls. Towards this end two real experiments were conducted. Results suggest that both modes of deliberation had an effect on participants as they induced changes in their opinions. Table 2 summarizes the changes found in both face-to-face as well online deliberations in terms of direction and valence of their impact on participants' attitudes about the five topics of deliberation.

Several fruitful insights could be made from our findings. First, the online deliberation proved to be more effective since it changed more attitudes compared to its face-to-face counterpart. This finding could be attributed to the fact that participants were young students who were keen on interacting with others via computers. Thus, an online environment can be regarded as a viable channel for deliberation, just like face-to-face settings.

Second, both face-to face as well as online deliberation caused more shifts in attitudes in the opposite direction than reinforcements of initial attitudes. This result indicates that the two modes did not induce group polarization. It is herein suggested that a computer-mediated environment could reduce the phenomenon of group polarization found in prior deliberation studies, thus relaxing the mechanism of social comparison where citizens tend to conform to the views of the majority. Moreover, even though both samples were largely homogeneous and consisted of like-minded respondents, results suggest that deliberators in both modes were exposed to competing views and a diversity of perspectives. Arguably, computer-mediated environments can deliver on the promise of an efficient deliberation which is the exchange of different viewpoints and arguments.

Third, the two deliberative conditions were quite different in regards to the valence of their impact on attitudes. Specifically, after face-to-face deliberation, participants held more negative views about the mediatization of polls and the impact of polls on citizens-government communication as well as on voting behavior. At the same time, face-to-face deliberation induced respondents to become more in favor of the accuracy and reliability of polls and the use of polls by politicians and parties during election campaigns. However, it should be noted that the negative impact of the face-to-face deliberation was found in more attitude statements (4 out of 7).

On the contrary, the effect of online deliberation on citizens' attitudes was mostly positive (9 out of 10). Specifically, after the computer-mediated deliberation, participants held more positive views about the accuracy and reliability of polls while they decreased their negative opinions about the relationship among pollsters, media, and politicians. This difference in the valence of impact on participants' attitudes might indicate that the mode of deliberation (i.e., face-to-face, online) could be an important factor that contributes to the outcome of deliberation. The aforementioned effects of deliberations on citizens' attitudes should be interpreted with care since the outcomes of deliberation are highly context specific depending on the issue under discussion [24].

In addition, it should be noted that we took special care so as to minimize the bias caused by the differences in several aspects of the two experimental conditions. For example, the briefing materials as well as the panel experts were identical in both deliberations. However, the two experiments differed in their duration as well as the number and the content of questions asked by participants during the deliberation. Specifically, online participants asked far more questions the three experts compared to their face-to-face counterparts. Moreover, the two samples differed in a small degree in regards to the gender, the semester of attendance and their level of political involvement. Another experimental condition that might impose bias to our results is the non-use of small group discussions. Based on the aforementioned, the findings of the study should be interpreted with care.

Our face-to-face and online projects differ from other deliberation experiments. Moreover, the mode of the online deliberation was asynchronous while the samples used in our deliberations were not representative since we relied on students. Another differential feature of our study is that we did not use control groups in order to compare attitudes of participants after deliberations with attitudes of respondents who did not participate in the deliberations.

Future research could focus on the impact of different aspects of online deliberation on attitude change. For example, by surveying participants during different moments of virtual deliberation (i.e., after reading the written material, after online discussion, after reading experts' answers) fruitful insights could be yielded about which specific feature of deliberation causes changes in opinions.

Acknowledgment. This research has been co-financed by the European Union (European Social Fund – ESF) and Greek national funds through the Operational Program "Education and Lifelong Learning" of the National Strategic Reference Framework (NSRF) - Research Funding Program: ARCHIMEDES III. Investing in knowledge society through the European Social Fund.

Appendix A

Table 2. Effects of face-to-face and online deliberation

	Pre-deliberation mean values		Post-deliberation mean values		T-value/significance	
	Offline	Online	Offline	Online	Offline	Online
A. Reliability-accuracy of opinion polls						
1. In general, the process of polling as conducted in Greece is reliable	2.88	3.06	2.83	3.04	0.542/ 0.589	0.177/ 0.860
2. Polls always produce reliable results	2.44	2.62	2.38	2.61	0.560/ 0.577	0.144/ 0.886
3. A sample of 1000–1500 people can accurately represent the universe of potential voters	2.20	2.20	2.49	2.52	−2.753/ 0.007*	−2.905/ 0.004*
4. Polls are an accurate snapshot of public opinions at a particular point in time	3.18	3.14	3.15	3.28	0.276/ 0.783	−1.317/ 0.189
5. Answers given by respondents in polls reflect their true beliefs	2.38	2.21	2.19	2.24	1.719/ 0.089	−0.277/ 0.782
6. Respondents will give their answers based on what they believe is the most socially acceptable/favorable or the most popular, rather than their true opinions	3.19	3.25	3.08	3.22	0.920/ 0.360	0.339/ 0.735
7. Respondent have the particular knowledge required to answer the questions of opinion polls	2.56	2.38	2.64	2.48	−0.776/ 0.440	−1.000/ 0.318
B. Data manipulation in public opinion polls by media organizations, pollsters and politicians						
1. Media organizations most of the times fairly present and publish the results of opinion polls	2.83	2.63	2.60	2.87	2.497/ 0.014*	−2.518/ 0.012*
2. Media organizations manipulate and publish selectively the results of opinion polls in order to satisfy the interests of their (sponsors)	3.66	3.86	3.61	3.69	0.540/ 0.590	2.029/ 0.043*
3. Media organizations manipulate and publish selectively the results of opinion polls in order to exert influence on public opinion	3.72	3.77	3.69	3.48	0.235/ 0.815	3.186/ 0.002*
4. Many polling organizations selectively report opinion polls results in order to influence public opinion in a certain direction	3.66	3.81	3.79	3.63	−1.365/ 0.176	2.037/ 0.043*
5. When the clients of opinion polls are either parties or politicians, then the chances of reporting results which favor them are increased	3.76	3.94	3.69	3.73	0.726/ 0.470	2.372/ 0.018*
6. Results of opinion polls are manipulated by the political offices of parties or candidates in order to influence public opinion	3.49	3.56	3.52	3.33	−0.336/ 0.738	2.421/ 0.016*
7. Polls reported often conceal the real opinion of respondents.	3.23	3.14	3.43	3.00	−1.751/ 0.083	1.526/ 0.128

(*Continued*)

Table 2. (*Continued*)

	Pre-deliberation mean values		Post-deliberation mean values		T-value/significance	
	Offline	Online	Offline	Online	Offline	Online
C. Use of public opinion polls by politicians in decision making process						
1. Politicians need surveys to pursue the right policies	3.50	3.65	3.39	3.43	1.043/ 0.300	2.450/ 0.015*
2. Politicians and political parties use public opinion polls to assist them to the development of their election campaign strategies	3.90	3.79	3.51	3.74	4.340/ 0.000*	0.537/ 0.592
3. Election campaigns are dominated by public opinion polls	3.75	3.60	3.37	3.76	3.556/ 0.001*	−1.743/ 0.082
4. Politicians use polls to specify the top issues which concern the electorate and set their political agendas	3.49	3.55	3.42	3.38	0.617/ 0.539	1.752/ 0.081
5. Politicians use polls to persuade the public for or against a certain political position	3.80	3.90	3.59	3.77	1.973/ 0.052	1.692/ 0.106
6. Politicians use polls to make the right political decisions	2.63	2.59	2.74	2.64	0.971/ 0.334	−0.523/ 0.601
7. Politicians use polls as a source of accurate information about the expectations and preferences of the electorate	3.18	3.03	3.00	3.30	1.495/ 0.138	−2.634/ 0.009*
D. Impact of polls on political participation						
1. Polls provide a way for citizens to stay informed about the top political issues and the opinions of the public towards them	3.55	3.51	3.37	3.50	1.804/ 0.075	0.152/ 0.879
2. Opinion polls facilitate a better communication between citizens and politicians	3.04	3.10	2.84	3.32	2.195/ 0.031*	−2.314/ 0.021*
3. Opinion polls serve as a communication channel between citizens and government and an indirect form of public participation	3.22	3.26	3.02	3.36	2.273/ 0.025*	−0.887/ 0.376
4. Polls create a more democratic society	3.07	3.00	3.06	3.13	0.118/ 0.906	−1.197/ 0.232
5. Through polls citizens can make their voices heard and participate in the policy making process	2.87	3.00	3.47	3.16	−1.325/ 0.189	−1.424/ 0.156
E. Impact of polls on voting behavior						
1. Results of election polls may affect the voting behavior of the public	3.74	3.79	3.73	3.88	0.127/ 0.899	−1.003/ 0.317
2. Polls affect undecided voters and help them vote	3.64	3.60	3.53	3.55	1.079/ 0.283	0.488/ 0.626
3. Polls may lead people to not vote for the party or candidate that appears to be losing the elections	3.37	3.45	3.47	3.42	−1.000/ 0.320	0.253/ 0.800
4. Polls may lead people to not vote for the party or candidate that appears to be winning the elections	3.24	3.25	3.50	3.39	−2.345/ 0.021*	−1.303/ 0.194
5. Polls may lead people to abstain from voting since they believe that their vote will not make a difference to the election outcome	3.34	3.46	3.44	3.48	0.791/ 0.431	−0.125/ 0.901

*Significant at the $p < 0.05$ level.

References

1. Page, B.I.: Who Deliberates?: Mass Media in Modern Democracy. University of Chicago Press, Chicago (1996)
2. Gastil, J.: Is face-to-face citizen deliberation a luxury or a necessity? Polit. Commun. **17**(4), 357–361 (2000)
3. Chambers, S.: Rhetoric and the public sphere: has deliberative democracy abandoned mass democracy?. Polit. Theory (2009). doi:10.1177/0090591709332336
4. Goodin, R.E., Dryzek, J.S.: Deliberative impacts: the macro-political uptake of mini-publics. Polit. Soc. **34**(2), 219–244 (2006)
5. Niemeyer, S.: The emancipatory effect of deliberation: empirical lessons from mini-publics. Polit. Soc. **39**(1), 103–140 (2011)
6. Wright, S., Street, J.: Democracy, deliberation and design: the case of online discussion forums. New Media Soc. **9**(5), 849–869 (2007)
7. Graham, T., Witschge, T.: In search of online deliberation: towards a new method for examining the quality of online discussions. Commun.-Sankt Augustin Berlin **28**(2), 173–204 (2003)
8. Zhou, X., Chan, Y.Y., Peng, Z.M.: Deliberativeness of online political discussion: a content analysis of the Guangzhou daily website. Journalism Stud. **9**(5), 759–770 (2008)
9. Mitra, A.: Marginal voices in cyberspace. New Media Soc. **3**(1), 29–48 (2001)
10. Janssen, D., Kies, R.: Online forums and deliberative democracy. Acta Política **40**(3), 317–335 (2004)
11. Papacharissi, Z.: Democracy online: civility, politeness, and the democratic potential of online political discussion groups. New Media Soc. **6**(2), 259 283 (2004)
12. Albrecht, S.: Whose voice is heard in online deliberation?: A study of participation and representation in political debates on the internet. Inf. Commun. Soc. **9**(1), 62–82 (2006)
13. Loveland, M.T., Popescu, D.: Democracy on the web: assessing the deliberative qualities of internet forums. Inf. Commun. Soc. **14**(5), 684–703 (2011)
14. Wilhelm, A.G.: Virtual sounding boards: how deliberative is on-line political discussion? Inf. Commun. Soc. **1**(3), 313–338 (1998)
15. Wright, S.: Politics as usual? Revolution, normalization and a new agenda for online deliberation. New Media Soc. **14**(2), 244–261 (2012)
16. Dahlberg, L.: The internet and democratic discourse: exploring the prospects of online deliberative forums extending the public sphere. Inf. Commun. Soc. **4**(4), 615–633 (2001)
17. Chambers, S.: Reasonable Democracy: Jürgen Habermas and the Politics of Discourse. Cornell University Press, Ithaca (1996)
18. Chambers, S.: Deliberative democratic theory. Annu. Rev. Polit. Sci. **6**(1), 307–326 (2003)
19. Iyengar, S., Luskin, R. C., Fishkin, J. S.: Facilitating informed public opinion: evidence from face-to-face and on-line deliberative polls. In: Annual Meeting of the American Political Science Association. Philadelphia (2003)
20. Rhee, J.W., Kim, E.: Deliberation on the net: lessons from a field experiment. In: Davies, T., Gangadharan, S.P. (eds.) Online Deliberation: Design, Research, and Practice, pp. 223–232. CSLI Publications, Stanford (2009)
21. Strandberg, K., Grönlund, K.: Online deliberation and its outcome—evidence from the virtual polity experiment. J. Inf. Technol. Polit. **9**(2), 167–184 (2012)
22. Price, V.: Citizens deliberating online: theory and some evidence. In: Davies, T., Noveck, B.S. (eds.) Online Deliberation: Research and Practice, pp. 37–58. Chicago University Press, Chicago (2006)

23. Luskin, R.C., Fishkin, J.S., Iyengar, S.: Considered opinions on U.S. foreign policy: face-to-face versus online deliberative polling. In: International Communication Association, New Orleans, LA (2004)
24. Min, S.J.: Online vs. face-to-face deliberation: effects on civic engagement. J. Comput. Mediated Commun. 12(4), 1369–1387 (2007)
25. Tucey, C.B.: Online vs. face-to-face deliberation on the global warming and stem cell issues. In: Annual Meeting of the Western Political Science Association, San Francisco (2010)
26. Muhlberger, P.: Attitude change in face-to-face and online political deliberation: conformity, information, or perspective taking?. In: Annual Meeting of the American Political Science Association, Washington, DC (2005)
27. Grönlund, K., Strandberg, K., Himmelroos, S.: The challenge of deliberative democracy online–a comparison of face-to-face and virtual experiments in citizen deliberation. Inf. Polity 14(3), 187–201 (2009)
28. Delli-Carpini, M.X., Cook, F.L., Jacobs, L.R.: Public deliberation, discursive participation, and citizen engagement: a review of the empirical literature. Annu. Rev. Polit. Sci. 7, 315–344 (2004)

A Privacy-Friendly Method to Reward Participants of Online-Surveys

Michael Herfert, Benjamin Lange, Annika Selzer$^{(\boxtimes)}$, and Ulrich Waldmann

Fraunhofer Institute for Secure Information Technology SIT, Rheinstraße 75,
64295 Darmstadt, Germany
{michael.herfert,benjamin.lange,annika.selzer,
ulrich.waldmann}@sit.fraunhofer.de
http://www.sit.fraunhofer.de

Abstract. Whoever conducts a survey usually wants a large number of participants in order to attain meaningful results. A method to increase the motivation of potential participants is offering a prize that is awarded to one of them. For that purpose the pollster usually collects the E-mail addresses or other personal data of the participants, enabling him to notify the winner. Collecting the participant's personal data may, however, conflict with the potential participant's privacy interests as well as the pollster's concern about dishonest answers participants may give to gain favor. Therefore, this paper presents solutions that enable the pollster to carry out a survey in an anonymous way while only collecting the winner's personal data. If the prize is a virtual good, then even the winner's identity is concealed.

Keywords: Data protection · Data reduction · Online survey · Privacy · Blind signatures · Scope-exclusive pseudonyms · Zero-knowledge proofs

1 Necessity for Privacy-Friendly Prizes

Surveys are often advertised as anonymous. On the other hand, pollsters usually want to have a large number of participants in order to attain meaningful results. Therefore, they seek to increase the potential participants motivation by giving away a prize. For that purpose the pollster usually collects participants E-mail addresses or other personal data to be able to send a winning notification to the prize-winner. Collecting the participants personal data may, however, remove[1] the anonymity of the survey and in doing so may conflict with potential participants privacy interests: If the potential participant holds a high degree of anonymity while participating in the survey, but loses this anonymity if he wants to win the prize, the motivating effect of the prize might be lost completely.

Therefore, this paper presents a solution that enables the pollster to award a prize in a privacy-friendly way. After the legal and technical requirements as

---

[1] Whether the anonymity is withdrawn or can be withdrawn depends on the form of data collection.

© Springer International Publishing Switzerland 2015
S.K. Katsikas and A.B. Sideridis (Eds.): E-Democracy 2015, CCIS 570, pp. 33–47, 2015.
DOI: 10.1007/978-3-319-27164-4_3

well as the objectives of the privacy-friendly solution have been introduced, a solution for a *closed user group* is presented. A closed user group is a group where the maximum number and identities of participants are known and limited by the pollster prior to the survey. An example of a closed user group is the set of employees of a company with its management being the pollster. Another example is the closed group of registered participants of a training course with the course organizer asking for anonymous feedback. After the description of the closed user group solution, a solution for *open user groups* will be described. An open user group is a group where the maximum number of participants is not known prior to the survey and where everybody is free to join the survey. Examples are common surveys via Internet, where an organizer could hardly identify participants without using an expensive and probably inadequate method. In addition to describing solutions for the two user groups, we will detail different variants of the solutions mentioned. Furthermore the experience with a privacy-friendly, paper-based variant will be shared. The paper ends with a description of the related work and a summary. We do not introduce new cryptographic primitives in this paper, we simply use the defined ones, such as blind signatures, scope-exclusive pseudonyms (aka. domain specific pseudonyms), and zero-knowledge proofs [3, 4, 10].

2   Legal Requirements

To protect all individuals, the collection and processing of personal data in Europe is regulated under statutory provisions on privacy, such as the Data Protection Directive 95/46/EC and the Directive on Privacy and Electronic Communications 2002/58/EC.[2] Personal data is any information concerning the personal or material circumstances of an identifiable individual, e.g. names, E-mail addresses and telephone numbers.

One of the basic principles of privacy is processing as little personal data as possible and converting personal data into pseudonymous or anonymous data whenever possible. Pseudonymized data is personal data where the identifying characteristics have been replaced with a label in order to preclude identification of the data subject or to render such identification substantially difficult. Pseudonymized data is normally protected by the directives mentioned above, since it is usually possible to restore personal references. In contrast, anonymized

---

[2] These Directives address the member states of the European Union and must be transposed into internal law. The following examples are based on the provisions of the Federal Data Protection Act, which transposes the regulations of the Directive 95/46/EC to German law. Since the transposition into internal law is fairly similar within Europe, one example of transposition is considered sufficiant for this paper. Please note, that it is planned to replace the mentioned Directive with a European General Data Protection Regulation. In contrast to European Directives, European Regulations do not need to be transposed into internal law. The draft can be found at http://ec.europa.eu/justice/data-protection/document/review2012/com_2012_11_en.pdf.

data is personal data that has been modified so that the information concerning personal circumstances can no longer be attributed to an individual who has been identified or is identifiable. The collection and processing of anonymized data is not protected by statutory provisions concerning privacy, since this data is considered the opposite of personal data.[3]

If an organization wants to collect and process personal data, the following principles need to be ensured:

- The processing of personal data shall be admissible only if permitted or prescribed by a statutory provision or if the data subject has consented.[4]
- The processing of personal data is allowed only for lawful purposes. The particular purpose must be determined in advance and cannot be changed later. Personal data which is not needed to fulfill the lawful purpose must not be processed.
- Personal data are to be processed in accordance with the aim of processing as little personal data as possible. In particular, personal data are to be pseudonymized or rendered anonymous as far as possible and deleted when they are not needed anymore to fulfill the lawful purpose they were collected for.[5]
- Organizations processing personal data either on their own behalf or on behalf of others shall take technical and organizational measures. Measures shall be required only if the effort involved is reasonable in relation to the desired level of protection.[6]
- Organizations processing personal data need to concede rights – such as provision of information, correction and erasure of data – to the data subjects.[7]

Consistently and ideally, the solution to be defined would collect no personal data at all. If this is not feasible for various reasons, e.g. the prize has to be delivered to a physical address, then only as little personal data as required for the specific purpose shall be collected. This may mean that only the winner would submit some personal data, which would be deleted immediately after use.

3 Objectives and Functional Requirements

The expectations for a privacy-friendly solution are similar to the general election principles (free, equal, secret, general and direct suffrage, known procedure) and can be summarized as follows:[8]

---

[3] Compare Sect. 3 I, VI, VIa of the Federal Data Protection Act.
[4] Compare Sect. 4 of the Federal Data Protection Act.
[5] Compare Sect. 3a of the Federal Data Protection Act.
[6] Compare Sect. 9 of the Federal Data Protection Act.
[7] Compare Sects. 19–21 and 33–35 of the Federal Data Protection Act.
[8] Cf. Common Criteria Protection Profile BSI-PP-0037, "Basic set of security requirements for Online Voting Products", https://www.bsi.bund.de/SharedDocs/Downloads/DE/BSI/Zertifizierung/ReportePP/pp0037b_engl_pdf.

Req-A **Free:** Nobody shall be forced to participate in the survey and the corresponding selection of the winner. The methods should provide anonymity and non-traceability in terms of whether a potential participant actually has or has not participated. This requirement might be optional, as even political elections commonly include an identity check of actual voters by a local election committee.

Req-B **Equal:** Each participant shall participate only once in both the survey and selection of the winner.

Req-C **Secret:** The survey must not include identification data of the participants. It shall not be possible to establish a link between the identity of the participant and his survey answers – even in the case of the winner.

Req-D **General:** No one should be excluded from participation. Unlike general elections our solution is only open to Internet users as the technical implementation requires a regular computer with Internet access. Nevertheless the implementation should not require special hardware (e.g. a chip card reader), high communication bandwidth, or computational complexity.

Req-E **Direct:** The survey answers and notification of the winner shall be directly transferred and protected from theft or manipulation.

Req-F **Known procedure:** The methods, algorithms, and selection process shall be transparent and should be openly verifiable even without in-depth expert knowledge.

The participant's anonymity according to Req-C and Req-D may be impaired by the fact that each communication via Internet includes the transfer of IP addresses and, therefore, may leave information to identify and track users. However, in case of a private Internet user, the transmitted IP data usually just reveals the Internet service provider (ISP) involved. Even in this case, the ISP might be asked by public authorities to reveal addresses of individual subscribers. Users can resort to anonymous proxies in order to prevent technical traces from being spread on the Internet. But the proxy providers may still log addresses. Onion routing was developed to realize effective anonymous communication by using constantly changing routes via encrypted proxy servers.[9] This paper does not address technical communication traces in the Internet but assumes that this problem can be solved.

4   Closed User Groups

In this section we describe a privacy-friendly method of undertaking an online survey that fulfills the requirements stated above. We concentrate on the case of a closed user group.[10] Thus, we assume that there is a fixed group of potential participants whose identities are known to the pollster. The identity data of a

---

[9] Tor is an example of a network software that anonymizes communication data based on onion routing, see: www.torproject.org.

[10] A generalization of this solution for an open user group is given in the next section.

user known by the pollster will be denoted as *id*. First we will provide a high-level description of our solution from a user's perspective. Afterwards, we will also give a more detailed technical description.

4.1   High-Level Description

Our solution is based on the idea of using special software for all interactions between a participant and the pollster. This software should be open source and freely available. Alternatively, it may be software that has been evaluated by a renowned and trusted evaluator. This gives participants good reasons to trust in the correct functionality and that the software does not contain any backdoor.[11] Since we are interested in solutions for a big number of surveys (e.g. regularly conducted surveys for employees of a company) installing a piece of software would be no major obstacle.[12] In the best-case scenario, there would be a widely used standard software for all kinds of privacy-friendly surveys that can be freely downloaded and used more than once. In the following description, we assume the participant interacts with the pollster using a piece of software. The procedure for participating in a survey consists of the following five steps:

The procedure for participating in a survey consists of the following five steps:

Step 1.   A potential user with identity *id* downloads the survey software from an independent source (e.g. research institute) or in the form of an open source tool provided by the pollster. After installing the software, the user registers using his identity *id*. This data is used to assure that only members of the closed group participate in the survey. In return, the user receives a blinded token T_1 that cannot be forged. The token is stored in the software and used to grant a participant access to the online survey. It is central to our solution that the token T_1 itself is not known to the pollster. This is achieved by cryptographic means using the concept of blind signatures [12]. Blind signatures ensure that the pollster can only see and deliver a "blinded" form of the token, while only the user can extract the real token. Intuitively speaking, the pollster embosses a sealed envelope without knowing the content, while only the user can extract the embossed piece of paper inside the envelope.[13] By using this procedure, the token only known by the user uncouples the eligibility to participate from the participant's identity.

Step 2.   If a user possesses a valid token T_1, he will be allowed to submit his survey answers. After submitting the survey answers, the participant receives another blinded token T_2 in return that is not known to the pollster.

---

[11] Of course this would also include a possibility to check the integrity of the downloaded software by using digital fingerprints etc.

[12] In other cases there might be better options like browser-based solutions (e.g. browser applets or java-script based functionality), since users could not be willing to install a software for participating in a single survey.

[13] See Sect. 4.2 for a more technical description.

Nobody can forge this token, and it can only be issued by the pollster. This token serves as a receipt for completed survey participation.

Step 3. If a participant chooses to take part in the random selection to win a prize, he (via the software) sends his token T_2 to the pollster. In turn he receives a picture (showing for example the Eiffel Tower) with a super-imposed visible number n. The pollster ensures that each participant has a different picture and that all superimposed numbers are different too. The pollster stores each link between a token T_2, the corresponding picture and superimposed number.

Step 4. The pollster randomly draws one T_2 token as the winner token out of the represented T_2 tokens. The pollster publishes the corresponding winner's picture but without the superimposed number.

Step 5. The winner discovers that his picture is the winner's picture. He reports this to the pollster and proves he is the winner by sharing his knowledge of the correct superimposed number. To avoid confusion, the pollster accepts only the first submitter of the correct number if the winner has – knowingly or unknowingly – shared the superimposed number with others.[14] The pollster gives the winner the prize. The winner may need to provide some personal data so that the pollster can give him the prize (Fig. 1).

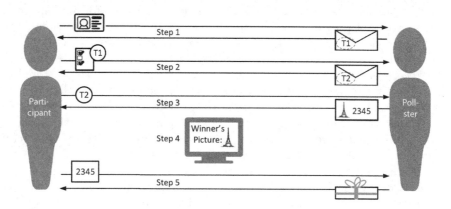

Fig. 1. Steps from the perspective of a winning participant

The first step can be seen as the "registration step" to give members of the group access to the online survey. Step 2 is the core of the procedure and concerned with anonymously submitting the survey. Steps 3–5 deal with the random selection and distribution of the prize.

---

[14] This risk can be avoided by the terms and conditions of the survey, e.g. "Only the first submitter of the winning raffle ticket wins the prize." Generally, setting terms and conditions for a raffle is highly recommended in order to inform possible participants about their eligibility, the time frame of the raffle, and a description of the prize.

4.2   Technical Description

We now give a technical description of the procedure described above and show that all requirements stated in Sect. 3 are fulfilled. Obviously, the requirements of free participation (Req-A) and the procedure (Req-F) are fulfilled, since we assume there will be free user interaction with the software and the software is reliable. Thus, we concentrate on the remaining requirements. Since Steps 4–5 are designed in a straight forward manner, we will only give a detailed description of Steps 1–3. These steps are the core of our solution to achieve the objectives stated above. The basic idea of Steps 1–3 is to separate the identity id known to the pollster, the survey submitted (which will be denoted as S in the following) and the lot used for random selection of a winner (consisting of a picture P with superimposed number n) cannot be linked together. This is achieved as follows (see Fig. 2):

Step	Participant		Pollster
1		$\xrightarrow{\quad id \quad}$	checks id
	extracts token T_1	$\xleftarrow{\text{blinded token } \tilde{T_1}}$	
2		$\xrightarrow{T_1,\ \text{survey } S}$	checks T_1, obtains S
	extracts token T_2	$\xleftarrow{\text{blinded token } \tilde{T_2}}$	
3		$\xrightarrow{\quad T_2 \quad}$	checks T_2
	obtains P, n	$\xleftarrow{\text{picture } P, \text{ serial number } n}$	

Fig. 2. Procedure for Steps 1–3 in closed groups

In Step 1 the user's identity id is replaced by a token T_1 that does not reveal any personal data. It is therefore essential that the pollster does not learn anything about the token T_1 issued to the participant. To achieve this, we use the technique of blind signatures (see e.g. [11,15] for details). The concept of blind signatures makes it possible that the given user information can be digitally signed by an entity (e.g. the pollster) without revealing this information. In our case, the survey software can generate a unique serial number m for the participant. Subsequently, it will request a digital signature on m from the pollster that will function as token T_1. The pollster blindly signs the serial number by a blind signature $\tilde{T_1}$ without learning m or the actual signature T_1. The user can extract T_1 from the blind signature $\tilde{T_1}$. This ensures that only the user knows his token T_1 and that T_1 cannot be linked to his id (Req-C).

In Step 2 the participant reveals his token T_1 to the pollster to gain access to the online survey. Since showing the same token multiple times can be detected by the pollster, this aims to ensures that every potential participant can only participate once (Req-B). After submitting the survey, the participant obtains another token T_2 by way of blind signatures (similar to Step 1). Thus the submitted cannot be linked to the identity of the user (Req-C).

In Step 3 the participant reveals his token T_2 to the pollster, ensuring that every user can participate in the random selection only once (Req-B). In return the participant receives a picture P with a superimposed serial number n. The serial number has to be chosen large enough that the probability of a cheater trying to guess the winning number is sufficiently small. The number, together with the blindly issued token T_2, makes it possible that the winner's identity cannot be linked to his survey answers (Req-C). It also aims to ensure that the notification of the winner is protected from theft or manipulation (Req-E).

5 Open User Groups

5.1 Introducing an Identity Provider

In an open user group, the identities of the potential participants are not known in advance. Therefore, the challenge is avoiding one user submitting multiple opinions. We must find an identity which is in a one-to-one relation to the user. An E-mail address is unique to a user, but a user may have multiple E-mail addresses; thus, an E-mail address is not sufficient.

A national government agency can act as an appropriate identity provider if it issues ID cards that support an electronic authentication mechanism. This is a very secure solution, because the government guarantees the one-to-one relation. Facebook is another example of an identity provider. By using the *Facebook connect* mechanism, it is possible to rely on the Facebook account of a user. This variant is less secure, because a person may have more than one account. Facebook estimated in June 2012 that 4.8 % of all accounts are made by users with multiple accounts.[15] On the other hand, Facebook has more than 1 billion users. This makes Facebook a suitable identity provider for many surveys. These are just two examples for identity providers. Of course using an identity provider has the drawback that the identity provider learns about someones interest to participate in a survey. But since we are mainly interested in solutions for more than a single survey (e.g. regularly conducted online surveys conducted by one or more agency), this gain of information is negligible. We stress, that in case of a large number of surveys the identity provider only learns about the *interest* of a person to participate in one or more of these surveys.

In the following section, we assume that an appropriate identity provider has been selected. The idea for an open user group is that the pollster issues a certain number of blinded tokens all at once. For that, Step 1 as defined in Sect. 4.2 will be replaced by Step 1' as follows (Fig. 3):

---

[15] https://www.sec.gov/Archives/edgar/data/1326801/000119312512325997/d371464 d10q.htm.

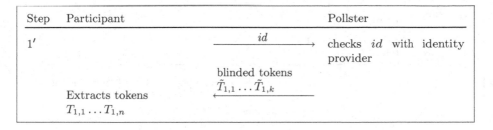

Fig. 3. Replacement for Step 1 (cf. Fig. 2) if an identity provider is involved

1′ The participant sends his *id*, which can be verified by the pollster in co-operation with the identity provider. The pollster responds by sending k blinded tokens.

For every survey the user wants to take, he sends the appropriate token $\tilde{T}_{1,i}$ in Step 2.

As an example, if a potential participant sees that a pollster advertises 50 surveys on his website, three of which are in his interest, he can ask the pollster for permission to join all the surveys. The pollster then registers the participant so that he cannot ask to join the same surveys again. He then hands out 50 blinded tokens to the participant, and each token is assigned to a specific survey. Following this step, the participant hands in three questionnaires by using the three relevant tokens. Since the tokens are blinded, the pollster does not know if the participant joined any of the 50 surveys.

The number of tokens issued can be adapted to the number of ongoing surveys in order to provide a high degree of privacy.

By using these sets of tokens, the pollster – in the present as well as in the future – learns that a potential participant, identified by his *id*, is interested in joining one or more surveys. However, he will not learn whether or not the potential participant actually used his tokens to join a survey, neither will he be able to connect the participation of one survey with the participation of another survey.

5.2   Introducing a Trustee

The drawback of the solution above is that the pollster may learn something about the interests of the user. To avoid this, we now define, in addition to the identity provider, the role of a *trustee* which issues *survey credentials* as described below. A survey credential is a token that enables a user to participate in surveys.

The trustee issues exactly one survey credential per person. The pollster must trust that this is really true. The system works as follows (Fig. 4):

Step A. The user generates a private cryptographic key and a commitment to this key. A key is a number or a tuple of numbers that is later used to derive pseudonyms. A commitment is a number or a tuple of numbers which documents that the user owns the private key without revealing

Step	Participant		Trustee
A	Generates *private key* and *commitment*		
B		$\xrightarrow{\text{id, commitment}}$	checks *id* with identity provider
		$\xleftarrow{\text{survey credential}}$	

Fig. 4. Protocol between participant and trustee.

the private key. A very simple example for a commitment to a number x is the hash value of x. The commitments used in our scheme are more complex but not detailed here[16] (see [3,4,10]).

Step B. The user sends the commitment to the trustee. He uses an identity mechanism as defined by the identity provider. The trustee responds by sending a *survey credential*. This is a cryptographic object which certifies that this user has asked for participation in surveys.

These steps have to be done once in the user's lifetime.

To participate to a concrete survey, user and pollster execute Step 1″, as defined below (Fig. 5), which is a modification of Step 1 as defined for closed user groups in Sect. 4.2.

Step	Participant		Pollster
1″		$\xleftarrow{\text{domain id}}$	publishes *domain id*
	Calculates *domain specific pseudonym* and *domain credential*	$\xrightarrow{\text{domain credential}}$	verifies credential
	Extracts token T_1	$\xleftarrow{\text{blinded token } \tilde{T}_1}$	

Fig. 5. Replacement for Step 1 (cf. Fig. 2) if a trustee is involved

1″ The pollster publishes a *domain identifier*. This is a string which is unique for this survey. For example, it may be a URL containing a domain which is under the pollster's control. The participant receives the domain identifier and constructs a *domain specific pseudonym*. This is a number which is calculated from the domain identifier and the user's private key. After that he

---

[16] As stated in Sect. 1 we do not introduce new cryptographic primitives in this paper, we simply use the ones defined.

creates a *domain credential*. This is a cryptographic object which says "this token has been made for the mentioned domain identifier and the owner of this token owns a survey credential". The user sends the *domain credential*. The pollster verifies this token in an interactive *Zero Knowledge Proof*, i.e. the user proves the correctness of the token based on his private key and survey credential without revealing either of these elements. Finally, the pollster sends the first blinded token $\tilde{T}_1$.

The forthcoming steps are identical to the closed user group scenario.

If the user tries to calculate a second domain credential, the pollster will detect this. The reason for this is he sees the domain specific pseudonym twice. Therefore, it is not possible to participate more than once.

If the same pollster offers another survey identified by a different domain identifier, then the same user will generate a completely different domain credential and nobody can link these tokens.

Compared to the variant without trustee (Sect. 5.1), this new solution is more secure. This is because the pollster knows nothing about the participant. If pollster and trustee work together in an illegal conspiracy, the participant's privacy is still protected, because the pollster learns nothing as a result of this conspiracy. On the other hand, the solution without trustee is easier to implement, because its mathematical background is less complicated.

The role of the trustee can be operated by the pollster. In this case the pollster knows which persons are interested in surveys. He does not know which person participates in which survey, and he does not know if a person has ever participated. This means the security of this variant is in between the variant without trustee and the variant with a trustee as a separated role. Again, we have omitted the mathematical details here, they can be found in [3,4,10].

6 Further Variants

There are further variants that can either replace or complement the above mentioned solutions. Those variants are described in the following sections.

6.1 Solution for the Case of Low Participation

In the solutions described above, low participation may result in two similar privacy risks: On the one hand, the completed questionnaire can be brought in connection with a particular person if only one person participated in the contest. If the pollster only receives one completed questionnaire after the survey, he knows that the questionnaire was completed by the prize winner of the survey. On the other hand, the pollster of a closed user group survey usually knows the participants personally and, therefore, might be able to guess who filled out a specific questionnaire if the participation was low. If a survey should, for example, show whether or not the employees want to change the company's caterer and the idea of changing the companies caterer has been introduced on the initiative of one of the employees, it is very likely that this employee will be a survey participant who votes for the change. If the number of participants is unexpectedly low and – on top of that – only one person voted for the change, one can be almost certain who filled out that form.[17] This is especially critical if the questionnaire contains questions about more than one subject: If the survey asks whether or not the cater should be changed as well as what the preferred food and costs of the food would be, the employer could find out about his employee's health conditions (e.g. Diabetes patients try to avoid sugar), religion (e.g. Muslims reject pork) or financial situation (e.g. Financially weak employees avoid expensive food).

To avoid these risks, a second trustee called *counter* is introduced. For every survey the counter creates a public/private key pair and publishes the public key on his website. A participant encrypts his survey with this key (Step 2 in Fig. 2), therefore the pollster can not reveal it. In addition, the participant sends in Step 1 his token T_1 to the counter. He uses an authentication scheme that identifies him as a member of the participants without specifying which member. After the pollster has received token T_1 in Step 2, he sends T_1 to the counter, too. For every pair of identical tokens, the counter increases the number of returned surveys. At the end, the counter checks if the number of returned surveys exceeds the minimum number of surveys, as negotiated with the pollster. If this is true, he sends the private key to the pollster. Otherwise, he does not send the private key and the pollster can not decrypt any survey. The potential participants should be informed prior to participation about the minimum number of participants, if such a lower limit exists. This may be important to decide whether to participate or not.

6.2   Solution with Winner's Anonymity

The previously described variants are based on a notification website that asks the winner for his contact details in order to send out the prize by post. However, collecting the winners contact details can be avoided by providing a digital prize. This can be done by directly placing a digital book, music file, or movie on the website that notifies the winner. Instead of asking the winner to fill in his contact details, the winner can simply download the file after entering the correct number (winning code).[18] Alternatively, the pollster could buy a coupon code for an online shop and place the coupon code on the website that notifies the winner. Then, the winner can copy the coupon code and redeem it in the corresponding online shop.

7   Experience with a Paper-Based Variant

At the beginning of this year, we gathered first experiences with a paper based variant of a privacy-friendly feedback questionnaire and prize with a closed user

---

[17] This risk usually decreases with more participants.

[18] In this case, it must be ensured that only the winner will be able to download the file and the digital prize will be passed on in accordance with the Terms of Use of the seller.

group that participated in an annual workshop.[19] In contrast to the surveys we carried out in the past, which had largely the same closed user group, the group handed in 80 % more questionnaires this year. Moreover, the answers to these questionnaires provided many more feedback details and personal (but anonymous) comments. The following section outlines this paper-based variant.

Each potential participant of the survey receives a questionnaire that he is supposed to fill out and return to the pollster. The participants personally throw the completed questionnaires into a voting box. Only those participants who have submitted their questionnaire are allowed to draw one raffle ticket in business card format from a second supervised box. The participants are asked to keep the ticket and the information imprinted on it private.

Each ticket shows a random image[20] on the front side and a "Quick Response Code" (QR-code) on the back. The QR-code contains the URL of the raffle website together with a 16-digit winning code. An additional short serial number on the back makes it easier to identify which raffle ticket has been drawn or left undrawn. The pollster keeps an electronic database of all raffle tickets and deletes all undrawn raffle tickets after the drawing.

After the survey the winning ticket with the associated image and winning code is randomly selected. Since the pollster has every potential participant's contact details, he can inform the participants by E-mail about the selected image and invite the winner to visit the page and enter the corresponding winning code. The winner can do this by simply scanning the QR-code with a smart phone or, alternatively, manually entering the URL and winning code. If the code entered was invalid, only a notice of participation will be shown. After entering the correct winning code, the winner is asked to fill in his name in order to receive the prize. Of course, it is also possible for the winner to submit the raffle ticket and identifying data exclusively by mail.

8   Related Work

To our knowledge, the combination of an online survey with a randomly selected and anonymous winner has not been given attention in previous work. There are different voting schemes that achieve free, equal, and anonymous elections [2,5–7,16,17]. However, these schemes cannot be applied for randomly selecting an anonymous winner. On the other hand, they often concentrate on other features that are not necessary in the simple case of online surveys. For instance, e-voting schemes often provide features as ballot casting assurance, universal verifiability, or coercion-freeness [5,17]. These were not needed in our scenario. Furthermore, these schemes commonly assume the existence of a voting machine, which is not practical in scenarios of online-voting [16,17]. Other online-voting schemes like Helios [1] do not provide full anonymity, since they reveal who already participated in an election.

---

[19] Due to attendee registration, we were able to contact each potential participant by mail.

[20] The images are selected from a database of the pollster.

Beside e-voting schemes there are cryptographic schemes which provide full anonymity. Scenarios with e-cash [9,12,13] have a number of parallels to the procedure described above. In particular the limited use of e-cash corresponds to the requirement to participate in an election or online survey only once. In spite of these similarities, schemes for e-cash are too limited to be used for combining participation in an online survey with the random selection of a winner. Other cryptographic schemes, like credential systems [8,10,12,14,18,19], can be used as building blocks in our solutions; but they do not provide the required features. In particular, credential systems are not designed to limit the amount of times credentials are used. The project ABC4Trust provides a framework for online surveys by using attribute based signatures[21]. However, the framework is complex and includes more parties than is desirable in a simple scenario of online surveys. Furthermore, none of the schemes mentioned above provides the simple possibility to combine online surveys with a prize being awarded anonymously.

9   Conclusion

Pollsters usually offer a prize to a randomly selected winner in order to increase the number of survey participants. In this paper we showed different methods for awarding these prizes in a privacy-friendly way, e.g. without collecting every participant's personal data.

All of the solutions mentioned above comply with the principle of converting personal data into pseudonymous or anonymous data whenever possible: By using tokens or a trusted third party, one's eligibility to participate is uncoupled from the identity of the participant. As a consequence, the pollster does not know which user filled out which questionnaire.

Furthermore the solutions comply with the principle of processing as little personal data as possible, because the pollster

- only needs to collect personal data such as the postal address from the prize winner and
- will not be able to know which questionnaire was filled out by the winner even after the winner has submitted his personal data in order to receive the prize.

Initial experiences with a paper-based variant of a privacy-friendly survey and prize have shown a dramatically increased number of survey participants: In contrast to years of experience with a regular feedback questionnaire (specifying name and E-mail address) and prizes within a closed user group, the same group handed in 80 % more questionnaires after the privacy-friendly variant mentioned above was introduced. Therefore, the implementation of privacy-friendly online surveys and prizes can be a great chance for a threefold improvement: Protecting privacy, increasing the number of participants, and improving the quality of responses.

---

[21] https://abc4trust.eu/.

References

1. Adida, B.: Helios: web-based open-audit voting. In: Proceedings of the 17th Conference on Security Symposium, pp. 335–348 (2008)
2. Bär, M., Henrich, C., Müller-Quade, J., Röhrich, S., Stüber, C.: Real world experiences with bingo voting and a comparison of usability. In: WOTE 2008 (2008)
3. Bender, J., Dagdelen, Ö., Fischlin, M., Kügler, D.: Domain-specific pseudonymous signatures for the german identity card. In: Gollmann, D., Freiling, F.C. (eds.) ISC 2012. LNCS, vol. 7483, pp. 104–119. Springer, Heidelberg (2012)
4. Bichsel, P., Camenisch, J., Dubovitskaya, M., Enderlein, R.R., Krenn, S., Krontiris, I., Lehmann, A., Neven, G., Nielsen, J.D., Paquin, C., Preiss, F.S., Rannenberg, K., Sabouri, A., Stausholm, M.: Architecture for attribute-based credential technologies - final version (2014)
5. Bohli, J.-M., Müller-Quade, J., Röhrich, S.: Bingo voting: secure and coercion-free voting using a trusted random number generator. In: Alkassar, A., Volkamer, M. (eds.) VOTE-ID 2007. LNCS, vol. 4896, pp. 111–124. Springer, Heidelberg (2007)
6. Bräunlich, K., Grimm, R.: Sozialwahlen via Internet mit Polyas. DuD 38(2), 82–85 (2014)
7. Bräunlich, K., Grimm, R., Kahlert, A., Richter, P., Roßnagel, A.: Bewertung von Internetwahlsystemen für Sozialwahlen. DuD 38(2), 75–81 (2014)
8. Camenisch, J., Groß, T.: Efficient attributes for anonymous credentials. In: Proceedings of the 15th ACM Conference on Computer and Communications Security, CCS 2008, pp. 345–356 (2008)
9. Camenisch, J., Hohenberger, S., Kohlweiss, M.: How to win the clone wars: efficient periodic n times anonymous authentication. In: Proceeding of the 13-th ACM Conference on Computer and Communications Security, CCS 2006, pp. 201–210 (2006)
10. Camenisch, J., Lysyanskaya, A.: An efficient system for non-transferable anonymous credentials with optional anonymity revocation. In: Pfitzmann, B. (ed.) EUROCRYPT 2001. LNCS, vol. 2045, pp. 93–118. Springer, Heidelberg (2001)
11. Chaum, D.: Blind signatures for untraceable payments. In: Advandes in Cryptology - CRYPTO 1982, pp. 199–203 (1983)
12. Chaum, D.: Security without identification: transaction systems to make big brother obsolete. Commun. ACM 28, 1030–1044 (1985)
13. Chaum, D., Fiat, A., Naor, M.: Untraceable electronic cash. In: Goldwasser, S. (ed.) CRYPTO 1988. LNCS, vol. 403, pp. 319–327. Springer, Heidelberg (1990)
14. Chen, L.: Access with pseudonyms. In: Dawson, E.P., Golić, J.D. (eds.) Cryptography: Policy and Algorithms 1995. LNCS, vol. 1029, pp. 232–243. Springer, Heidelberg (1996)
15. Peointcheval, D., Stern, J.: Provable secure blind signature schemes. In: Kim, K., Matsumoto, T. (eds.) ASIACRYPT 1996. LNCS, vol. 1163, pp. 252–265. Springer, Heidelberg (1996)
16. Gjøsteen, K.: The norwegian internet voting protocol. In: Kiayias, A., Lipmaa, H. (eds.) VoteID 2011. LNCS, vol. 7187, pp. 1–18. Springer, Heidelberg (2012)
17. Müller-Quade, J., Henrich, C.: Bingo voting. DuD 33(2), 102–106 (2009)
18. Papagiannopoulos, K., Alpar, G., Lueks, W.: Designated attribute proofs with the Camenisch-Lysyanskaya signature (2013)
19. Pashalidis, A.: Interdomain user authentication and privacy. Royal Holloway University of London, Technical report (2005)

Security and Privacy in New Computing Paradigms

Cloud Computing Security Requirements and a Methodology for Their Auditing

Dimitra Georgiou[✉] and Costas Lambrinoudakis

Secure Systems Laboratory, Department of Digital Systems,
School of Information and Communication Technologies,
University of Piraeus, Piraeus, Greece
dimitrageorgiou@ssl-unipi.gr, clam@unipi.gr

Abstract. Security is a crucial issue in cloud computing especially since a lot of stakeholders worldwide are involved. Achieving an acceptable security level in cloud environments is much harder when compared to other traditional IT systems due to specific cloud characteristics like: architecture, openness, multi-tenancy etc. Conventional security mechanisms are no longer suitable for applications and data in the cloud, since new security requirements have emerged. Furthermore, there is a clear need for a trusted security audit method for cloud providers.

This paper identifies the security requirements that are specific to cloud computing and highlights how these requirements link to the cloud security policy while illustrating the structure of a General Security Policy Model. Furthermore, it proposes a method that can be adopted by cloud providers for auditing the security of their systems.

Keywords: Cloud computing · Software-as-a-Service (SaaS) · Data security · Data loss security requirements · Trusted security audit method

1 Introduction

Although cloud security concerns have been mentioned as one of the top challenges to cloud adoption, it is not clear which security issues are specific to Cloud Computing. ISACA and Cloud Security Alliance presented guidelines to mitigate the security issues in cloud [1, 2]. Reddy et al. [3] introduced a detailed analysis of the cloud computing security issues and challenges focusing on the cloud computing types and the service delivery types. Ramgovid et al. [4] presented the management of Security in Cloud focusing in Gartner's list [5]. However, there are several questions that remain open like: Which are the security requirements that exist only in Cloud? and What is the structure of a security policy for cloud environments? and Does the user has to solely depend on the service provider for proper security measures?

By utilizing the general security policy proposed in [6], we are proposing a methodology for auditing the security level of a Cloud Provider.

The paper is structured as follows: Sect. 2 presents the cloud specific security threats, while Sect. 3 proposes a list of General Recommendations that should appear in every security policy of SaaS environments. Section 4, presents the proposed

© Springer International Publishing Switzerland 2015
S.K. Katsikas and A.B. Sideridis (Eds.): E-Democracy 2015, CCIS 570, pp. 51–61, 2015.
DOI: 10.1007/978-3-319-27164-4_4

model-methodology for auditing the security level of a cloud provider. Finally, Sect. 5 provides conclusions derived out of the survey undertaken in this paper.

2 Cloud Specific Security Threats

Cloud Computing is a mix of technologies that supports various stakeholders (Cloud Provider, Service Provider and Users). But how a cloud differs from other models and what exactly is the organizational impact when moving to a cloud is not yet clear. For the users Cloud Computing is a synthesis of computing services without any understanding of the technologies being used. For an organization it is a scale of different services for users to grow innovation and their business income. But the threats that an organization faces as it shifts to cloud computing environments are different. Figure 1 illustrates the risks that we will scope in our paper: Table 1 provides the nine cloud security risks according to the Cloud Security Alliance [7], while Table 2 provides more cloud-specific security threats.

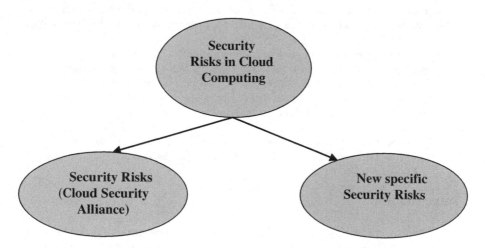

Fig. 1. Security risks in cloud computing

In Cloud Computing environment the threats are various and different according to the delivery models. In the previous tables we have discussed the risks in general focusing more on SaaS Cloud Providers. All these risks require substantial security attention. Cloud providers need to mitigate these security threats by adopting the appropriate security measures in accordance to a well formed cloud security policy. By addressing the aforementioned requirements cloud providers will earn the trust of their users.

The proposed methodology provides solutions for each threat and at the same time maps them with the provisions of the Cloud Security Policy.

Table 1. A list of cloud-specific security risks (cloud security alliance)

Nine security risks (cloud security alliance)	Description
Data breach	The data from various users and organizations reside together in a cloud server. If somebody breaches into the cloud then, the data of all users will be attacked
data loss	For both consumers and businesses, the prospect of permanently losing one's data is terrifying. Data loss may occur when a server dies without its owner having created a backup
Account hijacking	A process through which an individual's email account, computer account or any other account associated with a computing device or service is stolen or hijacked by a hacker
Insecure interfaces and API's	Cloud Computing providers expose a set of software interfaces or APIs that customers use to manage and interact with cloud services. The security and availability of general cloud services is dependent upon the security of these basic APIs. These interfaces must be designed to protect against both accidental and malicious attempts
Denial of service	Another common attack for Organizations that operate or use Internet connected services such as websites, or Cloud services need to be aware of threats that can disrupt service. A DoS attack makes your network unavailable to the intended users by flooding them with connection requests
Malicious insider	It's unpleasant to think that someone in your organization might be collecting a paycheck and planning to repay you with malice. But it does happen. Taking measures to protect yourself doesn't mean you don't trust the others. Systems that depend "solely on the cloud service provider for security are at great risk" from a malicious insider
Abuse of cloud services	This threat is more common in IaaS and in PaaS models. Hackers and other criminals take advantage of the convenient registration, simple procedures and relatively anonymous access to cloud services to launch various attacks
Insufficient knowledge	Rather than security issues, a lack of knowledge regarding cloud computing is stopping businesses that don't already use the service from taking the plunge. It is the main factor in preventing uptake.
Unintentional disclosure	This risk is the malicious or accidental disclosure of confidential or sensitive information. In a Cloud Computing environment it could be happen many times.

Table 2. Cloud-specific security threats to cloud computing

New specific security threats to cloud computing	Description
Data protection	Customers may not know where their data is being stored and there may be a risk of data being stored alongside other customers' information
Lack of standards	Several times Cloud Providers may perform similar in a different way. Security standards for cloud environments that have been developed by international organizations are necessary
International regulations	Providers and users must consider the legal issues related to the data that they collect, process and store
Third party control, subpoena and e-discovery	This is the most crucial concern in the cloud, since third party access can lead to loss of confidential information
Back up vulnerabilities	Providers must ensure that all sensitive data is backed up in order to facilitate quick recovery in case of disasters. Also, they should use strong encryption schemes to protect the backup data. The users need to separately encrypt their data and backups in order to avoid access by unauthorized parties
Cloud burst security	In cloud environments there are applications consisting of several virtual machines. Such bursting machines need strict security policies in order not to be vulnerable
Authentication and trust	Data in the cloud may be modified without user's permission. As such, data authenticity is very important and needs to be guaranteed
Lack of user control	In Cloud environments there is a potential lack of control and transparency since a third party holds the data
Cross border transfer of data	In this case the concern is if the protection level of the destination country is equivalent to that of the originating country. In cases where the destination country has laws that respect the conditions and requirements set by the domestic legal framework data can be transferred, otherwise the transfer is prohibited

3 General Recommendations for the Security Policies in Saas Environments

Although the security capabilities for a SaaS environment have developed, we argue that if the security policy of the cloud provider features some general recommendations that reflect the security requirements of an organization or/and a user, then the providers will mitigate the security risks and concerns. Thus if an organization chooses a SaaS provider that follows the following recommendations, it would be easier for a Third Party Auditor to check the security level of the Cloud Computing environment. **This ensures that the provision of all resources and the behavior of all users is in**

accordance with the recommendations set, and thus compliance issues are automatically avoided.

SaaS security recommendations
1. Invest in Education
2. Establish Cloud Strategy
3. Decide what goes to and under which control
4. Invest in Technologies that protect users' data
5. Audit the provider's services

1. **Invest in Education:** There is a need to identify the learning goals, the content structure and the learning experience of cloud computing in terms of senior high technology education, in order to help learners coping with this emerging technology. At the same time, the research result could be effectively applied on integrating emerging technology into formal technology education.
2. **Establish Cloud Strategy**: We would like to suggest a few basic steps that organizations can follow to define their cloud computing roadmap. This is not just about solving a problem, but moving a long-term strategic use of cloud computing that should bring long-term strategic value to the enterprise. The result of this will be a safe Cloud environment and a more easy way to test which Provider is more suitable for the users.
3. **Decide what goes to and under which control:** One of the biggest problems that security professionals face is to identify which control goes where. The user should not manage or control the underlying cloud, because it is not obligatory to have technical or managerial knowledge of Cloud. Organizations must choose the controls that meet users' specific needs. So if there are security certifications and accreditations, audit control will be an easy process and the Cloud Computing environment will be trusted.
4. **Invest in technologies that protect users' data:** If the Provider is not certified by some industry security certification authority for its software and hardware infrastructure, then the security control will be much more difficult. Users expect, through their SLA, to have a report that will inform them about the encryption solutions, intrusion detection and prevention solutions, data centers and all other technologies and mechanisms that the provider uses. Users need a secure and consistent "place" for their data.
5. **Audit the provider's services**: Organizations or Third Party Control must provide Cloud Service Providers with a way to make their security data available for potential customers. Organizations provide outsourcing services that affect the control environment of their customers. The key thing, to take away of this problem, is a conduct with a Cloud Auditor. The Cloud Auditor should have an audit plan, so that can be used as a guide. This plan should include policies and procedures. Because, the control of the Cloud Provider is difficult for the customer, the Cloud Auditor provides a standard way to present, automated statistics about performance and security. So, SaaS customers do not have to know the way of auditing. But only to select the safest Cloud Provider, according to the security functions by the Auditor.

It is necessary to agree on the way recommendations for the security policy are presented to the providers. They should be able to identify the recommendations that are relevant to the users' requirements and concerns. SaaS risks can be managed through this approach and cloud providers will be able to utilize systems with complex and dynamic environments more easily. Furthermore, the proposed approach will save time, effort and money to the providers.

4   Proposed Model-Methodology

The proposed model provides a solution to the security challenges of Cloud Computing. If Cloud Providers and Organizations follow this model, using the gates of the policy, they will succeed to have a secure cloud computing environment. More specifically, the Figure below illustrates the structure of the General Security Framework and the interdependencies among its components. The cloud provider or a third party auditor must follow/audit the four general categories (*Process-Functions Controls, Technology, HR, Legal and Compliances*) to avoid threats. In each category it is necessary to ensure/check what provisions are covered by the Cloud Provider according the following security measures- examples. A further analysis of what security controls should be linked to every security measure, will be provided. Until today the aforementioned audit process was rather difficult because there is no commonly agreed procedure or a common policy, and thus customers cannot easily rank their providers in terms of the security level that they support. The proposed Cloud Security Model addresses the relationships of security measures and places them in context with their relevant security controls and concerns.

Therefore, the proposed General Security Policy requires that **the third party auditor will audit** the following four categories:

Category 1 – Processes/Functions Controls: It must be ensured that the security measures adopted by the provider meet the requirements set by the Cloud Security Policy. Users expect to have available a report about Cloud Provider's operations, logs and industry security certifications, as well as the assurance of the auditor that the provider is doing these right.

Category 2 – Technology: The auditor should check what software and hardware technologies are used. What are the applications and the devices that users trust to store and possible share their data? Cloud providers may allow users' data to be transferred to another vendor or platform, growing the risks on the users' data.

Category 3 – HR: A great number of executives, managers and personnel are not familiar with what cloud computing means. There is a lack of awareness about cloud environments together with a lot of concerns about the various risks and the security of the data. Providers must aim to promote security, through education and sharing of good practices with the personnel. The auditor should check if the cloud provider is considering the provisions of this category.

Category 4 – Legal Requirements & Compliances: The auditor should check if the provisions of the legal framework under which data are stored and/or transferred are satisfied. Also the auditor should know in which country the data are located and

THREATS	CATEGORY (of threats)
Data Breach	LEGAL & COMPLIANCES
Data Loss	LEGAL & COMPLIANCES
Account Hijacking	TECHNOLOGY
Insecure Interfaces & API's	TECHNOLOGY
Denial of Service	TECHNOLOGY
Malicious Insider	PROCESS – FUNCTIONS CONTROLS
Abuse of Cloud Services	PROCESS – FUNCTIONS CONTROLS
Insufficient Knowledge	HR
Unintentional Disclosure	PROCESS – FUNCTIONS CONTROLS
Data Protection	LEGAL & COMPLIANCES
Luck of Standards	LEGAL & COMPLIANCES
International Regulations	LEGAL & COMPLIANCES
Subpoena and e-discovery	TECHNOLOGY
Third Party Control	LEGAL & COMPLIANCES
Back up vulnerabilities	TECHNOLOGY
Cloud Burst Security	TECHNOLOGY
Authentication and trust	TECHNOLOGY
Lack of user control	PROCESS – FUNCTIONS CONTROLS
Prohibition against cross border Transfer	TECHNOLOGY

Fig. 2. Linking threats with category

thus what are the regulations/restrictions for storing/processing/transferring that data. In this way the user can be assured that the storage/data processing that the cloud provider carries out is done in a lawful way.

Third party auditors can utilize this framework to understand the SaaS Provider's security context. All the previous threats are assigned to one of the four categories, which category is then associated with the necessary security measures and then is being linked with a set of rules that make up the Security Policy of the Cloud Provider. Figure 2 illustrates that relation between Threats and Categories while Fig. 3 depicts the proposed Model- Methodology.

In the previous Figure, we illustrate the solutions that are available for securing SaaS environments, in accordance to the proposed Security Policy. We have gathered the cloud computing threats and we have suggested measures addressing them.

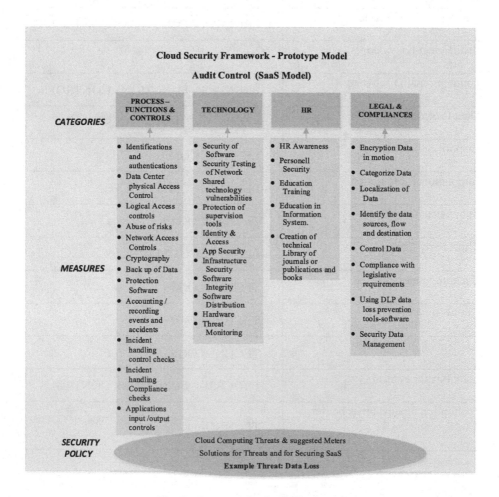

Fig. 3. Proposed SaaS security model

In the following case study- Example 1, we select the "Data Loss" threat, which has to do with the Legal & Compliances Category. This specific threat is crucial for Cloud Computing. In the analysis that follows we propose security measures that can be adopted in the cloud and then a set of Rules that will form our Security Policy.

Example 1. *Threat:* Data Loss
  Category: LEGAL REQUIREMENTS & COMPLIANCES
  Measures: With the exception of some general purpose measures, there are specific techniques and security mechanisms for Cloud Computing environments. The security measures associated with the aforementioned threat *are the following:*

1. Encryption of data in motion
2. Categorize data
3. Localization of data
4. Identify the data sources, flow and destination
5. Control data
6. Compliance with legislative requirements.
7. Using DLP Data Loss Prevention Tools-software

Security Policy Rules:

The security policy rules associated with the aforementioned threat and security measures follow:

1. **Encryption of data in motion**
   The encryption techniques should follow international best practice and should have broad acceptance by the international community as to their effectiveness. Data in transit need to be confidential.

   - For symmetric encryption to storage media or data transmissions, the appropriate algorithms and key lengths should be selected in accordance with the international authoritative bodies. (e.g. NIST)
   - Where a digital signature is required the laws of the country in which the provider is located should be adopted, as well as the decisions of the European Union

2. **Categorize data**
   Data should be classified according to the protection they need, according to the evaluation of their criticality through the risk analysis/assessment of the Cloud Provider.
   Top secret: information and vital data for the Cloud Provider, which any disclosure or unauthorized change will have direct impact on operations.
   Confidential: information and data relevant to the operation of the Cloud Provider which should be subject to strict controls. Sensitive information and data subject to laws protecting personal data, the disclosure of which need specific permissions/license.
   Reportable: information and data may be disclosed. The security requirements vary according to the category of the information owned. Each processing of

data must be guaranteed by procedural and technical resources that can be attributed to a specific individual. Therefore all critical actions will be strictly personalized access.

3. **Localization of data**

In Cloud Computing data travels over the Internet to and from one or more regions where the data centers are. The user of a cloud must know in which country the servers are located, how the data are processed and under which legislation. So, at any moment the provider should be able to inform its users about these issues. Data located in different countries, provinces or municipalities are subject to different legal frameworks. For this reason it is essential for the contract between the provider and the user to clearly state the geographic region of the servers.

4. **Identify the data sources, flow and destination**

Data should be accomplished. This process must include data discovery and data fingerprinting that provides a better understanding, who, where, when and in what format the information is being generated and in what devices it is being stored. In addition, identifying the cloud services being used and the type of data that is being transferred to the cloud is an important step during this process.

5. **Control Data**

In the absence of control data in a cloud environment, no activity is recorded which modify or delete users data. User should know how these data is handled. No information is stored like which nodes have joined, which programs have run, what changes are made. In addition, users want to know who from the providers have the data, where and in what way they are being processed.

6. **Compliance with legal requirements**

   - Recording and documentation of all legislative and regulatory obligations of the service and how all these obligations are addressed.
   - The privacy of the users should be ensured.
   - If sensitive personal data are collected, permission from the Data Protection Authority should be acquired.
   - Description of the procedures adopted for ensuring compliance with the legal requirements and regulations.

7. **Using Data Loss Prevention Tools-Software**

Data loss prevention (DLP) is a strategy for making sure that end users do not send sensitive or critical information outside the corporate network and prevent them by monitoring, detecting and blocking sensitive data while in-use (endpoint actions), in-motion (network traffic), and at-rest (data storage). Users also want DLPs to be used for describing software products that help a provider to control what data end users can transfer.

8. **Security Data Management**

When an outside party owns, controls, and manages resources, users should be assured that data remains private and secure, and that their organization is protected from damaging data breaches. Users want to be sure that data is not readable and that the provider offers strong key management. Cloud Providers should implement access policies which ensure that only authorized users can gain access to sensitive information.

5 Conclusions

Though there are a lot of researchers that have discussed about security issues in Cloud Computing, there are yet many challenges which have to be sorted out. The main issue is the creation of a Trusted Cloud Service Provider, that achieves the required assurance level and minimizes the risk in which organizations and users operate every day. In this paper we have proposed a Security Model that gives a solution to the security challenges of a SaaS Cloud Computing model. If the Cloud Providers follow the proposed model, using the gates of our policy, they will succeed to have a professional Security Audit and thus a high level of security in their cloud computing environment. In our paper we have addressed the Cloud Computing threats, we analyzed the most important security requirements mentioned by Cloud Providers and we suggested a set of rules for these threats. Our methodology can provide a solution for every threat by matching it with the appropriate measures and then linking these measures to the appropriate rules of the Security Policy. A case study of the Data Loss threat is presented, as it is the most important concern for Cloud Computing users.

References

1. ISACA: Cloud computing: business benefits with security, governance and assurance perspectives. In: White Paper Information Systems Audit and Control Association (2009)
2. Brunette, G., Mogull, R.: Security guidance for critical areas of focus in cloud computing. Technical report, Cloud Security Alliance (2009)
3. Reddy, R.K., Reddy, S.P.K., Sireesha, G., Seshadri, U.: The security issues of cloud computing over normal & IT sector. Int. J. Adv. Res. Comput. Sci. Softw. Eng. 2(3), 62–69 (2012)
4. Ramgovid, S., Eloff, M.M., Smith, E.: The management of security in cloud computing. In: Proceedings of 2010 IEEE International Conference on Cloud Computing (2010)
5. Brodkin, J: Gartner: seven cloud-computing security risks. In: Infoworld (2008)
6. Georgiou, D., Lambrinoudakis, C.: A security policy for cloud providers the software-as-a-service-problem. In: The Ninth International Conference on Internet Monitoring and Protection ICIMP (2014)
7. Cloud Security Alliance: The notorious nine: cloud computing top threats in 2013 (2013). http://www.cloudsecurityalliance.org/topthreats/

A Method for Privacy-Preserving
Context-Aware Mobile Recommendations

Nikolaos Polatidis[1], Christos K. Georgiadis[1], Elias Pimenidis[2(✉)],
and Emmanouil Stiakakis[1]

[1] Department of Applied Informatics,
University of Macedonia, Thessaloniki, Greece
{npolatidis,geor,stiakakis}@uom.edu.gr
[2] Department of Computer Science and Creative Technologies,
University of the West of England, Bristol, UK
Elias.Pimenidis@uwe.ac.uk

Abstract. Mobile recommender systems aim to solve the information overload
problem found by recommending products or services to users of mobile
smartphones or tables at any given point in time and in any possible location.
Mobile recommender systems are designed for the specific goal of mobile
recommendations, such as mobile commerce or tourism and are ported to a
mobile device for this purpose. They utilize a specific recommendation method,
like collaborative filtering or content-based filtering and use a considerable
amount of contextual information in order to provide more personalized recommendations. However due to privacy concerns users are not willing to provide the required personal information to make these systems usable. In
response to the privacy concerns of users we present a method of privacy
preserving context-aware mobile recommendations and show that it is both
practical and effective.

Keywords: Mobile recommender systems · Context-awareness · Privacy ·
Privacy-preserving systems

1 Introduction

The evolution of the concept of e-democracy and its related electronic government
services has led to information overload and privacy issues [21, 24]. The information
overload problem encountered in numerous online situations has given rise to the use
of recommender systems. Swiftly such systems have become necessary to the wider
public and at the same time have contributed heavily to an increase in privacy concerns
amongst service users. Recommender systems are algorithms and computer software
that are designed to provide suggestions for products or services that could be of
interest to a user of a website or an online application [2, 8]. They are considered to be
a subset of information retrieval systems whose job is to provide personalized recommendations to users and solve the information overload problem found in various
online environments. Recommender systems are valuable to users that do not have the
experience or the time to cope with the process of decision making while using the

© Springer International Publishing Switzerland 2015
S.K. Katsikas and A.B. Sideridis (Eds.): E-Democracy 2015, CCIS 570, pp. 62–74, 2015.
DOI: 10.1007/978-3-319-27164-4_5

web, particularly where a choice of products or services is available. Recent advances in the field of mobile computing and the rapid evolution of mobile devices such as smartphones and tablets, has led to need for advances in the field of mobile recommender systems [3, 12–14]. The access to a mobile recommender system at any given point in time and location is called ubiquity, thus an alternative term used to describe such systems is that of ubiquitous recommender systems [11]. Additionally the use of location data from Global Positioning System and the use of other contextual information, such as the time, weather information, physical conditions, social and others, have become common in mobile recommender systems [11, 17]. Nowadays there are an increasing number of e-services provided by governments that utilize a high amount of personal user data that need to be protected [22]. Examples of such are the location-aware applications and health services that can use mobile recommender systems [29, 30].

These new types of data have contributed in the creation of more personalized recommendations in mobile environments. It should be noted though that it is not clear whether a specific research domain of mobile recommender systems exists and that only specific goals are set for mobile recommendations, where a mobile application or website is designed and developed for a specific scenario [5, 12–14]. In this context different application domains exist, such as those for mobile commerce and tourism related services [5, 14]. Applications designed for any mobile recommendation domain share some common characteristics such as [5]: All run on a mobile device, such as a smartphone or a tablet, all provide some form of recommendation, all utilize some form of context and all rely on a wireless connection that could probably be slow.

Mobile context-aware recommender systems heavily rely on context to provide accurate and personalized recommendations in mobile environments. However typical privacy protection techniques such as the use of pseudonyms or the use of anonymity cannot be applied properly due to the fact that recommender systems rely on the use of personal data [15]. For example reference [7] is an approach to anonymous communication for location-based services that is based on use of dummies. Similar methods that have been used for privacy protection in location-based services include query enlargement techniques, progressive retrieval techniques and transformation based techniques [6]. These are different protection methods that can be adjusted to the context privacy problem found in mobile recommender systems. Privacy is an important part of context-aware mobile recommender systems that has not been properly exploited yet and, to the best of our knowledge, this is the first effort found in the literature to do that. In order to protect the user privacy at the context level the following contributions have been made:

- We have developed a method that aims to protect the user privacy in mobile recommender systems.
- It introduces an approach that is based on dummy context creation.
- It is experimentally evaluated, showing that it is both practical and effective.

The rest of the paper is organized as follows. Section 2 describes the factors affecting recommendations in mobile environments. Section 3 is the proposed privacy protection method. Section 4 is the evaluation of the aforementioned method, Sect. 5 is the related work section and Sect. 6 is the conclusions and future work.

2 Factors Affecting Mobile Recommender Systems

A number of factors exist that can affect mobile recommender systems and their ability to provide accurate personalized recommendations. These include the recommendation method, the context and privacy concerns [12, 13].

2.1 Recommendation Method

Recommender systems rely in some form of recommendation method to suggest the appropriate products or services to the user. The most important recommendation methods include [2]:

Collaborative filtering which is a method that recommends items to users that other users with similar ratings have liked them in the past. This works by asking each user to submit ratings for products or services and then searches between the ratings for similar users and provides the recommendations [2, 16]. Content-based filtering which is a method that uses a set of keywords supplied by the user that can be matched in the item's description [2, 8]. Finally, hybrid is a method that uses a combination of two or more recommendations methods [2, 8].

2.2 Context

Context is utilized by mobile recommender systems to provide more accurate and personalized recommendations. It is a type of data that is necessary to users that move constantly and their status changes. Different types of context can be employed in mobile scenarios and include, among others, location, time, weather and social presence. Contextual information is important for location-based recommendations [1, 10, 14]. Information can be collected either explicitly, by asking the user to provide data, or implicitly by collecting data from the mobile device and related sensors, such as the Global Positioning System [1, 11].

The context can be applied by using three different ways [1]: First, Contextual pre-filtering is a method where the contextual data is used to filter out irrelevant data from the dataset and then apply the recommendation method. Also, Contextual post-filtering is a method where the recommendation method takes places and then the irrelevant data are filtered out. Finally, Contextual modeling is a method where the recommendation method is designed in a way that the context is utilized within.

2.3 Privacy

Privacy in government to citizen services is considered an important factor and needs to be taken into consideration [23]. Mobile recommender systems offer the benefit of providing personalized recommendations to users of a context that constantly changes. On the other hand the ways that user data might be processed direct users towards a negative attitude, when it comes to supplying personal contextual information [10, 11]. Privacy protection techniques have relied mainly on location-based services [15] and do not take into consideration the whole concept of context. Privacy is an important factor that can be addressed properly using the right methods and makes it possible for the user to supply the required contextual information, thus making both the system usable and receive highly accurate personalized recommendations.

3 Proposed Method

Privacy is becoming increasingly important in mobile computing environments, including the field of recommender systems in such domains. However efforts have been made towards the location-based services problem, which is only one of the many parameters of context that can be found in context-aware mobile recommender systems. A method that protects the user privacy when context parameters are used for mobile recommendations is proposed. Mobile recommender systems are based on a regular recommendation algorithm such as collaborative filtering, content based filtering or a hybrid approach. Furthermore, as described in Sect. 2 a context filtering method needs to be applied in order to sort the recommendations and propose the ones that are more relevant according to the contextual parameters. In our method we use collaborative filtering with contextual post filtering with an overview of the recommendation process taking place at the server and shown in Fig. 1.

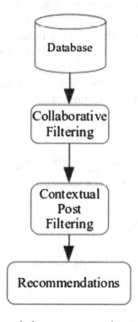

Fig. 1. Recommendation process service provider overview

3.1 Proposed Privacy Method

To protect the privacy of users requesting context aware recommendations we need to explain the architecture of the system and how it works efficiently.

Mobile Device: A mobile device could be a smartphone, tablet or another device that is portable and capable of utilizing location through the Global Positioning System or through a wireless network.

Secure Communication: It is assumed that a secure communication link is available at all times between the client (mobile device) and the server (service provider).

Service Provider: The service provider, or server, provides personalized recommendations to registered users of mobile devices.

A hybrid client-server recommendation approach is proposed in order to protect the privacy of the user and provide recommendations within a reasonable time. A mobile user submits a request to the server for recommendations. The ratings of all users are stored at the server, therefore collaborative filtering takes place at the server side. Furthermore, when the user makes a request both real and dummy contextual parameters are being sent, such as location, day type, weather, mood, physical and/or others to the service provider. For the recommendation approach to work algorithm 1 is called at the mobile device which shows a request submitted from a user to the server. The request includes a dummy creation for every context parameter. The next step is for the service provider to reply using Algorithm 2, which is the recommendation process that takes place at the server in typical client-server architectures. Consequently the real and false recommendations are being sent back to the mobile device in order to be sorted out and the real recommendations shown to the user. Moreover, Fig. 2 is the interaction between a user of a mobile device requesting recommendations and the service provider. The first step is for the mobile device to make a request to the server. Then the recommendation process takes place at the server. Then the server sends the real and fake recommendations to the mobile device. Finally, the mobile device throws away all the fake recommendations and presents the real to the user.

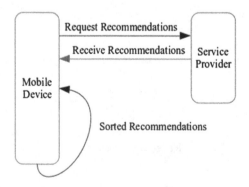

Fig. 2. Client-server interaction

Algorithm 1. Recommendation request (Mobile client)

Input: User id, Context parameters
Output: Recommendations /* *List of recommendations* */

Retrieve Location, Context_Parameters[n]
Generate Dummy_Location, Dummy_Context_Parameters[n]
/* *one fake context parameter for each real context parameter* */
Request /* to the service provider with parameters */ User id, Location,
Dummy_Location, Context_Parameters[n], Dummy_Context_Parameters[n]
/* *the service provider receives the request makes the recommendation as shown in*
algorithm 2 and provides the recommendations back to the client */
Receive Recommendations /* *real and false from the service provider* */
For (int i=0; i<Recommendations.size; i++**)**
      If
      i.hasParameter (Dummy_Location)
      Delete i;
      Else
      For (int j=1; j<=n; j++**)**
            If
            i.hasParameter (Dummy_Context_Parameters[j])
            Delete i;
            End If
      End For
      End If
End For
Return Recommendations

However, regarding Algorithm 1 it should be noted that the possibility of context disclosure by the context provider. For example within a given time frame the dummy context variables could be remain fixed in order to solve this issue.

4   Experimental Evaluation

For the experimental evaluation a Pentium i3 2.13 GHz with 4 GBs of RAM, running windows 8.1 was used. All the algorithms have been implemented in Java and used Collaborative filtering with contextual post filtering. Moreover a mobile smartphone running android 5.0 was used.

4.1   Real Dataset

For the evaluation part we have used the LDOS-CoMoDa context aware dataset [9]. This is a real dataset that apart from the usual user-rating scale from 1-5 for movies it also contains 12 contextual variables, which are described in Table 1. Furthermore, Table 2 is the statistical description of the dataset.

Algorithm 2. Recommendation process (Service provider)

Input: User id, Context parameters
Output: Recommendations

/* *Starts with collaborative filtering* */
Load User ratings
Load Similarity measure /* Pearson correlation similarity */
Provide Recommendations
/* *Contextual post filtering follows* */
For (int i=0; i<Recommendations.size; i++)
  If
  i.hasParameter != (Location || Dummy_Location)
  Delete i;
  Else
  For (int j=1; j<=n; j++)
    If
    i.hasParameter != (Context_Parameters[j] || Dummy_Context_Parameters[j])
    Delete i;
    End If
  End For
  End If
End For
Return Recommendations

Table 1. Description of Context Variables of LDOS-CoMoDa dataset

Context parameter	Values	Description of values
time	1 to 4	1 = morning, 2 = afternoon, 3 = evening, 4 = night
daytype	1 to 3	1 = working, 2 = weekend, 3 = holiday
season	1 to 4	1 = spring, 2 = summer, 3 = autumn, 4 = winter
location	1 to 3	1 = home, 2 = public, 3 = friend's house
weather	1 to 5	1 = sunny, 2 = rainy, 3 = stormy, 4 = snowy, 5 = cloudy
social	1 to 7	1 = alone, 2 = partner, 3 = friends, 4 = colleagues, 5 = parents, 6 = public, 7 = family
endEmo	1 to 7	1 = sad, 2 = happy, 3 = scared, 4 = surprised, 5 = angry, 6 = disgusted, 7 = neutral
dominantEmo	1 to 7	1 = sad, 2 = happy, 3 = scared, 4 = surprised, 5 = angry, 6 = disgusted, 7 = neutral

(*Continued*)

Table 1. (*Continued*)

Context parameter	Values	Description of values
mood	1 to 3	1 = positive, 2 = neutral, 3 = negative
physical	1 to 2	1 = healthy, 2 = ill
decision	1 to 2	1 = By user, 2 = By other
interaction	1 to 2	1 = first, 2 = number of int, after first

Table 2. Statistical description of LDOS-CoMoDa dataset

Description	Value
Users	95
Items	961
Ratings	1665
Average age of users	27
Countries	6
Cities	18
Maximum submitted ratings from one user	220
Minimum submitted ratings from one user	1

4.2 Performance Evaluation

User Bob is located at his home, which according to the description of the context parameters of the dataset is set to number 1. Moreover the time of the day is set to number 3 because it is evening time. The other available contextual parameters which are available are the social that is set to 1(alone) and mood which is set to 1(positive). Now, Bob wants to use his mobile application to recommend him a movie to watch, while he is at home. The following steps take place.

1. Bob starts the mobile application and makes the request.
2. The mobile application generates a random selects the location and randomly selects another location. In this case location 1 and 2 have been selected.
3. The time is not necessary to be protected. Therefore, the value remains to 3.
4. The social parameter is set to 1 and 3.
5. The mood parameter is set to 1 and 2.

All the information are being send to the service provider, which then provides movie recommendations according to ratings supplied by the users of the systems and with the use of collaborative filtering and by taking into consideration all the above contextual parameters described in steps 2 to 5.

Figure 3 shows the performance comparison when the service provider uses one contextual parameter for each type of context and when the second, dummy, parameter is introduced for every type of context. The number of the requested recommendations is set to 5, 10 and 20. We assumed that user with id no 23 in the dataset is Bob and that's how the experiment took place. However it should be noted that the collaborative

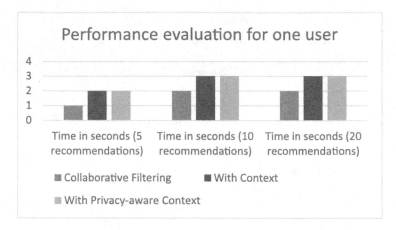

Fig. 3. Performance evaluation for one user

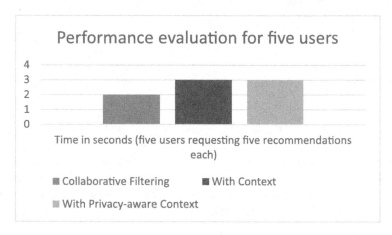

Fig. 4. Performance evaluation for five users

filtering method returned 14 relevant results with our provided settings and when the system requested 20. In all cases all the context parameters applied after the recommendations returned from the collaborative filtering algorithm.

Figure 4 shows the performance results when five users concurrently request for five recommendations each, whereas Fig. 5 shows the performance results for ten users requesting five recommendations each.

Furthermore, a performance evaluation regarding the transfer time is necessary and is shown in Table 3. Assuming that a number of data needs to be transferred from the service provider to the mobile client a wireless channel needs to be used. Supposing that two images for a recommended item are necessary and they are of 100 kb each and regular text which we have set to 100 Kb. Also note that rendering time and presentation in the mobile device was not included in these tests. Only transfer times between a computer and a

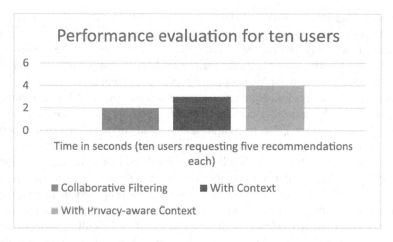

Fig. 5. Performance evaluation for ten users

Table 3. Transfer Time between the computer and the mobile device

Number of recommendations	Wireless speed	Size in megabytes	Transfer time in seconds
5	11 Mbits	1.5	4
10	11 Mbits	3	8
5	11 Mbits	1.5 (+10 % overhead)	5
10	11 Mbits	3 (+10 % overhead)	8

mobile device using a wireless network are included. Moreover, these times may vary depending on the number of concurrent requests to the server and any overheads included.

5 Related Work

There is a gap between recommender systems and mobile computing, where most the related work done is about protecting the personal data of a user, such as the ratings when referring to personalized recommendations or the location of the user when referring to mobile computing services. In our proposed method we aim to protect the privacy of the user using any type of contextual parameters for personalized mobile recommendations. Whereas, most of privacy-protection methods for location-based services perform well for protecting the location of a user when only non-personalized services are requested, our approach delivers recommendations in mobile environments without losing any accuracy and at the same time preserving the privacy of the user at the context level.

An example of preserving privacy in collaborative filtering is the use of distribution techniques that use an obfuscation scheme and a randomized dissemination protocol [18]. Also, the use of ratings perturbations is a well-known approach that is used in collaborative filtering for personal data protection [20]. Additionally, other privacy protection approaches exist in recommender systems such as [19] where the use of a semi-trusted third party is proposed. The data are split between the server and the semi-trusted third party, thus no single entity can derive sensitive information and the system can work only if these two separate parties collaborate.

Moreover, approaches in location based services have been developed to protect the location of the user but no other context parameters and for non-personalized services. For example in reference [7] a technique that is used for location privacy based on dummies is described. Similarly, in [25] an approach to location privacy is proposed and generates dummy locations based on a virtual grid or a circle. The approach requires only a lightweight front-end that can work tightly in a client-server model. Furthermore, in [26] a dummy generation algorithm is proposed in order to protect location privacy. In this approach various restrictions are taking place and assume that users do not stop regularly. However, it is stated that it is difficult to generate realistic dummies if the users stop regularly. In [27] two dummy based solutions are proposed to achieve k-anonymity for privacy-aware users. Also, in [28] a binomial mix-based solution is proposed which aims to protect privacy by using a centralized dummy generation mechanism that exploits the activities of each user to perform better in overall.

In [6] a number of different techniques are described for location privacy and include the use of query enlargement, which enlarge the position of the user to a larger set of positions and then send it to the service provider. Additionally the use of k-anonymous approaches is irrelevant in our case since these types of privacy-protection methods are dependent on the distribution of other users of the system. Besides the above, [4] is an approach to privacy preservation using adaptive and context-aware user interactions, although it is used in smart environments it is still important. Furthermore, the use of progressive retrieval techniques has been described by the same authors where the client iteratively retrieves results from the service provider without revealing its exact location. Also, the use of transformation based techniques is described in [7] that use cryptographic transformation, hence the service provider is not able to identify the exact location and only the client has the decryption functionality to derive the actual results.

6   Conclusions and Future Work

Various online services, including e/m-government, use technologies such as mobile recommender systems that aim to solve the information overload problem of users utilizing such a software system in their mobile device. Privacy though is an open issue and most privacy protection techniques have been based either on personal data, such as user ratings, protection or use third party systems for keeping private the exchange of information. We proposed a practical and effective method that aims to protect every aspect of contextual parameter found in context-aware mobile recommender systems, without the use of a third party. The proposed method automatically generates a set of dummies that are sent from the client to the server, with the real values hidden between the dummy ones. Then the system, with a small utility cost, provides a set of recommendations to the client without any privacy risks. On completion the client disregards the dummy recommendations, eliminating any surplus and/or confusing data. Although this method is practical, it could become more effective if the generated dummies become more realistic and the privacy protection element can be divided into multiple levels and become adaptive to each user, thus providing a lesser burden on the server. A clear case would be that of a user who does not have any privacy concerns. If the system is made aware of the user's position, then the server will be responding faster in providing recommendations as the load of the server will not be as heavy. Further performance evaluation tests will be necessary to fully support the proposed approach.

References

1. Adomavicius, G., Tuzhilin, A.: Context-aware recommender systems. In: Ricci, F., Rokach, L., Shapira, B., Kantor, P.B. (eds.) Recommender Systems Handbook, pp. 217–253. Springer, New York (2011)
2. Bobadilla, J., Ortega, F., Hernando, A., Gutiérrez, A.: Recommender systems survey. Knowl.-Based Syst. **46**, 109–132 (2013)
3. del Carmen Rodríguez-Hernández, M., Ilarri, S.: Towards a Context-Aware Mobile Recommendation Architecture. In: Awan, I., Younas, M., Franch, X., Quer, C. (eds.) MobiWIS 2014. LNCS, vol. 8640, pp. 56–70. Springer, Heidelberg (2014)
4. Pallapa, G., Di Francesco, M., Das, S.K.: Adaptive and context-aware privacy preservation schemes exploiting user interactions in pervasive environments. In: 2012 IEEE International Symposium on a World of Wireless, Mobile and Multimedia Networks (WoWMoM), pp. 1–6. IEEE, June 2012
5. Jannach, D., Zanker, M., Felfernig, A., Friedrich, G.: Recommender Systems: an Introduction. Cambridge University Press, Cambridge (2010)
6. Jensen, C.S., Lu, H., Yiu, M.L.: Location privacy techniques in client-server architectures. In: Bettini, C., Jajodia, S., Samarati, P., Wang, X.S. (eds.) Privacy in Location-Based Applications. LNCS, vol. 5599, pp. 31–58. Springer, Heidelberg (2009)
7. Kido, H., Yanagisawa, Y., Satoh, T.: An anonymous communication technique using dummies for location-based services. In: Proceedings of the International Conference on Pervasive Services, ICPS 2005. IEEE (2005)
8. Konstan, J.A., Riedl, J.: Recommender systems: from algorithms to user experience. User Model. User-Adap. Inter. **22**(1-2), 101–123 (2012)
9. Košir, A., Odic, A., Kunaver, M., Tkalcic, M., Tasic, J.F.: Database for contextual personalization. Elektrotehniški vestnik **78**(5), 270–274 (2011)
10. Liu, Q., Ma, H., Chen, E., Xiong, H.: A survey of context-aware mobile recommendations. Int. J. Inf. Technol. Decis. Mak. **12**(01), 139–172 (2013)
11. Mettouris, C., Papadopoulos, G.A.: Ubiquitous recommender systems. Computing **96**(3), 223–257 (2014)
12. Polatidis, N., Georgiadis, C.K.: Mobile recommender systems: An overview of technologies and challenges. In: 2013 Second International Conference on Informatics and Applications (ICIA). IEEE (2013)
13. Polatidis, N., Georgiadis, C.K.: Factors influencing the quality of the user experience in ubiquitous recommender systems. In: Streitz, N., Markopoulos, P. (eds.) DAPI 2014. LNCS, vol. 8530, pp. 369–379. Springer, Heidelberg (2014)
14. Ricci, F.: Mobile recommender systems. Inf. Technol. Tourism **12**(3), 205–231 (2010)

15. Scipioni, M.P.: Towards privacy-aware location-based recommender systems. In: IFIP Summer School 2011 (2011)
16. Shi, Y., Larson, M., Hanjalic, A.: Collaborative filtering beyond the user-item matrix: a survey of the state of the art and future challenges. ACM Comput. Surv. (CSUR) 47(1), 3 (2014)
17. Sun, Y., Chong, W.K., Han, Y.S., Rho, S., Man, K.L.: Key factors affecting user experience of mobile recommendation systems. In: Proceedings of the International MultiConference of Engineers and Computer Scientists, vol. 2 (2015)
18. Boutet, A., Frey, D., Guerraoui, R., Jégou, A., Kermarrec, A.M.: Privacy-preserving distributed collaborative filtering. In: Computing (2015). doi:10.1007/s00607-015-0451-z
19. Aïmeur, E., Brassard, G., Fernandez, J.M., Onana, F.S.M.: Alambic: a privacy-preserving recommender system for electronic commerce. Int. J. Inf. Secur. 7(5), 307–334 (2008)
20. Polat, H., Du, W.: Privacy-preserving collaborative filtering. Int. J. Electron. Commer. 9(4), 9–35 (2005)
21. Drogkaris, P., Gritzalis, S., Lambrinoudakis, C.: Employing privacy policies and preferences in modern e–government environments. Int. J. Electron. Gov. 6(2), 101–116 (2013)
22. Drogkaris, P., Gritzalis, A., Lambrinoudakis, C.: Empowering users to specify and manage their privacy preferences in e-Government environments. In: Kő, A., Francesconi, E. (eds.) EGOVIS 2014. LNCS, vol. 8650, pp. 237–245. Springer, Heidelberg (2014)
23. Enggong, L., Whitworth, B.: Are security and privacy equally important in influencing citizens to use e–consultation? Int. J. Electron. Gov. 6(2), 152–166 (2013)
24. Chadwick, A.: Web 2.0: new challenges for the study of e-democracy in an era of informational exuberance. ISJLP 5, 9 (2008)
25. Lu, H., Jensen, C.S., Yiu, M.L.: Pad: privacy-area aware, dummy-based location privacy in mobile services. In: Proceedings of the Seventh ACM International Workshop on Data Engineering for Wireless and Mobile Access, pp. 16–23. ACM, June 2008
26. Kato, R., Iwata, M., Hara, T., Suzuki, A., Xie, X., Arase, Y., Nishio, S.: A dummy-based anonymization method based on user trajectory with pauses. In: Proceedings of the 20th International Conference on Advances in Geographic Information Systems, pp. 249–258. ACM, November 2012
27. Niu, B., Zhang, Z., Li, X., Li, H.: Privacy-area aware dummy generation algorithms for location-based services. In: 2014 IEEE International Conference on Communications (ICC), pp. 957–962. IEEE, June 2014
28. Tran, M.T., Echizen, I., Duong, A.D.: Binomial-mix-based location anonymizer system with global dummy generation to preserve user location privacy in location-based services. In: ARES 2010 International Conference on Availability, Reliability, and Security, 2010, pp. 580–585. IEEE, February 2010
29. Kumar, M., Sinha, O.P.: M-government–mobile technology for e-government. In: International Conference on e-Government, India, pp. 294–301 (2007)
30. Georgiadis, C.K., Stiakakis, E.: Extending an e-Government service measurement framework to m-Governement services. In: 2010 Ninth International Conference on Mobile Business and 2010 Ninth Global Mobility Roundtable (ICMB-GMR), pp. 432–439. IEEE, June 2010

Privacy in Online Social Networks

Privacy and Facebook Universities Students' Communities for Confessions and Secrets: The Greek Case

Maria Sideri[1], Angeliki Kitsiou[2], Christos Kalloniatis[1(✉)],
and Stefanos Gritzalis[3]

[1] Cultural Informatics Laboratory, Department of Cultural Technology
and Communication, University of the Aegean, GR 81100 Lesvos, Greece
{msid, chkallon}@aegean.gr
[2] University of the Aegean, GR 81100 Lesvos, Greece
a.kitsiou@aegean.gr
[3] Information and Communication Systems Security Laboratory,
Department of Information and Communications Systems Engineering,
University of the Aegean, GR 83200 Samos, Greece
sgritz@aegean.gr

Abstract. Communities on Facebook (FB) provide their members with the opportunity to express themselves freely and share personal information using anonymity. It is known that people are reluctant to discuss vis-à-vis a number of personal issues in real life, since they fear types of informal control that may be exercised on them by other people. In digital life on the contrary, anonymity is thought to ensure privacy and enforce the disclosure of the most inner thoughts, feelings and concerns without the restrictions of informal social control. In this research, we examine the case of 20 newly formed networked FB students' communities. Although, the communities' goal is to enable students express freely, the research shows that members' speech is under criticism and their stated behaviors (online) are labeled according to the predominant social norms, highlighting standard types of informal social control, as well as latent types. The study is conducted by using the method of critical discourse analysis serving the creation of clear descriptive and explanatory categories, which resulted in our constructing two conceptual entity data models concerning administrators' and users' posts. FB communities websites not only do not meet the technical requirements regarding privacy but also new socio-technical aspects should be taken into consideration as personal information disclosure is violated. Our research indicates the necessity of new requirements that will fulfil privacy demands.

Keywords: Social media · Informal social control · Privacy · Anonymity · Conceptual model · Students' communities

1 Introduction

During the formation of the Network Society, as Castels [1] refers to the Information Society, plenty of networked communities have been formulated by using social media in order to distribute their own information, to get associated with other communities or

© Springer International Publishing Switzerland 2015
S.K. Katsikas and A.B. Sideridis (Eds.): E-Democracy 2015, CCIS 570, pp. 77–94, 2015.
DOI: 10.1007/978-3-319-27164-4_6

to join in activities of mutual interest [2]. The prevalence of social media affects social and cultural aspects of daily live, transforming the structure of people's social outlet. Although the forms of social outlet are changing, the information technology used still serves the objectives and social values, already established by the existing social, political and institutional constraints [3].

Social media and networking as a consequence of the development of social actors' activities in a structured system, contribute to the modulation of daily social practices. On the one hand social media enable easier access to communication and social interaction while on the other they constitute new fields of social conflict, characterized by different forms of social control [4]. Eriksen [5] notes that the derivative conflicts from the individuals' exposure to the "information flood", concerning security, predictability, sense of belonging, stable personal identity, cohesion, genuine unmediated experiences are all related to the exercise of social control. Respectively, the intensification of social control is achieved through sophisticated techniques, designed to gather or edit a huge amount of information, widespread on the Internet, for the entire population.

Authority is now exercised through controlling information [6], widespread via information technologies, where the quality of information is predefined and its meanings are shaped as a product of mediated experiences among the transmitters and the receivers [7, 8], enacting in social media. Taking into consideration that the state ceases to be the sole information operator, since multinational enterprises, handling information, transformed the public discourse from a consensus mechanism of critical dialogue to a consensus mechanism of manipulation [9], it is critical to understand the role of social media on the expansion of social control.

The rest of the paper is organized as follows. Section 2 addresses related work from domains such as privacy and informal social control, exercised in social media, in order to introduce the research question. Section 3 presents the research subject, the networked communities on Facebook created by students of Greek Universities, and their goals in advancing anonymity. Section 4 refers to the methodology followed as well as to the suggested conceptual entity data models, in which the research was relied. In Sect. 5 the results of our research concerning the disclosure of personal information are presented followed by a future entity data model. Finally, Sect. 6 recalls the main findings of the research and discusses future research objectives.

2 Related Work and Question Raised

It is well-acknowledged that the use of media for social control is an evolving conceptual frame during the last decades [10–12]. Chomsky [13] notes that a fundamental element of social control concerns the strategy of public's distraction from problems and determined policies through the technique of continuous deluge of insignificant information. With respect to this flood, social actors experience the contradictions of postmodernity, both individually and collectively, by retaining their internal fields of action based on the established values and rules as habitus [14] as well as by facing value-dilemmas about them, since the institutions guiding aids are not the only sovereign to coordinate their actions. In addition "*the discrimination boundaries among personal data and public accessible personal information are equally incon-spicuous, hereof multiplying the potential use and misuse of personal data"* [15] (p. 38), in order the social control to be expanded.

The concept of social control depends on the historical, political, economic, social and cultural parameters of each studied era [16]; a key feature of social control in Network Society is its expansion to behaviors that are classified as deviant, not only by the law, but also in informal ways by the predominant social values, patterns and standards. In other words, the social control that is now being exercised concerns the spontaneous compliance of people with the established principles and rules [17], through the process of "auto-disciplinary", as it was designated by Foucault [18].

Several researches [19–22] examine the case of social media through Benthams' panopticon framework. It is important to indicate that social control is exercised via interactive and interpersonal social activities and panopticon is expanded to more and more informal forms of social control, coming from everyone and addressing to everyone equally, altering thus the concept of privacy and surveillance both quantita-tively and qualitatively. In this context, informal social control predominates where little individualism or privacy exists [23]. Additionally, Cas [24] states that the disclosure of personal data in social media may have a profound impact on peoples' behavior and identity formation. A continuing process of self-determination and hetero-determination takes place due to the establishment of a complex communicative and symbolic reality, created in social media, where individuals constitute the fundamental nodes of an ongoing multi-communication composed by different cultural representation standards.

So, despite the fact of not being admitted or stated explicitly by the authority, contemporary social control focuses on monitoring everyday behavior [25], resulting from its expansion in more informal forms. What is gratify to note is that informal social control cannot be easily described, since it constitutes a part of peoples' daily interactions -*beliefs, social suggestions, ideologies, folklores, customs, religion, humor, sarcasm, satire, ridicule*- including nonverbal communication at the micro-level and hence it can hardly be standardized and categorized [26] (p. 112).

Aiming to identify and categorize the vastness and the ubiquity of informal social control exercised through social media, as well as its impact on the concept of privacy, it is really important to point out some specific features of this mechanism, using Foucault's framework about surveillance [18]. Social media, designated as a mecha-nism of informal social control, could be identified as a type of Foucault's [18] dis-cipline, without coinciding neither with an institution nor a mechanism of power. Social media, whose special feature is networking, turned to operate as a tool to expand cyber panopticon [27] and practice informal social control. Their function includes checking peoples' online moves, marking their online presence or absence, evaluating peoples' online behaviors, attitudes, actions and abilities, imposing online exclusion [28], equally for all. This equality to intangible surveillance provides social actors with a sense of security and supposed conformation of joint cognitive orientations, which leads them to trust their online profiles personal information which would be incom-prehensible to share in their actual personal interactions.

Therefore, social media reduce free self-determination as well as they limit privacy, while users have the illusion of privacy, which leads to boundary problems of the kind of information they should share [11]. Viégas [29] claims that there are differences between users' representations about how they feel for privacy and how they actually react to a privacy breach. Highlighting the existence of the privacy paradox phenomenon [11, 30, 31], it is important to say that the conceptualization of privacy is indicated by considerable variations among socio-cultural systems [32, 33]. Among all bounded approaches, it is crucial to note that privacy has been acknowledged as an important principle by all modern democracies [34] and it is in need of preservation [35]. But what kind of preservation does privacy need? Taking into consideration Bauman's note [36] that *"the information circulates the globe independently from its first transmitter"* (p. 33), as well as Foucault's [18] suggestion that authority depends on a set of internal mechanisms where individuals create themselves a relationship in which they are trapped, we focus on the formation of the concept of information privacy concerning the use of social media as public discourse field within informal social control is exercised. Posing the research question whether *"The disclosure of personal information in Facebook, as a field of informal social control, modulates the concept of information privacy"*, we examined the case of 20, newly formed, networked communities on Facebook, created by students of Greek Universities in relation to the disclosure either of their own personal information or other members' (students or academic staff) personal information.

3 The New Student Communities on Facebook

During 2014 a tendency occurred between students in Greek Universities to create new communities on Facebook. These communities which probably in the first place were set in Institutions of Athens expanded quickly to regional Institutions.

All of them have the well-known characteristics of communities on Facebook. Specifically participants have common interests -in this case students' identity sets the interest based community up to a point -, upload multimodal material -text and audiovisual-, comment on posts, using a written form of speech that resembles the spoken language –this is mentioned by Ong as "secondary orality" [37] - but has also abbreviations and emoticons. The first interesting issue about these communities is their name. Entitled *"Unmentionable"*, *"Confessions"*, *"Confidential"*, *"The cryptic of..."*, *"Revelations"*, *"Top secret"* or in a similar way, the words used originally set the community's targets. What are those? Although someone could think that these communities act as forum for dialogue, promoting interaction between student population on matters affecting them, their names-titles alone determine that they intend to act as environments of free speech or –correctly- of expression without restrictions. And this, in the first place, doesn't strike, since all social networking sites facilitate free communication, often restricted in vis-à-vis contact due to social rules. But in the case of these communities, it is not just the free expression among their members, but a speech on topics concerning personal information, especially emotional and erotic-sexual life and secrets, as recorded in the goals of each FB group. However, this doesn't mean that there are not posts about others topics such as exams, comments on politics and political parties. In this spectrum, these communities give their members space to talk about issues that in real life are hardly mentioned, as they provide –or thought to provide- anonymity and thus protection from social control.

4   Methodology

In Greece there are 23 Universities. In 14 of those, Facebook students' communities have been formulated in order to share secrets and innermost thoughts. In our exploratory research, we accessed the 11 of those 14 students communities on Facebook through all the posts from the moment of their beginning. We didn't assess the community named "Anolomogita" in Harokopio University of Athens and the homonym in University of Thessaly that are closed groups and assess is permitted only to members. The community of Athens University of Economics and Business was also not included due to lack of time. In some of these 11 institutions -those with a large number of students- communities are also organized based on faculties and departments. Our research included these cases too.

The study was conducted by using the method of critical discourse analysis, as a part of Qualitative Content Analysis, serving the creation of clear descriptive and explanatory categories, resulting from the users' posts, related to the plurality of data interpretations [38] as well as to the linguistic choices of research subjects [39]. This method is "open" to different interpretations and therefore characterized by flexibility [40]. The categories are also related to the significance and usefulness of data [41], as well as to latent messages [42]. As Rogers [43] indicates this method not only constitutes *"a description and interpretation of words on social context, but also explains why and how these operate"* (p. 2).

Furthermore, as Delbru et al. [44] indicate the abundance of web semi-structured data and the necessity for their structured analysis to be considered as vital to create a category system. Respectively, through a systematic, networked communities' posts check, we were led to recognizing, grouping and coding issues according to the purpose of our research, as well as to the assortment and creation of categories through a classification process, by which issues are evaluated appropriately and afterwards correlated [45]. Our category system was designated by defining communities' posts as units of measurement and analysis. The posts were distinguished to specific groups, characterized by common traits or properties, using qualitative criteria in order to achieve a strict observation of the posts' content and their communicative material, as well as their quantification. Mason [46] explains that the category system serves the accurate screening of analysis material and the taxa set, beyond the contribution to a discrete analysis, which lends research validity. The accuracy, validity and effectiveness of our classification is provided by the application of the following rules, with respect to Vamvoukas framework [47]: (i) **Objectivity**, (ii) **Exhaustivity**, (iii) **Correctness**, (iv) **Exclusivity** and Tsiolis and Babbie's framework [48, 49] about peer debriefing and test-retest reliability respectively.

This data classification process, followed a purposive sample procedure during which the necessary units (posts) were identified and selected -*290 posts were analyzed from approximately 3.000 posts*- and led us to the construction of two conceptual entity data models according to Han, Kamber and Pei's framework [50]. The conceptual entity data models –that stand for the aforementioned communities- the one oriented to the administrators' posts and the other to users' posts, allowed us to conduct a thematic typological analysis. Therefore, after identifying and defining the entities,

Table 1. FB Universities' communities

University	Name of community[a]	Friends	Beginning
University of Athens	EKPA Apokalipseis	3.401	2/2015
School of Philosophy, University of Athens	Filosofiko Aporrito	15.000	6/2014
School of Law and Political Sciences, University of Athens	Politiko Aporrito Reloaded	380	2/2015
Dept. of Mathematics, University of Athens	Ta math-es?	4.765	7/2014
Dept. of Pharmacy, University of Athens	Farmakeytiko Aporrito	800	11/2014
Dept. of Political Science and Public Administration, University of Athens	Ta Apokrifa toy Politikou	940	9/2014
Aristotle University of Thessaloniki	Anomologita A.U.Th.	20.000	11/2014
School of Agronomy, Aristotle University of Thessaloniki	Geoponimata A.U.Th.	678	12/2014
School of Engineering, Aristotle University of Thessaloniki	Politechnikes Sexomologiseis Thessalonikis	3.200	12/2014
Agricultural University of Athens	Geopo(r)nikes Exomoligiseis	3.400	11/2014
University of Piraeus	To Pa.Pirazei?	6.050	9/2014
Panteion University	Panteion Empisteytikon	5.600	9/2014
National Technical University of Athens	NTUA Wanna Know	3.230	1/2015
	EMPisteytiko	10.000	7/2014
University of Patras	Oyte toy Pa.Pa	8.075	1/2015
Dept. of Electrical and Computer Engineering, University of Patras	Electrologikon Aporriton	880	11/2014
Institutions of Crete (University of Crete, Technical University of Crete, Technological Educational Institute of Crete)	Pagkritio Aporrito - TOP Secret	240	3/2015
Technical University of Crete	Polytechniko Aporrito TUC	3.124	1/2015
University of Macedonia	Pa.Mak.edoniko Aporrito	1.730	11/2014
University of the Aegean	Anomologita University of the Aegean -Lesvos	1.325	3/2015

[a]The FB communities are entitled by Greek idioms related to the Universities', Faculties' or Departments' names, referring mainly to erotic-sexual life issues and therefore are not translated.

we proceeded with the determination of all interactions between the entities. The representational models of used data are illustrated by graphics so as to represent the entity framework infrastructure. The posts' speech was analyzed in order to underline parameters such as context, participants and meanings, aiming to detect language's ideological supports and record the relationships between language/text and social relations [51], as well as to reveal representations of privacy issues constructed through language. The categories are also interpreted by presenting short eye catching and inline passages of the posts, according to Richardson's framework [52]. Furthermore, it is important to note that our research is cross-sectional; studying the flow of posts in a particular period and in the specific social context oriented to the relationship among the analysis units (posts) (Table 1).

5 Results

Data organization in series, according to the semantic elements of the posts -as sections of the speech with respect to a concept- encapsulates their essential content and reveals the following concepts which are distinguished in two cognitive schemas. The first one concerns administrators' posts related to (i) Communities' goals, (ii) Confidential-ity-Anonymity (the two concepts are analyzed as one, because they are represented as identical by the administrators), (iii) Communities' function (where types of informal social control are indicated) while the second concerns users' posts related to (i) Dis-closure of personal information, (ii) Disclosure of other peoples' personal information, (iii) Context criticism (where types of informal social control are indicated). The structure of these two entity data models provides a broad view of those concepts that are included in order to encode the collected data, allowing the quantification of the results and their further comparison, subject to the equitable calculation of categorizing units. Additionally, each unit analysis allows information retrieved to be taking into account only once.

5.1 Administrators' Posts Entity Data Model

This Model consists of a major entity "Administrators' posts" and three minor entities "Communities' goals posts", "Confidentiality- Anonymity posts", "Communities'

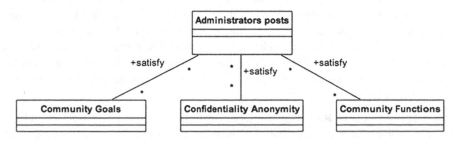

Fig. 1. Administrators' post entity data model

function posts", where major and minor entities are differentiated by their level. A Many-to-many (M:N) relationship among entities is indicated and represented by bidirectional bows which specify data distribution and the frequency of the analyzed entities -among 290 units' analysis, 20 % of them are the administrators' posts-highlighting the issues that have showed up, as being analyzed below (Fig. 1).

Administrators' Posts Referring to Communities' Goals: 6.55 % -(19). The identity of these communities is determined mainly by their goal, which in all cases is related to the provision of a place where members who belong to the same secondary social group can post whatever they want, every secret, anonymously. The goal of each community is set by its administrator from the beginning, as it is exemplified in Table 2 below:

Table 2. Quotes indicating communities' goals (Administrators' posts)

Geoponimata AUTh
"Dear Agriculturists, it's our turn to reveal, grumble, disapprove, fall in love... to pollinate and to sprout anonymous" (24/12/2014)

Politechnikes Sexomologiseis Thessalonikis
"There is finally a place for us to share peppery and spicy secrets. Every kind of confessions concerning mostly situations in our university. Trust your secret to us with confidence here" (28/12/2014)

Ta Apokrifa toy Politikou
"Only for the students of the Dept. of Political Science and Public Administration ... has entertainment purpose. Abusive comments towards students or teachers are prohibited"

Pa.Mak.edoniko Aporrito
A space for *"secrets, confessions and all the happenings of PA.MAK"* (05/02/2015)

To Pa.Pirazei?
A space for *"innermost thoughts and feelings".*

Anomologita University of the Aegean –Lesvos
"Fantastic page for anonymous confessions, now on our island. Anonymous, confidential, but above all without taboos! For every kind of frustration, taste, secret and gossip! Give pain free".

According to these statements, students are invited to express themselves freely. It is significant to note that a number of words or phrases such as "reveal", "secret", "confession", "innermost thoughts" and "without taboos" are used to describe the potential content of the posts. These words are chosen not only because of their power as semantic units, but mostly because of their symbolic power embedded in the real world, where secrets and innermost thoughts are not supposed to be expressed in public and confessions are not supposed to be made. So these FB communities promise their members the breaking of real life's restrictions providing a place for expression without taboos. It is in one case only where the administrator emphasizes on community entertainment purpose.

Administrators' Posts Referring to Confidentiality- Anonymity: 6.55 % -(19). Emphasis within these communities is given on confidentiality guaranteed and on anonymity, as exemplified in Table 3 below:

Table 3. Quotes regarding confidentiality-anonymity (Administrators' posts)

Politechnikes Sexomologiseis Thessalonikis
"Boys and girls, share your secret with us in strict confidence!" (05/03/2015)
Pagkritio Aporrito - TOP Secret
"Welcome to PAGKRITIO SECRET! Share your secret anonymously" (02/03/2015)
Polytechniko Aporrito TUC
"...share your secret anonymously (there is no IP record or anything)"(29/04/2015)
Ta math-es?
"Whisper anonymously your thoughts in the form below and we will share them with confidentiality"
Panteion Empisteytikon
"Anonymity and Confidentiality. A page for Panteion students, in which you can send us messages about the faculty (teacher quotes, incidents in the school), generally any message about things that you would never say in public. These messages will be posted as Panteion Confidential. Your names will not appear anywhere (not even us) so express yourself freely. Abusive comments are not allowed"

As it is known people are afraid of expressing inner thoughts and feelings in public and hesitate to confess secrets, due to the probability of social control exercised by other people, either by disapproval, laugh, sarcasm, rejection or any other form of control. Anonymity ("names will not appear") in social networking communities is supposed to prevent users from exposure to public opinion. As the success of every group depends on the extent of its members' interaction, the promotion and emphasis on anonymity – expressed in administrators' post by the noun "anonymous" or by the adverb "anonymously" – must be understood as an intense attempt to persuade students to participate in the community. The reference to "strict confidence" and "confidentiality" is on the other hand a way to establish trust primarily between members and administrator. Anonymity is correlated to confidence through a bidirectional relation, in which the latter one ensures the first and anonymity's attainment confirms the given trust.

Administrators' Posts about Communities' Function: 6.89 % -(20). In each community, the administrator –not known in the examined cases- often becomes recipient of comments usually disapproving either because he/she delays to upload members' posts or because members consider that he/she selects what it will be posted or less often because he/she posts without checking the content. Therefore, administrator and users are all expanded to informal social control, exercised among them. Posts are submitted to the administrator using a special form (google docs) where personal information is requested only in reference to the Department or Faculty attended and in some cases to the year of studies. The administrator should examine the content of the post –if it follows the rules of the community- and he/she uploads it using a pseudonym and a number following, that refers to the post. Below the post, the Department or Faculty appears as stated by the member (Table 4).

The communities' rules are clear from the beginning. Although, in these FB pages every member can express freely, it is not allowed to send "insulting messages", "personally attack" or "offend" another person. Offensive comments are not just those that refer to other people by their surname but also those that delineate them. Given the

Table 4. Quotes indicating communities' function

Community	Administrators' post about communities' function
Anomologita AUTh.	*"Because of unfortunate incidents in recent days, I put a couple of more specific rules for the good, as far as possible, operation of the group.* *(1) Posts are welcomed if sent through the electronic form, which maintains your anonymity. Please, no more messages in the inbox, besides personal observations or complaints.* *(2) Messages that are personal attack on individuals and affect their personality will be ignored.* *(3) If you find a post that offends you, someone you know, or generally ... not ..., ship it to the inbox as quickly as possible, to resolve the issue.* *(4) Do not send the same message two, three, four, eight times. It's not going to go up automatically and you simply manage to do nothing more than slow and snorlax the process.* *(5) Do not ask to be posted what you send, once sent. There is a written order of priority. Because of the number of posts, it may take a while.* *(6) The code names of posts will change after # 100"* (26/12/2014)
Pagkritio Aporrito – TOP Secret	*"CAUTION* • *offensive comments to people (by surnames) will not be published* • *posts concerning political parties and sports will not be published,* • *Try to keep up with the concept of "secret" and "confidential" sharing anything with others who don't know who you are* • *If someone finds that he/she is personally affected by a post, send a personal message to the page with the post's LINK and we will check it out.*(02/03/2015)
Geopornimata AUTh	*"after protests from fellow students .... the insulting messages, which affect persons (namely) directly will not be published ... Thanks and good confessions!"*
Politechnikes Sexomologiseis Thessalonikis	*"Posts which attack other persons consciously mentioning them or responding to them by name or delineating them, will not be posted..."* (14/01/2015)

presupposed anonymity of the members who post, the above mentioned rule is set to ensure the anonymity of other people mentioned in the posts and to regulate a proper social behavior online so as to guarantee the community's cohesion and sustainability.

5.2   Users' Posts Entity Data Model

This Model consists of a major entity "Users' posts" and three minor entities *"Disclosure of personal* information *posts"*, *"Disclosure of other peoples' personal* information *posts"*, *"Context criticism"*, where major and minor are differentiated by their level. A Many-to-many (M:N) relationship among the entities is indicated and represented by bidirectional bows, which specify the data distribution and the frequency of the analyzed entities- among 290 analysis units, 80 % of them are the users' posts-highlighting the issues that came up, as being analyzed below (Fig. 2):

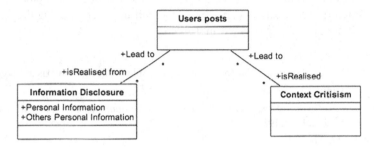

Fig. 2. Users' posts entity data model

Users' Posts Concerning Disclosure of Personal Information: 28.96 % (84). Our research showed cases that students' online behavior having to do with sharing personal information and specific details about their erotic-sexual life, differentiate from their actual behavior, without obvious motivation. It is really important to indicate that the replies to posts are named, without of course being able to ascertain whether the factual information is provided. Thirty-four per cent (34 %) of the reply posts we analyzed, showed the names of the students, coming into contradiction with the goals of the communities (Table 5).

Table 5. Quotes concerning disclosure of personal information (Users' posts)

Ta math-es?
Confessing his love to a woman and stating his will to have sex with her (25/05/2015) (post number 204)

NTUA Wanna Know
Confessing her love for a first year student and asking for help in order to find him (22/04/2015) (post number 537)

Filosofiko Aporrito
The student states that she does not prefer hugs with her boyfriend (31/05/2015) (post number 148)

Panteion Empisteytikon
Confessing that he/she prefers masturbating than having sex (22/12/2014) (post number 40)

Anomologita AUTh.
Confessing his/her problems about his/her relationship (31/05/2015) (post number 41)

Social networking sites play an important role to students' interaction and communication. Reed et al. [53] refer to Pascoe who reports that young people use social networking sites to express romantic feelings for their partners or to communicate with them. But this is not the case in the posts above, since they are not addressed to mates, but to other persons. Besides, there are two cases that the posts reveal erotic/sexual preferences (number 148 and 40) and not feelings.

Users' Posts Concerning Disclosure of Other Peoples' Personal Information: 25.17 % (73). Although the rule of non-reference in a person by name or descriptive features is clear and explicit in all pages, it is violated in some cases. Throughout our research, it became obvious that there are incidents where the post uploaded by the administrator referred to a person either by his/her full name or by using the first name and part of the surname, as presented in Table 6.

Table 6. Quotes concerning disclosure of other peoples' information (Users' posts)

Anomologita AUTh
Reference to a man (by name and surname), asking to communicate with him and have sex. (31/05/2015) (post number 249)
Geopornimata AUTh
Reference to a man (only by name) and his friends in order to have group sex.(01/06/2015) (post number 22)
Politechnikes Sexomologiseis Thessalonikis
Reference to a man (by name and part of his surname), asking if available for cybersex. (5/1/2015) (post number 17)
Ta math-es?
Reference to a woman (by name and surname) recording imagery for a specific attitude to sex (07/02/2015) (post number 204)
Anomologita University of the Aegean –Lesvos
Reference to a woman (by name) commenting her body and asking "how much is her fee for sex" (12/05/2015) (post number 94)
Reference to a woman (name and department) called whore (30/04/2015) (post number 45)

Many more are the cases that the person is described in detail by mentioning one or more clues such as physical characteristics, clothing, department, place and time of meeting, as exemplified in Table 7.

It is more than obvious that posts included in Tables 6 and 7 violate the rule of non offensive comments and reveal personal information. In some cases the comments are extremely abusive (e.g. post 94 in Table 6 or 405 in Table 7) and sexistic (e.g. post 45 in Table 6). These constitute a "problematic digital behavior" [54] exercised mainly through pressure either for acquaintance in the purpose of sex or for a specific sex attitude. What is interesting about these posts is that the administrator uploaded them although he/she had stated that offensive posts would be ignored. This didn't happen either because the administrators did not check the posts or because they didn't consider them insulting. Whatever the cause, they exposed publicly information concerning other people mentioned in the posts.

Table 7. Quotes concerning disclosure of other peoples' information (Users' posts)

Geopornimata AUTh
Reference to a man (by features: beard, dark red sweatshirt standing outside the auditorium) addressed as handsome (22/01/2015) (post number 23)
Politechnikes Sexomologiseis Thessalonikis
Reference to a man (by features: color of hair, beard, glasses, height, purple pants, every Thursday outside the canteen, probably doctoral candidate) characterized cute, whom the writer "wants to rape" (31/03/2015) (post number 405)
Pagkritio Aporrito - TOP Secret
Reference to a woman (by features: dress in animal print clothes, short, extremely fit back) (02/03/2015) (post number 7)
NTUA Wanna Know
Reference to a woman (by features: bus station, Tuesday, dark brown hair, a spot in cheek and big lips, light blue jeans...short black blouse and black bag) asking for acquaintance with her (19/05/2015) (post number 762)

Users' Posts Revealing Context Criticism: 22.41 % (65). Direct reactions by any student concerning the content of the posts are rarely seen. Relative examples of these are reported in Table 8. However, it is important to indicate that indirect reactions to the context showed up with high frequency, through sarcasm and humorous responses, highlighting another form of informal social control.

Table 8. Indicative context criticism quotes (Users' posts)

Anomologita University of the Aegean –Lesvos
The writer says that he/she got bored with posts about sexual life and that these posts are written by worthless people (direct criticism) (7/05/2015) (post number 58)
Panteion Empisteytikon
The writer questions if those who post are psychologically and spiritually healthy, as the page was created in order to provide students of Panteion with information but it turned out to be a porn page (direct criticism) (26/09/2014) (post number 213)
The student says that the page is to cause laugh according to the description of its goal and that there are groups for each department, where the posts' content is different. (direct criticism) (Reply to post 213-26/09/2014)
Anomologita AUTh.
The writer criticizes another student's character, as well as his/her social origin, due to previous post. (direct criticism) (31/05/2015) (post number 38)
Pa.Mak.edoniko Aporrito
Characterizing another student as pervert due to his/her reveal of having sex with his/her cousin (direct criticism) (Reply to post 101-05/02/2015)

5.3   Other Findings and Future Research

It is also worth mentioning some additional findings, which indicate that the members check and criticize the administrators. This happens in respect to delays on behalf of the administrator to upload (e.g. post on page Pa.Mak.edoniko Aporrito, 13/1/2015 and post on page Anomologita University of the Aegean –Lesvos, 04/05/2015).

The anonymity of the administrator causes questions about him/her and speculations about his/her age, sex, school that attends. This is another interesting issue, as members want to find out who the administrator is, violating anonymity that protects them. The administrator of "Anomologita" in Aristotle University states, during an interview for a blog, that *"it's fun that in "Anomologita" members speculate a certain identity for the administrator concerning sex and faculty"*. The same concern about administrator's sex exists also in Anomologita University of the Aegean –Lesvos (post number 69, 4/5/2015).

Our entity data models, coupled with the critical discourse analysis used, have established a linear process, including identification, examination, classification and analysis of the specific FB networked communities' speech. Throughout this process, we have to take into consideration that more information requirements are needed, in order to guide us to continue it by developing a more complex/diverse model in the future. Our conceptual entity data models can be used as the foundation for a logical data model, which will bear the correlations of analyzed information, indicated by critical discourse analysis, in order to decompose the relationships between the major entity types as well as the minor found. Therefore, the logical data model will include the entire relationships among entities, specifying primary keys and attributes for each entity, while it will dynamically define new discrete-valued attributes providing the critical discourse analysis within more complex information areas.

6   Discussion-Conclusions

The conducted analysis related to the referred FB communities, based on Foucault's framework [18] and on the argument for exercised informal social control in Facebook, brings up that the concept of information privacy is being modulated. Although all communities define their target as members' free expression with an emphasis on secrets and confessions, it is indicated in many cases that this expression was under criticism and the members' stated behaviors (online) were labeled according to the predominant social norms, highlighting standard types of informal social control (direct reactions), as well as latent types (indirect reactions such as sarcasm or humor), supporting Bergalli's and Sumner's [26] thesis about its exercise.

However, during online interaction, when informal social control takes place as in real life, members seem to bother less as they undergo the procedure of "auto-disciplinary". In some cases users feel they can share even the most inner information about their erotic-sexual life, expanding the concept of privacy; it seems though that some privacy/sexual taboos (sex with family members) cannot be overcome. In these cases, as anonymity precludes consideration of personal information, the focus was on the content of the suspensions.

It is obvious that there are rules of behavior in virtual communities and these rules are imposed by the administrator, who is also being monitored by users, highlighting once again the function of an extending cyber-panopticon in qualitative and quantitative way. These communities, promising confidentiality, aim at facilitating a trustful communication between members. Simultaneously, the communities promising members' anonymity basically release what to offline ground could hardly be said, since people fear informal social control applied as a "punishment" in cases of derogation from the rules of proper social behavior, as defined by each society over time. Nevertheless, confidentiality and anonymity are circumvented either by users revealing personal information or other users' personal information, while informal social control is fully exercised. The belief of being invisible and anonymous raises dangers for the members, as their individual rights to control and use personal information are restricted.

The most significant issues arising from this research concerning information privacy are related to the system's function (Facebook) and users' willingness to reveal personal information in order to participate in these communities. The latter derives from the fact that people try to compromise and adapt to the expectations of the group or community of reference, showing a specific behavior, mostly determined by the representation of group's expectations, *"in order to avoid the pain of deviance and exclusion from the group"* [27]. So through this study it is obvious that the social media websites and FB in particular not only does not meet the technical requirements regarding privacy protection (data traceability, user awareness about third party cloud providers, unauthorised disclosure of personal information) but also new socio-technical aspects should be introduced for formulating the multifaceted concept of privacy. An extended research is mandatory to reveal the set of parameters that users consider when using social media and how aware about their privacy protection really are. Users trust is based also on the protection of their privacy thus it is very important to identify which are the necessary technical and social factors that have an impact on their behavior. Users could be helped to address privacy issues, if the shaped information systems provided them with mechanisms and interfaces allowing them understand their function and if they were incorporated into their practices, values and sensibilities [55].

Although, no claims are being made about generalizing the results, our exploratory research provides a unique method studying both informal social control and privacy in Facebook. Respectively, supporting that privacy paradox concerns the erotic-sexual life of FB Universities' Communities users, our research reveals users' representations about primary and secondary disclosure of erotic-sexual personal information and therefore sets new perspectives about forms of exercised informal social control in Facebook concerning privacy.

Our research could be extended in several ways. The communities we dealt with are created recently. What was the cause and what was the reason for their appearance during this period is an interesting topic worth exploring in the future. Additionally, using the method of Critical Discourse Analysis and the entity data models we introduced, research could be extended in order to identify behavioral patterns in Facebook communities and/or reveal incentives for the provision of information.

References

1. Castells, M.: The Rise of the Network Society. Blackwell Publ, Cambridge (2004)
2. Albert, S., Flournoy, D.M., LeBrasseur, R.: Networked Communities: Strategies for Digital Collaboration. Information Science Reference, USA (2009)
3. Naxakis, C.: The theology of development. Some specific thoughts about its ideological foundations. *Epitheorisi Koinonikon Epistimon*, vol. 95, pp. 53–68 (1998). (in Greek)
4. Mooney, L., Knox, D., Schacht, C.: Understanding Social Problems. Thomson Learning Inc., USA (2007)
5. Eriksen, T.H.: Tyranny of the Moment. Fast and Slow Time in the Information Age. Pluto Press, London (2001)
6. Fuchs, C.: New media, web. 2.0 and surveillance. Sociol. Compass **5**(2), 134–147 (2011)
7. Thompson, J.B.: The Media and Modernity. Polity Press, Cambridge (1995)
8. Melucci, A.: Social Theory in the Information Era. Trotta Editorial, Spain (2002)
9. Habermas, J.: The Theory of Communicative Action: Lifeworld and System: A Critique of Functionalist Reason, vol. 2. Beacon Press, Boston (1987)
10. Lyon, D.: Surveillance as Social Sorting. Privacy, Risk and Digital Discrimination. Routledge, London (2003)
11. Barnes, S.B.: A privacy paradox: social networking in the United States. First Monday **11** (9), 4 (2006)
12. Fuchs, C.: Social Media: a Critical Introduction. Sage, Thousand Oaks (2014)
13. Chomsky, N.: Media Control: The Spectacular Achievements of Propaganda. Seven Stories Press, New York (2011)
14. Bourdieu, P.: The forms of social capital. In: Richardson, J.G. (ed.) Handbook of Theory and Research for the Sociology of Education, pp. 241–258. Greenwood, New York (1985)
15. Mitrou, L.: Law in Information Society. Sakkoulas, Athens-Thessaloniki (2002). (in Greek)
16. Lambropoulou, E.: Internal Security and Control Society. Kritiki, Athens (2001). (in Greek)
17. Chriss, J.J.: Social Control: An Introduction. Polity Press, Cambridge (2013)
18. Foucault, M.: Discipline and Punish: The Birth of the Prison. Vintage Books, New York (1979)
19. Mitrou, L., Kandias, M., Stavrou, V., Gritzalis, D.; Social media profiling: a panopticon or omniopticon tool?. In: Proceedings of the 6th Biannual Surveillance and Society Conference (24–26 April 2014)
20. Norris, C.: From personal to digital: CCTV, the panopticon and the technological mediation of suspicion and social control. In: Lyon, D. (ed.) Surveillance and Social Sorting: Privacy Risk and Automated Discrimination, pp. 249–281. Routledge, London (2003)
21. Lyon, D.: The Electronic Eye: the Rise of Surveillance Society-Computers and Social Control in Context. Wiley, UK (2013)
22. Kandias, M., Mitrou, L., Stavrou, V., Gritzalis, D.: Which side are you on? A new panopticon vs. privacy. In: Proceedings of 2013 International Conference on Security and Cryptography (SECRYPT), Reykjavik, Iceland (29–31 July 2013)
23. Anleu, S.L.R.: The role of civil sanctions in social control: a socio-legal examination. Crime Prev. Stud. **9**, 21–43 (1998)
24. Cas, I.: Ubiquitous computing, privacy and data protection: options and limitations to reconcile the unprecedented contradictions. In: Gutwirth, S., Poullet, Y., De Hert, P., Leenes, R. (eds.) Computers, Privacy and Data Protection: An Element of Choice, pp. 139–169. Springer, Netherlands (2011)
25. Chaidou, A.: Minors, Drugs, Social Controls. Nomiki Bibliothiki, Athens (2003). (in Greek)

26. Bergalli, R., Sumner, C.: Social Control and Political Order. European Perspectives at the end of the Century. Sage, UK (1997)
27. Ragnedda, M.: Social control and surveillance in the society of consumers. Int. J. Sociol. Anthropol. **3**(6), 180–188 (2011)
28. Van Dijck, J.: The Culture of Connectivity: a Critical History of Social Media. Oxford University Press, UK (2013)
29. Viégas, F.B.: Blogger's expectations of privacy and accountability: an initial survey. J. Comput.-Mediated Commun. **10**(3), 1–31 (2005)
30. Norberg, P.A., Horne, D., Horne, D.: The privacy paradox: personal information disclosure intentions versus behaviors. J. Consum. Aff. **41**(1), 100–126 (2007)
31. D'Souza, G., Phelps, J.E.: The privacy paradox: the case of secondary disclosure. Rev. Mark. Sci. **7**(4), 1–29 (2009)
32. Solove, D.J.: A taxonomy of privacy. Law Rev. **154**(3), 477–560 (2006)
33. Islam, M.B., Watson, J., Iannella, R., Geva, S.: What I Want for my Social Network Privacy. NICTA, Australia (2014)
34. Henderson, S.E.: Expectations of privacy in social media. Mississippi Coll. Law Rev. **31**, 227–247 (2012)
35. Cohen, J.E.: What privacy is for. Harvard Law Rev. **126**(7), 1904–1933 (2013)
36. Bauman, Z.: Globalization: The Human Consequences. Columbia University Press, New York (1998)
37. Ong, W.: Orality and Literacy: The Technologizing of the Word. Crete University Press, Heraclion (1997). (in Greek)
38. Stemler, S.: An overview of content analysis. Pract. Assess. Res. Eval. **7**(17), 137–146 (2001)
39. Fairclough, N.: Critical Discourse Analysis. The Critical Study of Language. Longman, London (1995)
40. Van Dijk, T.A.: Ideology. A Multidisciplinary Approach. Sage, London (1998)
41. Gooch, G.D., Jansson, G., Mikaelsson, R.: Focus groups in Motala Ström. In: Kangur, K. (ed.) Focus Groups and Citizen Juries: River Dialogue Experiences in Enhancing Public Participation in Water Management. Peipsi Center for Transboundary Cooperation, Estonia (2005)
42. Hancock, B.: Trent Focus for Research and Development in Primary Health Care: an Introduction to Qualitative Research, p. 1998. Trent Focus, UK (1998)
43. Rogers, R.: An Introduction to Critical Discourse Analysis in Education. Lawrence Erlbaum, NJ (2004)
44. Delbru, R., Campinas, S., Tummarello, G.: Searching web data: an entity retrieval and high performance indexing model. J. Web Semant. **10**, 33–58 (2012)
45. Whitley, R., Crawford, M.: Qualitative research in psychiatry. Can. J. Psychiatry **50**, 108–114 (2005)
46. Mason, J.: Qualitative Researching. Sage, London (2002)
47. Vamvoukas, M.: Introduction to Pshycopaidagogic Research and Methodology. Grigoris, Athens (2002). (in Greek)
48. Tsiolis, G.: Methods and Techniques of Analysis in Qualitative Social Research. Kritiki, Athens (2014). (in greek)
49. Babbie, E.: Introduction to Social Research. Kritiki, Athens (2011). (in greek)
50. Han, J., Kamber, M., Pei, J.: Data Mining: Concepts and Techniques. Morgan Kaufmann Publ, USA (2012)
51. Teo, P.: Racism in the news: a critical discourse analysis of news reporting in two Australian newspapers. Discourse Soc. **11**(1), 7–49 (2000)
52. Richardson, L.: Writing Strategies: Reaching Diverse Audiences. Sage, USA (1990)

53. Reed, L.A., Tolman, R.M., Safyer, P.: Too close for comfort: attachment insecurity and electronic intrusion in college students' dating relationships. Comput. Hum. Behav. **50**, 431–438 (2015)
54. Bennett, D.C., Guran, E.I., Ramos, M.C., Margdin, G.: College students' electronic victimization in friendships and dating relationships: anticipated distress and associations with risky behaviors. Violence Vict. **26**(4), 410–429 (2011)
55. Nguyen, D.H., Mynatt, E.D.: Privacy mirrors: understanding and shaping socio-technical ubiquitous computing systems. Georgia Institute of Technology, technical report GIT-GVU-02-16 (2002)

Tagged Data Breaches in Online Social Networks

Alexandra K. Michota[✉] and Sokratis K. Katsikas

Systems Security Laboratory, Department of Digital Systems, School of Information
and Communication Technologies, University of Piraeus, 150 Androutsou St.,
18532 Piraeus, Greece
{amichota,ska}@unipi.gr

Abstract. Tagged information in Online Social Networks (OSNs) is considered to be the basis of the semantic network that connects online resources based on their characteristics, and not only their URLs. The semantic interoperability creates difficulties in enforcing privacy control mechanisms that will solve authorization conflicts when accessing the tagged sharing content. In this paper we investigate whether the visibility levels in tagged content are applied according to the OSN users' intentions. Based on the visibility choices that are offered by the privacy setting menus in OSNs, we performed all the possible visibility combinations in a two-level social relationship scale for different user profiles and we examined whether these settings provide the requested privacy-aware access control mechanisms in social networks or whether there exist security gaps that let users' Personal Identifiable Information (PII) exposed to unintended audiences. The results indicate that the protection of OSN users' tagged PII lacks privacy controls that can fully protect the tagged sharing content and that the current mechanisms support access control for selected pieces of resources with selected groups of users.

Keywords: Tag · Sharing content · PII · Privacy · Visibility · Data breaches

1 Introduction

The main purpose of collaborative tagging is to loosely classify resources based on end-user's feedback, expressed in the form of free-text labels such as tags. The novelty of such an approach to content categorization has been seen, in recent years, as a challenging research topic.

Tags are also known as id-tags. Id-tags give the ability to the users to add labels over pictures to indicate which users appear in them. Therefore, each id-tag essentially corresponds to a unique user id. By leveraging id-tags, one can easily identify the potential owners in a given picture. Hence, users can upload content into their own or others' timeline; they can also tag other users who appear in the content. Each tag is an explicit reference that connects to the user's timeline.

Tagging means assigning unrestricted keywords to all kinds of content. It becomes social when tags are shared among OSN users and different users are allowed to tag the same content item. The ability to tag in Facebook OSN extends to linking any person,

© Springer International Publishing Switzerland 2015
S.K. Katsikas and A.B. Sideridis (Eds.): E-Democracy 2015, CCIS 570, pp. 95–106, 2015.
DOI: 10.1007/978-3-319-27164-4_7

page, or place to anything that is posted, including status updates, comments, or app activity [1].

OSNs allow the users to be policy administrators of the protection of user data [2]. Users can restrict data sharing to a set of people they choose to give them access to their PII. Nevertheless, interlinking profile information may be risky. The possibility to identify users across systems based on their tag-based profiles has been of great research interest. [3] Tagged data includes information such as captions, comments and photo tags; marked regions that identify people on the photo. Even if the OSN users in a photo are not explicitly identified by photo tags, the combination of publicly available data and face recognition services can be used to infer someone's identity [4]. Collateral damage is the terminology that is used to describe this kind of problems. OSN users unintentionally put their friends or even their own privacy at risk when performing actions on OSNs such as in Facebook [5].

With the current tagging control mechanisms, the content "owner" has access rights over the privacy of the tagged content, while the tagged user cannot control the visibility of this data type beyond denying the related link with reference to her profile, by "removing the tag". Privacy conflicts that lead to data leakage by letting users' PII exposed to unknown audiences occur due to the fact that multiple connected users may have different privacy limitations over their sharing, on one hand, and due to the lack of collaborative privacy controls on the other [6, 7].

In this paper we focus on examining the privacy of tagged photos in Facebook. The paper is structured as follows: The tagged content types are presented in Sect. 2. Section 3 describes the privacy control mechanisms that are offered in OSNs for the protection of tagged data. Then, the scenarios we examined are described and the results are analyzed, in Sect. 4. Finally, the paper concludes with Sect. 5.

2   Tagged Content Types

In Facebook, when you tag someone, you create a link to his or her profile. The post you tag the person in may also be added to that person's timeline. A "friend" who "tags" a newcomer in a photo, engages the newcomer in a chat session, or refers to the newcomer in a public status update. In all of these cases, the friend directly engages the newcomer with some content, and the new user may be both more likely to notice the content and come to understand the value of participation. This may lead to long-term engagement on the part of the newcomer. These singling-out actions may also highlight some social connection between newcomers and their friends, potentially providing an added effect of in-group membership [8].

Unlike tagging in other social systems like Flickr or de.licio.us, where members use descriptive terms like "sunset" or "cool", tagging in Facebook is the linking of a face in a photo with a registered user. Friends tag photos by clicking on a face and selecting a name from a list of their friends. Tagged photos are then linked to the tagged person's profile. Tagging may occur in any photo, not necessarily one posted by the newcomer; thus, it is a way for friends to both demonstrate a feature of the site, and to draw newcomers into photo viewing and sharing. Some newcomers tag themselves. These are known as self-tags. [9]

The content items are classified as follows:

Status Tagging: Friends that an OSN user tags in her status updates will receive a notification and they are linked to this post. They will also have the option to remove tags of themselves from her posts.

Photo Tagging: Image tagging on the web has recently become extremely popular. The popular photo sharing and tagging service in Flickr and the photo tagging application in Facebook are the most characteristic examples.

Geo Tagging: This is the process of adding geographical identification metadata to various media such as a geotagged photographs or videos, websites, SMS messages, QR Codes or RSS feeds; it is a form of geospatial metadata. This data usually consists of latitude and longitude coordinates, but they can also include altitude, bearing, distance, accuracy data, and location names. Location Based Services (LBSs) share users' related content such as location information. Facebook's version of geotagging lets users tag their location on status updates or photos. [10]

Hashtag: This tagged content consists of a keyword or a keyphrase that is preceded by a hash mark (#). Hashtags are used as titles for topics of common interests among OSN users, and facilitate the search for them. An OSN user can add one or more hashtags to her status updates or to her photos; these are then indexed by the social network she has logged in and they are searchable by other users. Once an OSN user clicks on one hashtag, a new page that aggregates all the related content that is accompanied by the same hashtagged keyword will open. Twitter is the social network that introduced the hashtag that facilitates finding the trending topics. Facebook hashtags drive its users to a page that aggregates all the related posts; this content may be visible to specific audiences depending on the privacy restrictions that have been applied by the users. Hashtagging on Instagram is very useful when users are looking for photos similar to the ones that they have taken.

3   Privacy in Tagged Content

Different privacy options are offered by OSNs. OSNs provide access control mechanisms allowing users to make PII contained in their own profiles accessible to people they trust. The most popular privacy limitation for OSN users' tagged information is removing a tag. But these mechanisms have not been proved to be very protective of the users' PII, due to the fact that in many cases data leakage problems have been noticed.

More specifically, removing a tag simply removes the name tag from the photo, but the photo still remains visible in the News feed and Search areas. Hence it is necessary to develop an access control mechanism including all the authorization requirements from multiple users. Each of the controllers of the content can set her privacy settings and can specify who can see the content. If two users disagree on whom the shared data is to be exposed to, then a privacy conflict occurs. Therefore, a mechanism is required to identify the privacy conflicting segments and to resolve those privacy conflicts.

When a user wishes to review the privacy settings of her tagged sharing content in Facebook, she must visit the "Timeline and Tagging" setting page in order to limit the audience who can have access to her tagged information. "Timeline Review" controls are offered in Facebook, giving the user the opportunity to manually approve or reject posts she is tagged in, before they go on her timeline. In the second part of the "Timeline and Tagging" settings, the "Who can see things on my timeline" page, a user can choose who can see posts she has been tagged in on her timeline. The offered options are the same for each Facebook content type, namely "Fiends", "Public", "Only me" and "Custom"; although the user can customize the tagged content visibility level, the content item is shared by default with anyone tagged in this post.

In case that a user has uploaded a photo and then she has applied tagging services, she has the choice to decide whether she will share it with the friends of tagged users or not. When someone is tagged in a photo, he has no right to change its visibility level but she can decide whether this photo is allowed to appear on her timeline or not. It should be noted that the person who uploaded a photo chooses the audience for that photo. There is also the option for a Facebook user to hide a tagged content from her timeline. When a user hides a photo or post she is tagged in from her timeline, or adjusts appropriately her "Timeline and Tagging" privacy setting, this only limits who can see the content on her timeline. The photo or post is still visible to the audience it is shared with in other places on Facebook, such as News Feed or Search.

In June 2011, Facebook users may have noticed a box appearing on the right of their home page called "Photos are better with friends". This was a new way for users being made aware about features that were added to Facebook such as the "Photo Tag Suggest". The tag suggestion service uses facial recognition in order to help the users easily identify a friend in a photo and share that content with them. When a user turns off tag suggestions by using the "Timeline and Tagging" setting page, Facebook will not suggest that people tag her when photos look like her. The template that was created to enable the tag suggestions feature will also be deleted. However friends will still be able to tag photos of her. The tagging tools offered by Facebook, including grouping photos that look similar and suggesting friends who might be in them, are meant to make it easier for a user to share her memories and experiences with her friends. [11]

Privacy limitations about who knows OSN users' location are offered by OSNs that support LBSs. OSN users can share their location only with those they trust. For instance, in a service like "Facebook Places", registered users can create separate lists and, by using privacy controls, they can restrict its access to location status up-dates, messages, and photos. They can also disable the option that allows others to share their location (check you in). Another option lets the users set their location data so that it is not publicly available or searchable.

When Instagram is used via mobile devices, in case a user takes a photo while connected via Wi-Fi or 3G, her phone logs the coordinates where the photo was taken. Using that information, a user can add that photo to a "Photo Map". This is an easy way to add context to photos, document travels and see photos other Instagram users have taken nearby. By default, adding location or adding the photo to "Photo Map" is turned off for all photos a user uploads to Instagram. This means that no photos will appear on the user's "Photo Map" without her explicit permission. However if a user shares this photo on Facebook, this photo will be visible by her friends by default. A user can explore the "Photo Maps" of people with public profiles and people with private profiles who have approved her as a follower.

Summing up, both sharing content owners and tagged users need to manage their identity and control appearance to different, sometimes overlapping groups.

Hashtag-related privacy settings are vague in comparison with the ones discussed above. If an OSN user publishes a post on her profile to friends only, and the post contains a hashtag, the hashtag will be clickable and will open up to display all other posts on Facebook containing that hashtag. However, only friends can see friends-only posts that show up in hashtag searches. Even when friends include hashtags in comments on another user's friends-only thread, her post is still private and visible just to her friends. With hashtags shared in private groups, that clickable hashtag will open to show public posts with that tag but posts from the private group are only available to group members. Individual comments on threads do not surface in hashtag searches.

Sharing via other OSNs creates privacy concerns about the visibility of the tagged content. If someone with a private profile shares a photo or video on a social network like Instagram, the image will be visible on that network and the permalink will be active. In other words, the photo will be publicly accessible by anyone who has access to its direct link. Sharing a photo or video on a social network does not mean that the image will be visible in Instagram. Users' accounts will still appear private to those who are not approved followers. Privacy & Safety Center specifies that a user can make her posts private in the Instagram profile so only approved followers can see them. Once a user makes her posts private, people will have to send her a follow request if they want to see her posts, her followers list or her following list.

Even though a user puts her account on private, many people can still see her photos, especially if she connects her Instagram to other social networks. More specifically, we examined the privacy of a Facebook post by sharing an Instagram picture on it. Clicking on the related link, direct access is given to the picture, as the default privacy for this content item defines that it is visible to user's friends. Even though we tried to see what other pictures this person had shared on Instagram by clicking on that person's Instagram account, we did not succeed, as it was set on private. This was logical as no one can see any other pictures, unless she requested to follow her. Hence, we conclude that the link that OSN users see in any OSN that supports registration via impersonation is clickable and guides straight to the specific Instagram picture, for any of the million registered users of the corresponding OSN to see.

It is necessary for any OSN user to check the privacy settings on the connected accounts. For instance, if a user has her Instagram connected to Facebook, she should make sure her sharing settings on Facebook are not set to "Public" but to for "Friends". This setting can be applied via the Instagram app in her Facebook applications settings where she can set the visibility per app.

4   Scenarios

In order to investigate whether the visibility options for the tagged sharing content items are applied according to the privacy settings that have been set by the users, we used real user profiles on Facebook, which is the social network that supports all the content types for the tagged information. In this study, we chose to investigate the privacy of tagged photos not only because this is the most used tagged content type, but also because it is the content item on which every user can tag each type of information she likes, such as profile names, location, comments that are addressed to specific person and hashtags; we examined the case of tagging a user's profile in a photo that was uploaded in Facebook.

We present a variety of scenarios from Facebook to illustrate several issues regarding privacy controls to users' tagged content. In order to protect the users' identity, we use the terms "User *" instead of real names. In Facebook, they have their own profiles, which contain their private information, uploaded resources and other types of resources.

We do not consider a specific friendlist for our study. We only chose one mutual friend of User A and User B to examine the visibility levels of the following custom settings that were applied by User B. Hence, User C is defined as a mutual friend of User A and User B. User D belongs to the User B's friendlist, while User E to the User A's friends. Users F and G are friends of the User A's and B's friends. Friends of tagged are defined as the friends of the friend that a user has tagged in the content. The friends of friends class also includes the friends of tagged by default. Figure 1 depicts a social graph that shows how the users that we have included in our study are connected.

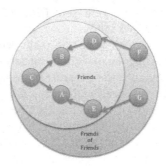

Fig. 1. Social graph I

In this study, we used a two level scale social relationship management. The first one is the fine-grained level that gives to the data owner the possibility to share its content with her friends; the second level is the social circle; it allows the owner to create a social circle because of her friends. In this level, the friends of her friends develop a relationship with the data owner and they grant indirect and partial access to her resources.

We assume that User A is socially connected with User B in Facebook. Recently, User A went to an event with User B and uploaded a picture of that event in her profile. User A would like to share this photo with her friends and tagged User B in the photo they were together.

Scenario 1: User A, who is the data owner, i.e. the person who uploaded the photo and then she tagged it, chooses the photo to be viewed by her friends. She has also chosen by default this photo to be visible by the friends of tagged people. As seen in Table 1, the exception to the rule that this may not happen is due to a possible custom setting that User B may have applied. Settings such as "Only me", "Apart from User C" or "Only User C" can limit the User B's audience visibility. Even if User B would like to make the tagged photo visible to the friends of her friends, this is not possible, as the data owner has granted access only to their friends.

Table 1. Scenario 1 - Visibility combinations for the tagged photo

Data Subjects	User A		User B	Profile User A	Profile User B
	Friends		Friends	User A's Friends	User A's & B's Friends
	Friends		Public	User A's Friends	User A's & B's Friends
	Friends		Only me	User A's Friends	User B
Visibility Level	Friends	Custom	Friends of Friends	User A's Friends	User A's & B's Friends
	Friends		Friends apart from User C	User A's Friends	User A's & B's Friends apart from User C
	Friends		Friends of Friends apart from User C	User A's Friends	User A's & B's Friends apart from User C
	Friends		Only User C	User A's Friends	User B, C
Content Type	Uploaded Photo	Tagged Photo		Timeline User A	Timeline User B

Scenario 2: We consider that User A changed the visibility of her photo from "Friends" to "Public". The public option has two different meanings for the Facebook audience. In case a user has turned on the setting for profile link with search engines, it is easy for everyone over the web to find the user's timeline in search results. If then she changes this setting to off, it may take a while for search engines to stop showing the link to her timeline. If the second setting were her first choice, only registered users in Facebook could have access to her profile. We assume herein that this choice had been made.

As it can be seen in Table 2, the sharing content is visible to everyone on User A's timeline. The audience to which the content on timeline B is made visible is defined according to the privacy settings that User B has applied. In this case, there are no limitations from the User A's side. For instance, when User B chooses the tagged photo to be visible to the friends of her friends, her request can be fulfilled as there are no limitations from User A's side.

To sum up, the audience who can have access to the tagged photo is mainly defined by the choices of User B, due to the fact that the content owner had chosen the photo to be visible to everyone.

Scenario 3: User A applies the "Only me" option for the visibility of the tagged photo. According to the Table 3, only User A and B can have access to the photo regardless of the privacy settings that User B has already applied for her tagged content.

Scenario 4: User A does not want to share the photo with specific registered users, so she customizes her privacy settings according to her special preferences.

Table 2. Scenario 2 - Visibility combinations for the tagged photo

Data Subjects	User A	User B		Profile User A	Profile User B
Visibility Level	Public		Friends	Everyone/Public	User A & B's Friends
	Public		Public	Everyone/Public	Everyone/Public
	Public		Only me	Everyone/Public	User B
	Public	Custom	Friends of Friends	Everyone/Public	User A's & B's Friends & Friends of User B's Friends
	Public		Friends apart from User C	Everyone/Public	User A & B's Friends apart from User C
	Public		Friends of Friends apart from User C	Everyone/Public	User A's & B's Friends & Friends of User B's Friends apart from User C
	Public		Only User C	Everyone/Public	User B, C
Content Type	Uploaded Photo	Tagged Photo		Timeline User A	Timeline User B

Table 3. Scenario 3 - Visibility combinations for the tagged photo

Data Subjects	User A	User B		Profile User A	Profile User B
Visibility Level	Only me		Friends	User A	User A, B
	Only me		Public	User A	User A, B
	Only me		Only me	User A	User B
	Only me	Custom	Friends of Friends	User A	User A, B
	Only me		Friends apart from User C	User A	User A, B
	Only me		Friends of Friends apart from User C	User A	User A, B
	Only me		Only User C	User A	User B
Content Type	Uploaded Photo	Tagged Photo		Timeline User A	Timeline User B

Scenario 4A: We assume that User A chose her photo to be visible to her friends without including the friends of tagged. In this case, as shown in Table 4, either User B has chosen "Friends" or "Friends of friends" or "Public" for her tagged content visibility, the photo can be viewed by User A's and B's friends; although User A has chosen User B's friends not to see the tagged photo on timeline B, their mutual friends have access to it. Hence, User C, who is a mutual friend of A and B, can see the tagged photo on both timelines. In case User B has limited the visibility of the photo in order to be visible only by her, User C and all their mutual friends will continue seeing and having access on the tagged photo only through User A's timeline. The photo will not be visible by User C on User B's timeline. User C will not have access at all to this photo on condition that User B has excluded her from the friendlist that is authorized to see all her tagged content.

Scenario 4B: First, as shown in Table 5, we assume that User A set the option "Friends of friends without friends of tagged" and second, as shown in Table 6, we assume that she set the option "Friends of friends" including User B's friends to the audience that was authorized to see the photo.

Table 4. Scenario 4A - Visibility combinations for the tagged photo

Data Subjects	User A	User B		Profile User A	Profile User B
Visibility Level	Friends (without friends of tagged)	Friends		User A's Friends	User A & Mutual Friends of Users A & B
	Friends (without friends of tagged)	Public		User A's Friends	User A & Mutual Friends of Users A & B
	Friends (without friends of tagged)	Only me		User A's Friends	User B
	Friends (without friends of tagged)	Custom	Friends of Friends	User A's Friends	User A & Mutual Friends of Users A & B
	Friends (without friends of tagged)		Friends apart from User C	User A's Friends	User A & Mutual Friends of Users A & B apart from User C
	Friends (without friends of tagged)		Friends of Friends apart from User C	User A's Friends	User A & Mutual Friends of Users A & B apart from User C
	Friends (without friends of tagged)		Only User C	User A's Friends	User B, C
Content Type	Uploaded Photo	Tagged Photo		Timeline User A	Timeline User B

Table 5. Scenario 4B (i) - Visibility combinations for the tagged photo

Data Subjects	User A	User B		Profile User A	Profile User B
Visibility Level	Friends of Friends (without friends of tagged)	Custom	Friends of Friends	User A's Friends and Friends of her Friends	User A's & B's Friends & Friends of Users B's Friends
	Friends of Friends (without friends of tagged)		Friends apart from User C	User A's Friends and Friends of her Friends	User A's & B's Friends apart from User C
	Friends of Friends (without friends of tagged)		Friends of Friends apart from User C	User A's Friends and Friends of her Friends	User A's & B's Friends & Friends of Users B's Friends apart from User C
	Friends of Friends (without friends of tagged)		Only User C	User A's Friends and Friends of her Friends	User B, C
Content Type	Uploaded Photo	Tagged Photo		Timeline User A	Timeline User B

When User A set the option "Friends of friends without friends of tagged" for the photo she uploaded and User B has set the privacy option "Friends of friends" for the tagged content when added on her timeline. User A's friends and friends of her friends can see the photo, like it or comment on it. Having excluded the friends of tagged, User A does not allow User B's friends to have access to it. Based on the Table 5, although User A has limited her content's visibility, not only their mutual friends but also all the User B's friends can see the photo on both timelines.

Table 6 shows similar visibility results with Table 5, when User A and B set the privacy option "Friends of friends" for the specific photo. Moreover, User B has applied limitations on her timeline, regardless of the privacy settings of User A, who is the content owner.

Table 6. Scenario 4B (ii) - Visibility combinations for the tagged photo

Data Subjects	User A	User B		Profile User A	Profile User B
Visibility Level	Friends of Friends	Custom	Friends of Friends	User A's Friends and Friends of her Friends	User A's & B's Friends & Friends of Users B's Friends
	Friends of Friends		Friends apart from User C	User A's Friends and Friends of her Friends	User A's & B's Friends apart from User C
	Friends of Friends		Friends of Friends apart from User C	User A's Friends and Friends of her Friends	User A's & B's Friends & Friends of Users B's Friends apart from User C
	Friends of Friends		Only User C	User A's Friends and Friends of her Friends	User B, C
Content Type	Uploaded Photo	Tagged Photo		Timeline User A	Timeline User B

Whether or not the friends of User B's friends will have access to the tagged photo depends on the way they are connected on Facebook. Hence, we examine two special cases that are presented below:

First, as shown in Fig. 2, we assume that User H is a mutual friend of User A's and B's friends. Due to the fact that User H belongs to the lists of User A's and User B's friends of friends, she can see the photo on both timelines.

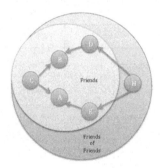

Fig. 2. Social graph II

Second, we assume that User H belongs only to User A's friends of friends. Thus, we confirmed that User H does not see the tagged photo on User B's timeline.

To sum up, privacy gaps are highlighted, even when the users have applied strict privacy settings. We examined whether the friends of tagged can see the photo that the data owner uploaded even if she had excluded them from the authorized audience she chose to see it. Furthermore, friends of both users' mutual friends and friends who belong to their "Friends of friends" lists can also have access to this photo although privacy limitations had been put in place.

Scenario 4C: We assume that User A has set the option "Friends without friends of tagged apart from User C" for the photo she uploaded. As it can be seen in Table 7, regardless of the settings that User B has defined for the tagged photo among "Friends",

"Friends of friends" and "Public", even if she has excluded their mutual friends e.g. User C, User A finally decides who will be authorized to have access to the content. Due to the fact that User A is the content owner and she has omitted User C from her audience, User C is not allowed to see the photo on either timeline.

Table 7. Scenario 4C - Visibility combinations for the tagged photo

Data Subjects	User A		User B	Profile User A	Profile User B
Visibility Level	Friends (without friends of tagged) apart from User C	Custom	Friends of Friends	User A's Friends apart from User C	User A's Friends & Mutual Friends of User A & B apart from User C
	Friends (without friends of tagged) apart from User C		Friends apart from User C	User A's Friends apart from User C	User A & Mutual Friends of User A & B friends apart from User C
	Friends (without friends of tagged) apart from User C		Friends of Friends apart from User C	User A's Friends apart from User C	User A's Friends & Mutual Friends of User A & B apart from User C
	Friends (without friends of tagged) apart from User C		Only User C	User A's Friends apart from User C	User B
Content Type	Uploaded Photo	Tagged Photo		Timeline User A	Timeline User B

We also examined the case when User A has set the option "Friends of friends without friends of tagged apart from User C" for the photo she uploaded. The only difference with Scenario 4C is that when User A augments her audience for her photo, User B's audience will also be augmented to include a part of Friends of User B's friends to the authorized audience that has access to the photo.

Scenario 5: Profile tags are visible only on the content item that is shared to the OSN we have logged in. Having logged in on User A's Instagram account, she uploaded and tagged User B who belongs to her followers on the same photo and then she also shared it in Facebook. We observed that the tags she added on that photo were not visible in Facebook. In case she would like the photo to be tagged on Facebook, she should tag her friend again in it. The only tagged content items that are visible when sharing a tagged photo in other OSNs are the hashtags.

5 Conclusions

The aim of this paper was to examine the privacy of tagged photos in Facebook. The study revealed that the privacy options as defined by the Facebook users seem not to fully implement the requested privacy limitations for the tagged sharing content. In conclusion, the results of our analysis indicate that in Facebook privacy gaps exist that let the users' PII exposed to unauthorized audience, even if the users had limited its visibility.

The weaknesses we identified in current privacy options increase the need to provide users with more flexible mechanisms to control the visibility of their PII in OSNs. In order to enhance the privacy visibility levels in Facebook, privacy preferences should be added that will aim at minimizing the possibilities for data breaches and will let the users choose the audience who will have access to their shared content. The users' privacy intentions should be taken into account when privacy setting menus are designed, providing simple and precise privacy controls that will be stable, independent from the social relationship management and adequate to limit unauthorized users from accessing their data.

References

1. Rangiha, M.E., Karakostas, B.: Social business process management and social tagging. In: Proceedings of Org2 Workshop - Towards Organization 2.0: Advancements in Enterprise Social Networks (In conjunction with the 15th International Conference on Web Information Systems Engineering – WISE 2014), Thessaloniki, Greece (2014)
2. Hu, H., Ahn, G.-J., Jorgensen, J.: Multiparty access control for online social networks: model and mechanisms. Int J. IEEE Trans. Knowl. Data Eng. Arch. **25**(7), 1614–1627 (2013)
3. Iofciu, T., Fankhauser, P., Abel, F., Bischoff, K.: Identifying users across social tagging systems. In: Proceedings of 5th International AAAI Conference on Weblogs and Social Media - ICWSM, Barcelona, Spain (2011)
4. Gross, R., Acquisti, A., Stutzman, F.: Faces of facebook: privacy in the age of augmented reality. In: BlackHat, USA (2011)
5. Krishnamurthy, B.: I know what you will do next summer. ACM SIGCOMM Comput. Commun. Rev. **40**(5), 65–70 (2010)
6. Madejski, M., Johnson, M., Bellovin, S.: The failure of online social network privacy settings. Technical report CUCS-010-11, Columbia University, NY, USA (2011)
7. Squicciarini, A., Shehab, M., Paci, F.: Collective privacy management in social networks. In: Proceedings of the 18th International Conference on World Wide Web, pp. 521–530. ACM (2009)
8. Hogg, M.: Social categorization, depersonalization, and group behavior. In: Hogg, M., Tinsdale, T.S. (eds.) Blackwell Handbook of Social Psychology: Group Processes, pp. 57–85. Blackwell, Malden (2001)
9. Lampe, C., Ellison, N., Steinfeld, C.: A familiar Face(book): profile elements as signals in an online social network. In: Proceedings of CHI 2007, pp. 435–444. ACM Press (2007)
10. Chow, C.-Y., Bao, J., Mokbel, M.F.: Towards location-based social networking services. In: Proceedings of the 2nd ACM SIGSPATIAL International Workshop on Location Based Social Networks (LBSN 2010), pp. 31–38. ACM, New York, USA (2010)
11. Facebook. www.facebook.com

E-Government and E-Participation

The Role of Computer Simulation Tools in Improving the Quality of Life in Small Settlements of the Czech Republic

Vojtěch Merunka[1,2](✉)

[1] Department of Information Engineering, Faculty of Economics and Management,
Czech University of Life Sciences in Prague, Prague, Czech Republic
[2] Department of Software Engineering, Faculty of Nuclear Sciences and Physical
Engineering, Czech Technical University in Prague, Prague, Czech Republic
vmerunka@gmail.com

Abstract. The paper addresses the problem of low participation of residents of small settlements in the territorial planning processes. Low participation causes dissatisfaction with democracy in local government and decreases the quality of life. The paper presents a solution which consists in the use of computer simulation tools to increase the level of knowledge of the persons concerned, which makes the effect of increased participation. This hypothesis was confirmed experimentally by our project in settlements of Central Bohemia.

Keywords: Territorial planning · Quality of life · Participation · Process modeling · Process simulation · Training and education

1 Introduction

In our project we used computer simulation tools for the transfer of knowledge from experts to representatives of local governments to achieve higher level of participation of residents of small settlements in the *territorial planning processes*.

1.1 Territorial Planning

Territorial (e.g. urban or spatial) planning is a strategic tool for any construction and development activities in the landscape. Territorial planning can fulfill the requirements of sustainable development in two ways: To create *promotive* conditions for the desired development directions and also *restrictively*, because it prevents from disparity development, and protects irreplaceable values.

The basis of the institutional dimension of sustainability concepts in the territorial plan is its *clarity*, *transparency*, and *acceptance* of its concept of community life in a settlement. Therefore, it is necessary to allow and encourage the *active participation of citizens* in these planning decisions that have a direct impact on quality of life of affected citizens. These impacts we can summarize in the following five points as:

© Springer International Publishing Switzerland 2015
S.K. Katsikas and A.B. Sideridis (Eds.): E-Democracy 2015, CCIS 570, pp. 109–123, 2015.
DOI: 10.1007/978-3-319-27164-4_8

1. Territorial plan is a practical tool for *addressing issues* of citizens and other local actors on the quality of life in the village. A plan is in fact, the document, after which discussion and approval, enables the implementation of both private and public works in the area.
2. Territorial planning is one of the ways to facilitate *decision making* of mayors and other members of the local government in order to solve problems that may to appear. One of them is the issue of *suburbanization* (e.g. *urban sprawl*) happened in suburban landscape. [9] There is a need to ensure the proper behavior local citizens in order to maintain the cultural and historical value of the settlement and the landscape.
3. Approved and realized territorial plan supports *public-private initiatives*. For example: construction, business, maintaining the landscape value, protection from flooding, and raising the technical level of individual buildings.
4. Territorial Plan is the basic document, on the basis of which, the local government can *get funds* (subsidies) to improve their environment. A territorial plan is a very important technical tool to affect the quality of life in the village. Territorial plan therefore can be considered a small village law. These activities of local government bring the potential to improve the quality of decision-making, enhancing the level of knowledge of local actors and knowledge transfer.
5. Territorial planning is defined by law and its implementing regulations in the form of text in the paragraph structure. This is yet related to the experience of individual experts (mostly landscape designers, architects...) acquired through their practice. But these *important skills are not formally recognized and described*. Therefore, it is difficult to transfer this knowledge from experts to concerned people of local government and local community.

The territorial planning (from the perspective of its impact on the specific life situations) is not concerned by public. Citizens and other local actors do not understand it sufficiently. There are also related subsequent processes of zoning and building permition, which depend on the territorial planning. In addition, the Czech Republic, several amendments to the relevant law during the consolidation of Czech legislation with EU legislation have been performed. All these changes and modifications are not fully getting into the legal awareness of people. Local citizens involved in these processes lack knowledge about the real impact of territorial planning on their life situations. They do not know how these processes can be used in their favour, and how these territorial activities affect the quality of both private and public life in the settlement. Local citizens are only dependent on the biased interpretation of various professionals from external companies representing their own interests.

1.2   Quality of Life

Maslow's hierarchy of needs is a theory in psychology proposed by Abraham Maslow in his 1943 paper "A Theory of Human Motivation" in Psychological Review [13]:

(1) *Physological needs* (e.g. drinks, food, heating, dwelling...).
(2) *Safety needs.*
(3) *Love and belongings needs.*
(4) *Esteem needs* (e.g. to feel respected, to be accepted and respected by others).
(5) *Self-realization and self-trancendence needs* (e.g. to feel be valuable for the others, spirituality).

The democracy is the human organization system that tries to ensure the integrity of personal interests and the interests of the whole community and deeply depends on the presence of (4) and (5). Of course, the paradox is that many people worth of self-realization, they are only motivated by lower physiological needs, ease and comfort.

Generally, the lower-lying needs (1,2,3) are the necessary condition for less urgent and developmentally higher needs (4,5). However, this is sometimes impossible in non-democratic conditions, where satisfaction of higher needs can help in extreme human life situations (emergency shortage, hardship, prison...) to substitute the missing lower needs.

1.3 Society in the Digital Era

This paper also reflects the phenomenon of contemporary society, which is the existence of social networks and digital world, as described by Laura Robinson [17] who argues that in contemporary society is an important not only self-realization of individual persons in the real material world but also their *involvement in the digital world*. Thus, if IT will support the knowledge transfer and transparency of information about real-life situations through their virtual representation in the online world, then we can expect a better participation rate of individuals using these digital technologies to the real material world. Level of understanding, literacy and the ability of individuals to participate in public administration, according to Hancock [10], belongs to the important indicators of personal quality of life and the level of democracy of modern society.

2 Hypothesis

The general objective of this project is an interdisciplinary approach linking insight to local government in terms of process visualization of selected agendas of territorial planning and building development with social development of rural areas in order to improve the quality of life.

Hypothesis of our project is based on the assumption of usefulness of *endogenous approach*[1] when improving the quality of life in small settlements in the segment of territorial planning and building development by increasing local citizen participation in these processes. We took advantage of the existing relationship between the rate of participation in the processes of territorial planning and building development and the quality of life, as it speaks respective authors

---

[1] Help by own resources of the entire community.

[4,12,16] and how they are also built international conventions, particularly the *Aarhus Convention* [2] and the *European Charter of Regional and Spatial Planning*. [5]

3 Project

Our project has been started in January 2012 and ended in December 2014.

1. We mapped the state of knowledge about territorial planning and building development among the inhabitants of small municipalities in the Central Bohemian Region.
2. We have proposed a new computer-based method of working with process-oriented knowledge for representatives of small municipalities and other local actors.
3. We have verified the benefits of our newly proposed method and we have found the participation enhancement as a possible tool to improve the quality of life in the dimension of citizen participation in the processes of the municipality for the purpose of self-realization through citizen involvement in the community development and the optimum balance between private and public interests within the community.

3.1 Explored Area

Our exploration covered the processes of territorial planning and building development in perspective of citizen participation in these processes as a factor determining the quality of life in rural areas. The studied area was selected based on the following conditions:

1. Central Bohemian region sufficiently uses IT; Computer equipment and Internet access were not a problem. This area is a reference model of the Czech e-government. Also, these municipalities are included in developing areas around the capital city of Prague by the development policy of the Czech Republic and the principles of territorial development of Central Bohemian district. Central Bohemian region is the only region of the Czech Republic which developed and fulfilled successful operating and developing the project the public e-Government CZ.04.1.05/2.2.00.5/3173 called "My Office - Bohemia Online". According to the data from the Czech Statistical Office, the use of IT both in individuals and households is between 60 % and 100 % of total population.
2. Municipalities belong to small rural communities (total population well below 2.000 and total area between 4 and 19 quadrate kilometers).[2]
3. For the purposes of the additional experiment, there were selected municipalities of two most important categories in the Czech Republic: *developing rural areas* and *non-developing areas of neighborly type.*

---

[2] The smallest village had only 88 citizens and 4 quadrate kilometers. The Czech Republic (like France) is characteristic by a large number of very small villages.

3.2   Used Metod and Tool

There is obvious an analogy between enterprise business processes and governmental processes in our method. In the Czech environment, this option has been firstly discussed by Duben et al. [8]

If we accept the premise that where the business has a product for a customer who is the reason and purpose of the process, so there we have, in the case of public administration, a *life situation* as "a product" (for example, to obtain a building permit, to obtain a subsidy...) and a *citizen* as "a customer." Business process models show the sequence of events as they happen through time in the form of a graphical diagram. In this diagram, we can indicate the activities and statuses of all participants and communications (including messaging, material, or documentation flows) between these participants and the links between these activities and states under different conditions. Process modelling is the proven and practical method used also for organizational consulting (finding participants and descriptions of roles processes, knowledge transfer). Computer-based process modelling allows to perform the analysis and design of systems for the active participation of the participants (interviews, workshops...). Our idea of using business process models for description the local government and public administration agendas was already published in [14,15].

For the purposes of mapping life situations, we have chosen (see Table 1) the methodology BORM approach which was developed as a collaborative work of Czech Technical University and Loughborough University as tested in several business projects of the international advisory and consulting company Deloitte. [11]

We have prepared a set of knowledge maps and simulation models of business processes created using special computer software for knowledge modeling and simulation. We have created process models showing four agendas to get *building permits*. In addition, we identified yet three procedural areas, which included in particular the agenda of *planning*, *re-planning*, and *land management* (which result is *zoning*). The total number of process models was 7. (see an example at Fig. 1) Project investigators tried to improve the decision-making processes mayors and other participants in local government. The research objective was to encourage local actors for knowledge transfer and improve the level of knowledge in dealing with life situations. During the project, the research team chose the Crat.CASE [6] as the best modeling tool.

3.3   First Survey - Before Training

Before introducing our visual models to people, we performed the first survey based on the questionnaire having 40 questions about details of processes in four areas of participation of the public and addressed to 463 people (an example of the questionnaire is at Fig. 2 on the following page). These 40 questions were of 4 following groups:

1. New territorial plan for a village (*planning*).

Table 1. Selection of the optimal process modelling method.

Method	Theoretical background	Advantages	Disadvantages
EPC – Aris	Petri nets	Widespread method in Europe It has a quality modeling tool	A complex method that does not respect the standards Very expensive modeling tool
UML Activity Diagram or BPMN	Flow-Chart	International standard. Numerous modeling tools, as well as free or cheap	Too focused on information technology, difficult to understand
UML state-chart	FSM Automata	International standard. Numerous modeling tools, as well as free or cheap	Too focused on information technology, difficult to understand
BORM	**Composed FSM Automata**	**Shows the behavior of the participants and the process flow as their dialogue.**	**It is not one of the widely known methods.**
Workflow Diagrams	Flow-Chart	Simple method	Rarely used in Europe. There is no consistent standard and therefore ambiguous interpretations

2. Change of an territorial plan of a village (*re-planning*).
3. Territorial decission of a village (*land management*).
4. Building permission.

The questions were about the knowledge of particular documentation and internal situations inside of these processes and about existing participation in these situations expressed in two ordinal scales of frequency (*daily, weekly, monthly, once per year, less than once per year, never*) and quality (*very good, good, something, very little, nothing*). We stressed the details of particular processes about concrete states and situations, where one can comment, ask or consult something in a process. This is very important, because legislation precisely defines situations, where concrete process participants have chance to participate.

The percentage of missing responses ranged only between 0 % and 2 %. The communities were chosen to best represent the two largest categories of Czech villages (as already explained). Obtained data were processed using the statistical program SPSS. Collected results were very alarming as shown in Table 2.

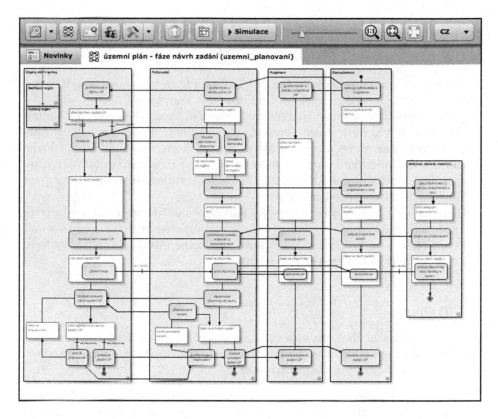

Fig. 1. Process model example.

Table 2. Existing process knowledge.

Process	Full knowledge	Partial knowledge	No knowledge
New territorial plan (participants involved, procedure, necessary documents...)	3 %	18 %	**79 %**
Territorial plan change (participants involved, procedure, necessary documents...)	4 %	16 %	**80 %**
Territorial decission (participants involved, procedure, necessary documents...)	4 %	19 %	**77 %**
Building premission (participants involved, procedure, necessary documents...)	9 %	38 %	**53 %**

In addition, respondents were asked about their own level of participation in these process areas. To each of the four process areas, respondents answered whether they themselves sometimes involved in the process or to become involved, specifically when and how often.

The result showed:

1. There is no difference between the small villages from two categories. Respondents from both categories do not differ in this knowledge.
2. Respondents do not know content and reason of these processes. This ignorance is reflected both in the sense that respondents do not know what particular activities these processes are composed from, and they do not know who are the individual participants and actors of these particular activities. They have only a vague idea about the documentation related to the inputs and outputs of discussed processes.
3. There is also a very low expected participation to the future. Majority (approaching 90 %) of respondents never participated in these processes and do not plan to participate in these processes in the future. Respondents were not motivated to change their passivity.

3.4   Training

We must emphasize that we expect to work with our method twice manner possible, like for example, it is the difference between the driving a car by a user and the design of car by a car constructor:

1. The first is the *user level*. Users are participating people from small villages who only work with finished visual models of processes. This user has no need to create any new visual processes but only must understand processes in order to get the necessary new knowledge. According to our experience from interviews with 57 people, explanation of method is very short, typically between 5 and 30 min.
2. The second level is the *expert level* of people (urbanists or architects or other professionals) who have sufficient domain knowledge and actively uses our method. It means that he can create visualizations of new processes and verify them. Such knowledge, of course, requires a good professional and more time than the first level. But, because the issue of territorial planning and building development is clearly codified in the relevant legislation, which is uniform for the entire territory of the Czech Republic, we expect that even if the broad deployment of our methods in practice, there is no need to educate and train some specialists. The greater task, in this case of wider deployment, would be about assure technical infrastructure, in concrete terms, for example, printing handbooks, organization of trainings, IT maintenance, and installation of proper computer servers and management of necessary user accounts for those who would remotely (from their own computers) work with our models.

Our method for visualization of territorial planning and building development processes can also be described as a method which, through visualization of the participants and their communications, describes *life situations*. The very notion of a *life situation* is in the humanities known and used, but rather only as the

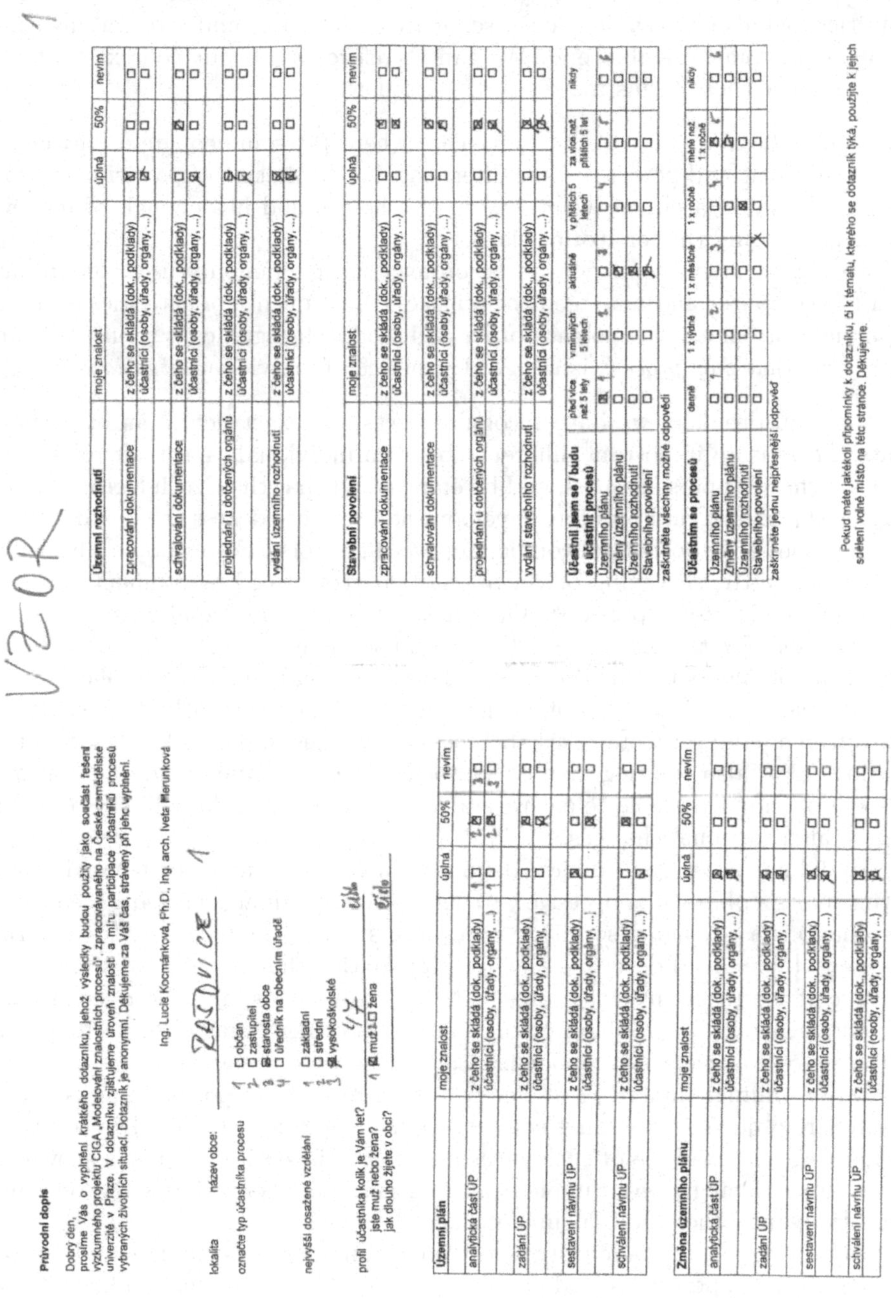

Fig. 2. Questionnaire example.

axiom than an exactly defined term. This means that the term *life situation* can either represent only some spatio-temporal moment within more complex activities and also the whole causal sequence of activities and interactions that results until some valuable end. We can therefore say in our context that we need to define these terms more exactly as follows:

- By the *situation*, we consider only case where (at some concrete particular time moment and place) is some interrelated constellation of participants (for example, when a citizen wants to build a house, and has enough of money, but is opposing the territorial plan).
- By the *process*, we consider (in accordance with commonly used definitions in the computer and management sciences) the sequence of activities of more participants that relate to each other and produce a significant result. We can also say that this *process* is a logical sequence of individual *situations*.

A second problem, we have recognized, was the exact definition of participants. There is an important difference between individuals and their roles that are performed by persons. It should be emphasized that the Czech legislation on territorial planning and building development does not address the possibility of crossing roles or hypothetical conflicts between the roles. For example, the same person can be the surveying officer at the Department of Environment and the owner of the discussed property. Or a member of the municipal council, which is responsible for the creation of the document, may, as any other citizen, to give their comments to this document. This situation is further complicated by the problem of low level of professionalization and inconsistently defined rights and duties of civil servants (clerks). Frequent changes in offices leadership after elections have also the negative effect to the quality of public administration. There is often not possible to ensure sufficient continuity in the fulfillment of the agenda after personal changes.

We did not use only graphical diagrams, but also auxiliary text-based tools. In the analysis phase, it is necessary to define the individual processing scenarios. A scenario is a textual description of a process where the structured text form (such as a table form) describes the default situation that the process starts, one or more of the resultant situations that the process ends, and the roles of participants in the process. This textual description of the behavior of participants in the process are so-called modeling cards that were designed in the late 80 s by Ward Cunningham and Kent Beck [3] as a learning tool for designing classes of software objects in teaching computer science and are still used in software engineering. An example of such cards describing the entire process is shown in Fig. 3 on the facing page. Supplemental information also includes the relevant legislation, and other used documentation.

Craft.CASE tool [6] allows two very important things for understanding the progress of the operations and thereby gaining a better understanding of the process:

1. It is a *visual simulation* of the process, step by step, where the colour gradually affixed each stage of the process.

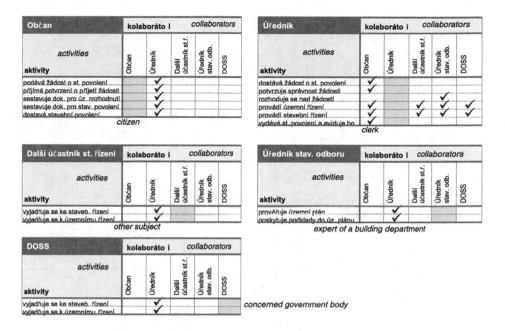

Fig. 3. Modelling cards example.

2. In addition to the feature of a visual simulation, it is possible to work with a *remote dialogue* with another user or consultant or designer in the form of a talk similar to the social network (e.g. Facebook), as shown in the Fig. 4 on the next page.

3.5   Second Survey - After Training

Our method was verified through *semi-structured interviews*, which were attended by 57 people successively from the same 13 communities, such as municipalities which were in the first survey. They were mostly motivated citizens from the ranks of a municipal council or other agile people in a village. For each community, it was 2–5 people who were recruiting by the *snow-ball* technique, in which our first informant led us to other members of the groups selected in a progressive manner. The *semi-structured interview* is a partly controlled interview, when there is prepared in advance a set of questions that need to be answered, but their order may vary. The interviewer may alter the wording of these questions based on the knowledge of the respondent, and may also ask for additional questions. This form of testing our method was based on the idea that the opinions and ideas of the respondents will be better expressed in these interviews than in a fixed questionnaire.

Each interview lasted a maximum of 20 min, but it is necessary to add to this time also time spent for the demonstration of our method, so that the total

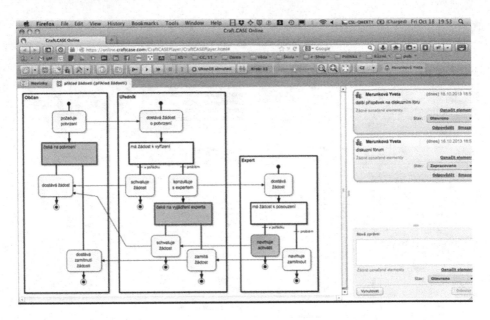

Fig. 4. Example of a remote dialogue between users.

time for each respondent ranged from about 10 min to about 50 min. Because respondents disagreed with video camera and audio recording on a dictaphone, there was created a paper sheet with preformed major three issues:

1. The first set of prepared questions was involved, as in the previous survey, to the current level of knowledge about the processes of territorial planning and building development before the application of our method. The difference was in the content of the questions that were more focused at the subsequent classification of the existing level of knowledge by the CMM approach[3], which can be used for quality assesment of public administration processes. [7]

   (a) Do you have sufficient information on these processes, their participants, relevant legislation, documentation, so that you could initiate such a process and instruct your fellows how and where to participate?

   (b) Do you think that your fellows have sufficient information on these processes, their participant's etc. so that they can provide information on how and where they can involve?

   (c) Do you think that the quality of execution of these processes is primarily dependent on the knowledge and skills of the municipal council?

   (d) You have in your community some extraordinary person whom you can ask for expert knowledge? Do you think it is good that the success of the processes depends on this important person and you do not need to understand?

---

[3] Capability-Maturity Model with scale of five levels: *chaotic*, *repeatable*, *defined*, *managed*, and *optimizing*.

(e) Do you think that the processes performed in your community formerly in a "fire fighting" way would be in performed in the same unaware way if repeated again?

2. In the second set of questions, we focused on the training of the new method.
   (a) How much time did you spend to understand this method?
   (b) Do you find this method interesting and useful in comparison with just reading texts of the relevant laws?
   (c) Did you know that these processes are so structured? Did you expected these processes are easier or more difficult?
   (d) Now, if you know more about these process, do you remember some event from the past in which you would behave differently?
   (e) Do you want to add something you are missing in our method?

3. Finally, we asked for the effect of the new knowledge about the processes of territorial planing and buiding developement.
   (a) Will you more involve in these processes, comment on them and respond to them?
   (b) Do you know how these processes can be better used for your personal benefit and for the benefit of your community?
   (c) Do you think that these processes can be used to improve life in your community to allow not only for the development but also preventing problems and conflicts?
   (d) Do you think that experts and people outside your community (investors, government bodies...) who participated formerly in your processes, did they inform you objectively and in agreement with your interest?
   (e) Do you think that now you can perform these processes with less uncertainty than before?

3.6   Results

The most important results are in Table 3. These results make our method successful.

Table 3. Selected results.

54 people confirmed that our method is useful, it allows them to better understand the context and enhances their future involvement in processes.	95 %
3 people commented neutrally, our method does not help them.	5 %
No respondent indicated that they assume a new method even more complicated causing wrong orientation in processes.	0 %

Besides this method evaluation, we obtained yet another interesting results:

- Processes were carried out flexibly and ad-hoc. Citizens were "event-driven" by the competent external authorities (39 respondents, 68 %).
- From the past, citizens remember one or more situations, in which they could behave differently, but they did not have sufficient knowledge (39 respondents, 68 %).
- About the method and simulation tool, citizens would like to add new functionality of document repository and timing and tracking of specific process in order to display who and why decided. Also, personal contacts would be valuable (26 respondents, 46 %).
- In the past, citizens were misinformed by biased officials and other external authorities (38 respondents, 67 %).

However, it should be noted that an important and decisive motivation factor of citizens' participation in these processes is development and maintenance of their own immovable property, which depends on their particular economic situation, and cannot be easily improved only through better process knowledge. Therefore, the citizens' interest was focused mainly on understanding and possibilities of their role in private building permit process, but public interests have had lower priority.

4   Conclusion

Submitted work is interdisciplinary and is narrowly focused on one particular problem area of territorial planning and building development. Proposed method can concretely support the traditional concept of e-democracy as the broadly positive influence of information technology in today's "modern" public administration and their necessity for regional and social development, thus contributing to greater dynamism and adaptability of citizens and representatives of small municipalities, their better participation, which brings greater fulfillment of those involved and the consequent improvement in quality of life through increased intangible wealth (knowledge).

It is obvious that even if our proposed method was accepted and confirmed as a useful tool, it requires some effort from its users. We met also with the view that easier than learning a new method would be to use some external consulting services, such as advice by some relevant territorial planning authority. This is certainly a possible solution, but we prefer to solve problems in the way of this old saying: *"Give a hungry man a fish and you feed him for one day only. But when you learn him fishing, you feed him forever."*

The author would like to acknowledge the support of the research grant SGS14/209/OHK4/3T/14 and NAKI MK-S-3421/2011 OVV.

References

1. van der Aalst, W.M.P.: Business process simulation revisited. In: Barjis, J. (ed.) EOMAS 2010. LNBIP, vol. 63, pp. 1–14. Springer, Heidelberg (2010)
2. The Aarhus convention, European commission, environment and law (2015). http://ec.europa.eu/environment/aarhus. Accessed 06 July 2015
3. Beck, K., Cunningham, W.: A laboratory for teaching object oriented thinking. In: ACM SIGPLAN Notices, vol. 24, no. 10, pp. 1–6, New York (2012). ISBN 0-89791-333-7
4. Beierle, T.C., Cayford, J.: Democracy in Practice: Public Participation in Environmental Decisions. Resources for the Future, Washington (2002)
5. CEMAT Conference: European Regional Planning Strategy, Chapter 4 - Citizens Participation in Regional/Spacial Planning, vol. 69, pp. 172–198. Council of Europe, Strasbourg (1992). ISBN 92-871-1995-3
6. Craft.CASE modelling tool (2015). http://www.craftcase.com. Accessed 30 June 2015
7. Christiansson M.T.: A Common process model to improve e-service solutions - the municipality case. In: Proceedings of the 11th European Conference on e-Government ECEG 2011, Ljubljana, Slovenia (2011)
8. Duben, J.; Merunka, V.; Lukáš, M.: Modelling of public agendas, project for muncipality of Cheb (in Czech). Institute for Governemental Information Systems, Prague (1997)
9. European environment agency: Urban Sprawl in Europe - the ignored challenge. EEA Report No 10/2006. EEA, Copenhagen (2006). ISSN 1725-9177, ISBN 92 9167-887-2
10. Hancock, T.: Quality of life indicators and the DHC (2001). http://www.ontla.on. ca/library/repository/mon/24002/299271.pdf
11. Knott, R.P., Merunka, V., Polák, J.: The BORM Methodology: A Third-generation Fully Object-oriented Methodology, Knowledge-based Systems, vol. 3, no. 10. Elsevier Science Publishing, New York (2003)
12. Madden, K., Schwartz, A.: How to turn a place around - project for public spaces, New York (2000). ISBN 0970632401
13. Maslow, A.H.: A theory of human motivation. Psychol. Rev. **50**(4), 370–396 (1943)
14. Merunka, V., Merunková, I.: Modeling and visualization of urban planning and building development processes for local government of small settlements. In: Barjis, J., Pergl, R. (eds.) EOMAS 2014. LNBIP, vol. 191, pp. 59–73. Springer, Heidelberg (2014)
15. Merunka, V., Merunková, I.: Local government processes of small settlements in the Czech Republic. In: Sideridis, A.B., Yialouris, C.P., Kardasiadou, Z., Zorkadis, V. (eds.) e-Democracy 2013. CCIS, vol. 441, pp. 103–112. Springer, Heidelberg (2014)
16. Posas, P., Fisher, T.B.: Organisational behaviour and public decision making in the environmental assessment context. In: Environmental Assessment Lecturers' Handbook, Road, pp. 93–115 (2008)
17. Robinson, L.: The cyberself: symbolic interaction in the digital age. New Media Soc. **9**, 93–110 (2007)

Citizen e-Empowerment in Greek and Czech Municipalities

Maria Ntaliani[1]([⊠]), Constantina Costopoulou[1], Sotiris Karetsos[1],
and Martin Molhanec[2]

[1] Informatics Laboratory, Department of Agricultural Economics and
Rural Development, Agricultural University of Athens, Athens, Greece
{ntaliani,tina,karetsos}@aua.gr
[2] Department of E-Technology,
Czech Technical University in Prague, Prague, Czech Republic
molhanec@fel.cvut.cz

Abstract. This paper studies the concept of electronic empowerment from the citizenship view, which refers to citizens' political participation, accessibility and their ability to supervise government decisions. Especially, the study focuses on local government for two case studies, namely the municipalities in Greece and the Czech Republic. Firstly, the paper describes existing models and indices for electronic empowerment measurement. The Citizen Web Empowerment Index has been used for the two case studies to estimate the level of citizen electronic empowerment. Next, the paper presents the analysis results of the measurements, showing that both countries are at low to moderate level of e-empowerment.

Keywords: Electronic participation · Citizen empowerment · Local government · Municipality · Portals

1 Introduction

Electronic participation (e-participation) is directly related to democracy. The imperative need to improve and extend representative democracy has evinced the role of local government. Emerging demands for participation at local governments reflect the need for increased control over their decisions, as well as for transparency and accountability (Alonso 2009). According to United Nations (United Nations E-Government Survey 2014), e-participation relates to the process of engaging citizens through Information and Communication Technologies (ICTs) in policy and decision-making in order to make an inclusive, participatory and collaborative public administration. Sæbø et al. (2008) state that e-participation regards the extension and transformation of participation in societal democratic and consultative processes mediated by ICTs, and is distinguished into government driven participation and citizen-driven participation, referring to the government or the citizens respectively as the main drivers for achieving it.

E-participation comprises an expansion of a government's toolbox for reaching out to engaging with citizens and communities, as well as specifying their requirements for policies and services, and cannot replace traditional forms of public participation

© Springer International Publishing Switzerland 2015
S.K. Katsikas and A.B. Sideridis (Eds.): E-Democracy 2015, CCIS 570, pp. 124–133, 2015.
DOI: 10.1007/978-3-319-27164-4_9

(e.g. face-to-face meetings, paper-based communications, telephone calls, physical bulletin boards) (UN 2014). Globally, various models have been proposed aiming at mapping the development or maturity of e-participation. These models vary from three to five levels of e-participation. The ultimate goal of the models is to empower citizens in society.

Generally speaking, empowerment connects individual strengths and competencies, natural helping systems and proactive behavior to social policy and social change (Rappapon 1984). Distinct theories of empowerment have been developed for the processes that occur at the individual, group and organizational levels, and in the wider community. The advancements of Internet and Web 2.0 technologies have given a new dimension to empowerment, namely electronic empowerment (e-empowerment). According to Amichai-Hamburger et al. (2008), e-empowerment can be viewed from four levels, namely the personal; the interpersonal; the group; and citizenship levels. E-empowerment comprises the higher maturity level of e-participation models. In this paper, the citizenship level of e-empowerment is studied.

In the Machintosh model (2004), the e-empowerment stage is defined as "using technology to empower citizens and support active participation and facilitate bottom-up ideas to influence the political agenda. Citizens are considered as producers for policies rather than just consumers as in the previous levels". In Wimmer's model (2007), it is stated that e-empowerment facilitates the transfer of influence, control, and policy making to citizens. Alshibly and Chiong (2015) relate the concept of citizen empowerment with increased control over the production of desired public outcomes and the prevention of undesired outcomes.

The objective of this paper is to present the findings of the evaluation of the degree of citizen empowerment in local municipality portals in Greece and the Czech Republic. The presented cases have been selected because these two countries have similar demographics and economic level. More specifically, the population of Greece is 10.8 million, while the population of the Czech Republic is 10.5 million people. Greece holds the 50th place and the Czech Republic holds the 51st in the GDP ranking. Regarding the Human Development Index, Greece is ranked 29th and the Czech Republic 28th.

In this context, the paper is structured as follows: the second section provides an overview of models and indices of citizen e-empowerment measurement. The third section presents an index entitled "Citizens Web Empowerment Index" (CWEI), which has been used for the two case studies. The fourth section provides the major findings of the measurements, and the last section concludes the work and provides directions for future research.

2   Background

A number of models for e-participation have been proposed in literature, such as the Machintosh (2004), the Wimmer (2007), the Tambouris et al. (2007), the Al-Dalou and Abu-Shanab (2013), the United Nations E-Government Survey (2014) and the Alshibly and Chiong (2015) models. In the following, two of these models, the mostly related with the e-empowerment concept, as well as an index for measuring e-empowerment are described. The first e-participation model has been developed by individual researchers and has been widely accepted by the research community; and the second has been developed by the UN and has been applied at a worldwide scale. Also, the CWEI index has been developed by researchers and has been selected in this study since it is specialized for e-empowerment.

The first model for e-participation has been proposed by Tambouris et al. (2007) and it is a combination of five evolutionary stages as follows:

- **e-Informing** is a one-way communication that provides citizens with online information concerning policies and citizenship;
- **e-Consulting** is a limited two-way communication for collecting public comments, opinions, ideas and alternatives;
- **e-Involving** is about engaging online citizens to ensure that public feedback is understood and taken into account;
- **e-Collaborating** is a higher level two-way channel among public and government, helping citizens to develop alternatives and to identify solutions;
- **e-Empowerment** is the delegation of final decision-making rights to the public, and implementing what citizens decide.

The UN use a three-level model of e-participation that shifts from "passive" to "active" engagement of people leading to their real empowerment. This model is based on the E-Participation Index (EPI), which is a qualitative assessment based on the availability and relevancy of participatory services available on government websites. It deals with the use of electronic services to facilitate provision of information to the public (e-information), interaction with stakeholders (e-consultation) and engagement in decision-making processes (e-decision making), as mentioned below:

- **e-Information** refers to the online provision of public information and access to information upon demand to citizens;
- **e-Consultation** concerns whether citizens' feedback is taken into account in public policies, practices and services;
- **e-Decision Making** regards citizens' co-production in service components and delivery modalities, where the citizens perform the role of partner rather than the customer.

The goal of EPI index is to depict the e-participation performance of countries relative to one another at a particular time instance. Therefore, the comparative ranking of countries can just be used as an indicative of the broad trends in promoting citizen engagement (United Nations E-Government Survey 2014). According to the UN, in 2014 the Republic of Korea and the Netherlands have conquered the first place reaching the EPI value of 1. Uruguay is in the third place with EPI equal to 0.98, followed by Japan, France and the United Kingdom all together sharing the fourth place with their EPIs reaching 0.96. Then, Australia and Chile share the 7th place with 0.94 and USA is ranking 9th with 0.98. Greece holds the 17th place at 0.80, and the Czech Republic ranks 122nd with EPI equal to 0.25.

However, the need for further evaluation and measurement of e-empowerment has emerged. Towards this direction, Bellio and Buccoliero (2013) have proposed the CWEI index that focuses on the evaluation of portals provided by public agencies.

In particular, the CWEI has been used for measuring the degree of citizen web empowerment firstly in 104 Italian city portals, and secondly in 42 local government portals from 20 different European countries. In the second case, the cities were all members of the Major Cities of Europe group (Buccoliero and Bellio 2010; Bellio and Buccoliero 2014). In this work, in order to measure citizen empowerment provided by municipalities, the CWEI has been adopted and is analytically presented in the next section. This index has been chosen because it can be directly implemented and has already been used in literature for measuring citizen empowerment for the case of municipalities. Moreover, in literature there is no other index exclusively measuring e-empowerment.

3 Citizen Web Empowerment Index

The CWEI index is multidimensional and composed of a number of sub-indicators for measuring the various aspects of citizens' participation through the Web. It consists of a number of characteristics, the presence of which depicts the structure and the provision of information and services of the portals. The characteristics are included into four categories, namely "e-information", "Web 2.0 tools and services", "e-consultation" and "e-decision making process". It has to be noted that the "Web strategy evaluation" characteristic in "Web 2.0 tools and services" category, has not been taken into account because it refers to country evaluation rather than local governments. Also, in previous efforts, the maximum theoretical value of the index used was 100. In this work, this theoretical value has not been followed. Instead, every characteristic has been rated on a scale of 1-5, corresponding to a scale from total absence to complete provision, providing a qualitative assessment on citizenship e-empowerment. Below, the categories and their characteristics are analytically described for the case of municipalities.

e-Information: regards information on the structure of the public agency and its policies, without or upon demand. It includes the following characteristics:

- *Government structure:* information on the municipality's internal organizational structure (departments, agencies, employees).
- *Segmentation or life events:* analytical information on the particular department of the municipality one has to contact for particular life event or business situation.
- *Contact details:* information for communicating with the municipality administration and employees (address, telephone number, email, and fax).
- *Policies and procedures:* data on policies and procedures followed and relevant legislation.
- *Budget:* information on the municipality budget and its allocation for particular activities.
- *City Council minutes:* availability of memoirs of the City Council meetings.
- *Newsletter and/or Web magazine:* existence of an online publication for informing citizens on public issues (e.g. news, contests).

Web 2.0 tools and services: refer to social networking tools and mobile applications used by the public agency to enhance citizen empowerment. It includes the following characteristics:

- *Blog:* existence of a separate blog for the City Council.
- *Forum and chat:* allowing citizens to create a dialogue among them and the municipality for the city's issues.
- *Social network presence:* Facebook, Flickr, Youtube, Skype, Twitter.
- *Mobile services:* services and applications for mobile devices.
- *Web TV:* municipality broadcasts through Internet TV (e.g. Council meetings).
- *Open data strategy:* the municipality's strategy and time schedule for providing trusted data to the citizens.

e-Consultation: concerns information and services that facilitate the direct expression of citizens' opinion to the municipality. It includes the following characteristics:

- *Online polls and surveys:* allowing citizens to express themselves and provide a valuable feedback for the municipality.
- *Online complaints:* existence of online forms or services for enabling citizens in submitting their complaints.
- *Reputation systems:* systems for collecting, computing and publishing reputation scores based on citizens' opinions and perceptions on municipality issues (e.g. quality of provided services).
- *Mayor's direct online relation with citizens:* services for establishing the Mayor's direct online relation with citizens (e.g. personal website and its content).

e-Decision Making Process: refers to the ways citizens' opinion is reflected in decision making processes. These ways achieve the co-design and co-production of services from public agencies and their citizens. It includes the following characteristics:

- *Evidence for citizen opinion consideration:* it assesses evidences that the municipality considers the opinion of citizens in decision making processes (e.g. through e-voting systems).
- *Evidence for complaint consideration:* it gives evidence on what decisions have been taken starting from the consultation process (e.g. publication of online poll and subsequent actions taken).

4   Case Studies: Municipalities in Greece and the Czech Republic

This section presents the results from the CWEI measurement for two case studies, namely the municipalities in Greece and the Czech Republic.

4.1   Greek Case Study

Greece's local government is divided into three levels of administration. The first level is composed of 325 municipalities, which constitute of municipal units, and these in turn of communities; the second level consists of 13 regions; and the third of 7 decentralized administrations. The decentralized administrations are governed by the general secretary appointed by the Greek Government. The regions and municipalities are fully self-governed.

In 1998, the administrative system changed with the implementation of Kapodistrias plan. Before and after the Kapodistrias reform, the difference between municipalities and communities was merely a matter of size. Municipalities were big and urban whereas communities were small, single villages. From 5,775 (441 municipalities and 5,382 communities), the reform reduced them to 1,033 (900 municipalities and 133 communities) (Wikipedia 2015). From 1 January 2011, in accordance with the Kallikratis programme, the administrative system of Greece was drastically overhauled. The Programme of Kallikratis reduced furthermore the number of municipalities to just 325.

From 325 municipalities 319 have been examined according to the CWEI index, since six of them do not have a website or their website is under construction, these are the municipalities of Zacharo, the island of Leipsoi, the island of Serifos, Fourni islands, Oichalia and Sithonia. The measurement of CWEI has taken place from April till May 2015. The characteristics of the index have been evaluated by citizens. Regarding the "e-information" category the following results have been found:

- *Government structure:* only 1 % provides none information on the municipality organizational structure; 5 % has a few; 40 % has average; 37 % has much; and 17 % has very much.
- *Segmentation or life events:* 9 % has none; 19 % has a few; 49 % has average; 18 % has much; and 6 % has very much.
- *Contact details:* 3 % has none information for communicating with the municipality administration and employees; 9 % has a few; 38 % has average; 30 % has much; and 20 % has very much.
- *Policies and procedures:* 17 % has none data on policies and procedures followed and relevant legislation; 46 % has a few; 25 % has average; 8 % has much; and 3 % has very much.
- *Budget:* 83 % has none information on the municipality budget; 4 % has a few; 4 % has average; 3 % has much; and 6 % has very much.
- *City Council minutes:* 64 % has available information on memoirs of the City Council meetings; 20 % has a few; 7 % has average; 5 % has much; and 4 % has very much.
- *Newsletter and/or Web magazine:* 54 municipalities (17 %) have only a newsletter and 10 (3 %) only a Web magazine. 249 municipalities (78 %) have neither of the two and only 4 (1 %) have both.

Figure 1 presents the values assigned to the characteristics of the "e-information" category for the Greek municipalities. It is noted that the "Newsletter and/or Web magazine" is not illustrated since its value field is different.

Regarding the "Web 2.0 tools and services" category the following results have been found:

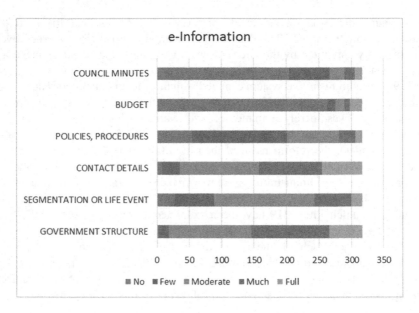

Fig. 1. e-Information Measurement

- *Blog, Forum or Chat:* 9 (3 %) municipalities have only a separate blog; 27 (8 %) municipalities do not have a blog but have either a forum or a chat; 283 (89 %) do not have a forum or a chat.
- *Social network presence:* 97 municipalities have Facebook, 8 have Flickr, 54 have Youtube, none has Skype, 66 have Twitter, 6 have Instragram, 2 have LinkedIn and 204 have none social network. It is noted that in this measurement each municipality could select more than one social network.
- *Mobile services:* 81 % has no applications for mobile devices; 16 % has only RSS; 1 % has only mobile applications; and 2 % has RSS and mobile applications.
- *Web TV:* 8 % has a Web TV to communicate information.
- *Open data strategy:* 60 % has not at all information for the municipality's strategy and time schedule; 16 % has a few; 11 % has average; 36 % has much; and 19 % has very much.

Regarding the "e-Consultation" category the following results have been found:

- *Online polls and surveys:* 91 % of the municipalities has none, 8 % has only polls and 1 % has both polls and surveys.
- *Online complaints:* 66 % of the municipalities has online forms for enabling citizens in submitting their complaints.
- *Reputation systems:* 94 % has no reputation systems.
- *Mayor's direct online relation with citizens:* 58 % has services for establishing the Mayor's direct online relation with citizens.

Regarding the "e-Decision Making Process" category, the following results have been found:

- *Evidence for citizen opinion consideration:* 88 % has not at all such evidence; 6 % has a few; 4 % has average; 1 % has much; and 1 has % very much.
- *Evidence for complaint consideration:* 88 % has not at all such evidence; 6 % has a few; 4 % has average; 1 % has much; and 1 has % very much.

4.2 Czech Case Study

The Czech Republic has a decentralised administration with 13 regions and 6,249 municipalities. Each municipality is run by a mayor, and the head of corporate towns is a lord mayor. Regions are administrated by a marshal; only in the capital city of Prague is this position reserved for Prague's lord mayor.

In this case study, due to the vast number of Czech municipalities, a representative sample has been selected. This sample includes three types of communities. The first type concerns municipalities that are parts of the city of Prague. There have been selected the following three parts of Prague: Prague 1, Prague 8 and Prague 10, which represent the 25, 106 and 108 thousand of inhabitants respectively. The second type refers to larger towns, the centres of the district. There have been selected Pardubice, Beroun and Olomouc, representing 89, 19 and 100 thousand of inhabitants respectively. The last type concerns small local towns. There have been selected Žd'ár and Sázavou, Bruntál and Kdyně, representing 21, 16 and 5 thousand of inhabitants respectively.

The measurement of CWEI took place at the end of June 2015. Regarding the "e-information" category the following results have been found: All except one, the smallest village, all municipalities meet at the highest level. This is due to the fact that the law obliges municipalities to publish much obligatory information, including the budget.

Concerning the "Web 2.0 tools and services" category the following results have been found: Most municipalities use Facebook and also provide RSS feed subscription for news. Many municipalities also provide their news through SMS. Some municipalities also have their website in a form adapted for mobile devices. Chat, blog and forum are usually not provided.

Regarding the "e-Consultation" category the following results have been found: a standard possibility to submit a complaint using an online form is provided. For the contact with the Mayor email and telephone is used. Sometimes the possibility of e-voting for municipal affairs is offered.

Referring to the "e-Decision Making Process" category the following results have been found: it is possible to say that there is good evidence that the town hall responding to complaints, at least they always have an obligation to provide the complainant with an answer. The possibility of public participation in strategic plans via the Internet is not yet generally realized.

5   Conclusions

This study investigates Greek and Czech citizen e-empowerment in local governmental web portals through a qualitative assessment. It is based on the CWEI index, which is focused on measuring e-empowerment. According to literature, various efforts for measuring e-participation have been made around the world. E-empowerment comprises the final level of e-participation maturity and CWEI comprises the only one specialized index for e-empowerment.

According to the results, the overall citizenship e-empowerment progress can be considered to be average in both countries. In the case of Greece, the "e-information" category presents advanced levels of availability of its characteristics. The category "Web 2.0 tools and services" present low to moderate levels of provision. An exception is the governmental system called "Diavgeia" which is obligatory used for the publishing of any administrative action which causes direct or indirect costs. The "e-consultation" and "e-decision making process" are lacking behind, with low levels of provision of their characteristics. However, they are progressively increasing in municipality websites.

In the case of the Czech Republic, since the sample is quite small, we can express only general remarks. Especially for larger municipalities, they have professionally created websites at a very good interface level. A common problem, however, is that every municipality has a slightly different structure of its website. It is therefore difficult to find certain information in the municipality website, although it exists.

Nowadays, with the rapid evolution of the capabilities of tablets and smartphones, as well as the advent of Web 2.0 technologies citizenship e-empowerment must be reconsidered. For example, social media has a particularly appealing potential for e-participation. Users can be empowered by social media, since it gives them a collaboration platform to communicate (Magro 2012). In both case studies, the use of social media has been proved to be low to moderate. In our point of view, local governments do not have a strategy for exploiting the feedback provided through their interactions with citizens via social media. The use of this feedback can support the progress of citizens' e-participation and more specifically e-empowerment. In the next years, citizens will be progressively empowered to play a far more active role in their local government policies and practices, using social media.

In the spirit of looking forward, future work will include firstly the CWEI measurement of all Czech municipalities in order to depict more accurately e-empowerment progress and secondly, the development of a framework that will determine a short and a long term strategy for using citizens' feedback by local governments, which will ultimately succeed e-government innovation. Concluding, there is much to be done for succeeding full citizen e-empowerment; but the more a society succeeds e-empowerment the more it succeeds e-democracy establishment.

References

Alonso, A.I.: E-participation and local governance: a case study. Theoret. Empirical Res. Urban Manage. 3(12), 49–62 (2009)

Al-Dalou, R., Abu-Shanab, E.: E-Participation Levels and Technologies. In: Proceedings of 6th International Conference on Information Technology (ICIT 2013), pp. 8–10 (2013)

Alshibly, H., Chiong, R.: Customer empowerment: does it influence electronic government success? a citizen-centric perspective. Electronic Commerce Research and Applications (2015) 16 June 2015, in press

Amichai-Hamburger, Y., McKenna, K.Y., Tal, S.A.: E-empowerment: empowerment by the internet. Comput. Hum. Behav. **24**(5), 1776–1789 (2008)

Bellio, E., Buccoliero, L.: Citizen Web Empowerment across Italian Cities: a benchmarking approach. Citizen E-Participation in Urban Governance: Crowdsourcing and Collaborative Creativity: Crowdsourcing and Collaborative Creativity, 284 (2013)

Bellio, E., Buccoliero, L.: Digital marketing strategies in Italy: the path towards citizen cities web empowerment. In: Obaidat, M.S., Filipe, J. (eds.) ICETE 2013. CCIS, vol. 456, pp. 142–159. Springer, Heidelberg (2014)

Buccoliero, L., Bellio, E.: Citizens web empowerment in European municipalities. J. e-Gov. **33** (4), 225–236 (2010)

Machintosh, A.: Characterizing e-Participation in policy-making. In: Proceedings of the Thirty-Seventh Annual Hawaii International Conference on System Sciences (HICSS 2004) (2004)

Magro, M.J.: A review of social media use in e-Government. Adm. Sci. **2**(2), 148–161 (2012)

Rappapon, J.: Studies in empowerment: introduction to the issue. Prev. Hum. Serv. **3**(2–3), 1–7 (1984)

Sæbø, Ø., Rose, J., Flak, L.S.: The shape of e-Participation: characterizing an emerging research area. Gov. Inf. Q. **25**(3), 400–428 (2008)

Tambouris, E., Liotas, N., Kaliviotis, D., Tarabanis, K.: A framework for scoping e-Participation. In: 8th Annual International Digital Government Research Conference, pp. 288–289 (2007)

United Nations e-Government Survey, (2014). http://unpan3.un.org/egovkb/Portals/egovkb/Documents/un/2014-Survey/E-Gov_Complete_Survey-2014.pdf

Wikipedia.: Kapodistrias reform (2015). https://en.wikipedia.org/wiki/Kapodistrias_reform

Wimmer, M.A.: Ontology for an e-participation virtual resource centre. In: Proceedings of 1st International Conference on Theory and Practice of Electronic Governance, pp. 89–98 (2007)

Local E-Government and E-Democracy: An Evaluation of Greek Municipalities

Georgios Lappas[1(✉)], Amalia Triantafillidou[1], Prodromos Yannas[2], and Alexandros Kleftodimos[1]

[1] Digital Media and Communication,
Technological Education Institute of Western Macedonia, Kastoria, Greece
{lappas, a.triantafylidou,
kleftodimos}@kastoria.teikoz.gr
[2] Business Administration,
Piraeus University of Applied Sciences, Aigaleo, Greece
prodyannas@teipir.gr

Abstract. The purpose of this study is the development of a citizen-centric framework for the evaluation of local e-government projects that is validated in the context of Greek municipalities. The proposed model consists of four categories, 14 factors/indices and 83 criteria. The framework incorporates the different aspects of e-government as well as e-democracy. To develop and validate the model two research undertakings were conducted: one survey that captured citizens' opinions about the important e-government features and a website analysis to inquire about the level of e-government sophistication of Greek local government websites. Results of citizens' survey served as input for the weighting of the model metrics. The analysis of the Greek municipal websites indicated that municipalities performed moderately well with regard to the disclosure of one-way information while they scored low in the provision of online services for citizens and businesses and the opportunities offered for citizens' interaction and participation.

Keywords: E-government · E-democracy · Evaluation model · Citizen-centric · Greek local governments

1 Introduction

Public authorities around the globe, at the local as well as at the national level are utilizing ICTs in order to communicate and interact with their stakeholders (e.g., citizens, businesses, associations, media, etc.). However, e-government implementation requires a large amount of funds [1]. Hence, it becomes imperative for e-government managers to monitor and evaluate the performance of their projects in order to be able to measure the return of e-government investment [2]. Given that the primary goal of e-government is to provide online services friendly to citizens that enhance their participation and engagement [3], the value benefits accruing to citizens should be a main concern of any e-government evaluation exercise. As [4] note there is a lack of studies that evaluate e-government projects based on the public value derived from citizens. Hence, the purpose of the present study is twofold. First, to propose a framework for the evaluation of e-government at the local level that is based on citizens' preferences

© Springer International Publishing Switzerland 2015
S.K. Katsikas and A.B. Sideridis (Eds.): E-Democracy 2015, CCIS 570, pp. 134–150, 2015.
DOI: 10.1007/978-3-319-27164-4_10

and second to apply the proposed evaluation model in the context of Greek municipal government websites. It should be noted that the proposed model incorporates e-government as well as e-democracy features. E-government deals with the passive provision of information and online services to citizens and businesses [5] whereas e-democracy moves to more active forms of citizens' participation and engagement in the decision making process of governmental agencies [6]. Herein, e-democracy and e-government are considered as two separate constructs that serve different purposes but are intertwined. In particular, e-democracy can be regarded as an offshoot of e-government [7] at the highest and most sophisticated attainable level [8] of e-government. Thus, e-democracy can be conceived as one of the final stages of the development and maturity process of e-government models [9].

2 Issues and Challenges of E-Government Evaluation Models

In the past years a number of studies have focused on the evaluation of e-government initiatives. However, as [10] indicate most of these evaluation frameworks have proven to be immature due to the complex task of assessing the performance of e-government projects. A limitation of the current evaluation models is their emphasis on the supply side of e-government [11]. Specifically, these models assess performance based on the features incorporated in the portals of public authorities without paying attention to the demand side: that is the expectations and needs of citizens who are the primary users of online public services.

Another methodological shortcoming stems from the bias generated from the subjective judgments of researchers. Specifically, in several studies, the evaluation frameworks were based on a set of criteria in which researchers' assigned weights based on their experience [11, 12]. Another challenge in evaluating e-government projects is related to the missing component of e-democracy. Although, most e-government evaluation frameworks assess performance in terms of information dissemination and other available online transactions, they fail to incorporate e-democracy or e-participation metrics [11]. The framework proposed by [12] included metrics that evaluated the level of citizen participation. These metrics tested whether municipal websites include features that enable citizens' engagement (i.e., comment boxes, chat rooms, online discussion forums, scheduled e-meetings, online polls, etc.).

Reference [11] also incorporated in their evaluation model an e-participation category that included three sub-factors namely, information, consultation and active participation. Specifically, information factor assessed whether a portal publishes documents regarding local policies. The consultation factor examined if websites included applications that allowed online consultations about important local issues. The active participation factor included metrics that assessed whether local governments' portal (a) incorporated chats, blogs, and e-forums, (b) conducted online polls of local issues, (c) allowed citizens to create a new discussion topic on the portal's forum, and (d) provided citizens with the opportunity to propose new agenda topics to be discussed in the upcoming council meetings. Reference [13] measured the channels of e-participation offered by municipalities in Mexico. Specifically, e-participation was evaluated by examining if websites included (a) the names of officials and their contact information (b) discussion fora, (c) blogs, (d) discussion tables, (e) online surveys, (f) e-voting tools, (g) reports of consultations and discussions. In a similar vein, [4] included in their evaluation framework a citizen engagement factor that measured whether local government portals incorporate online tools for (a) online submission of citizens' proposals about local services enhancement, (b) online surveys concerning citizens' satisfaction, (c) live broadcasts of council meetings, (d) direct communication with mayor and members of council meetings.

Based on the preceding analysis, it can be argued that the few e-government evaluation schemes that incorporate e-participation measures are not consistent in the way they evaluate e-participation. Some of the measures include several criteria to assess e-participation [12] while others treat e-participation as a multi-dimensional construct [11]. However, e-participation by its nature is a multi-faceted construct [14], thus e-government models should take into the different aspects that comprise e-participation. Given the above deficiencies found in the e-government evaluation models it becomes evident that a more holistic assessment of e-government is needed.

3   Research Methodology

In order to develop and validate our proposed evaluation model we took the following steps. First we conducted a literature review to identify the criteria-metrics that will comprise our model. Hence, most of the metrics included in the model were extracted from prior academic studies [12, 13, 15, 16] to ensure that the criteria used are theoretically valid. Moreover, the proposed model included items that originated from an analysis of several municipal websites in Greece in order to assure that the model was adjusted to the Greek local government context. The identified criteria were then grouped into factors. Special care was taken to develop the e-democracy/e-participation factors. These factors and their metrics were based on the studies of [17–19] that outline the different modes of e-participation. It should be noted that the derived factors of our model were organized around four main categories based on the various stages of e-government [20]. After determining the metrics, factors and categories that were to be included in the evaluation model, the next step was to assign weights of importance.

3.1   The Proposed Model

The proposed model consisted of four categories namely: informational, transactional, interaction-participation, and integration. Specifically, informational category captures the provision of information through one-way communication by municipal websites. This category includes the following factors: (1) information for citizens, (2) information about tourists, (3) information about the mayor and council members, (4) information about municipal projects, and (5) information about city council meetings.

The transactional category refers to the way municipalities utilize ICTs to help citizens as well as businesses to complete several transactions online [21]. This category is divided in two factors: (1) Transactions for citizens, and (2) transactions for businesses. The third category is named interaction-participation and is a combination of the two categories - two-way communication and political participation - proposed by [21]. This category is intended to capture the mechanisms and applications used by municipalities to enhance e-democracy. The factors of this category are based on several modes of e-participation found in the literature [17–19]. E-participation modes can be used as proxies for capturing e-democracy features [8]. Hence, the interaction-participation category includes the following factors: (1) e-consultation, (2) e-deliberation, (3) e-discourse, (4) e-petition, (5) e-voting, and (6) e-polling. Finally, the fourth category - integration - is similar to the transformation stage of e-government proposed by the Gartner Group [22] where local governments use their webpage to provide personalized information and services to citizens. This category is not divided in other factors. Like the interaction-participation category, the integration category can be seen as scaling up the e-government model to e-democracy. In total our instrument consisted of 83 criteria organized around 14 factors/indices.

3.2 Testing Reliability and Assigning Weights

The next step in the development process of our evaluation model was to assign relative weights to each criterion. As already noted, in order to retain objectivity in weighting the factors and adopt a citizen-centric approach, an online survey was conducted to assess citizens' perceived importance of the 83 criteria. This way, weighting was based on citizens' perceptions regarding the importance they attribute to each criterion.

The online survey took place from April to May of 2015 using the snowballing sampling technique. Snowball sampling is a "chain referral approach" where subjects recruit their friends, family members and acquaintances by using their social network contacts. The initial "seed" sampling units were students of the Technological Education Institute of Western Macedonia, Greece. It should be noted that students attending a course were to receive extra credit if they forwarded the online questionnaire to their social network contacts. Students were strongly advised to forward the online survey to individuals who were not students.

The online questionnaire consisted of the 83 criteria/items of our instrument. Respondents were prompted to indicate how important they perceived each of the 83 items to be included in a municipal website. Responses to all items were obtained using 5 point scales ranging from 1: not important at all to 5: very important.

In total, 395 respondents answered the online questionnaire. Regarding the characteristics of the sample, 57.5 % were females and 42.5 % were males. Most of them aged between 18 to 35 years old (65 %) and were single (60.8 %). 27.8 % of the respondents had completed secondary education while 33.9 % had a bachelor's degree. Only, 16.7 % were students. 71.6 % of participants had visited a municipal website at least one time in the past and 147 out of the 283 users of municipal websites (51.9 %) reported that they visit municipal websites at least 1 time during a month.

To examine the validity of the instrument, the reliability of the scales/factors was assessed using Cronbach's alpha coefficient. All of the 10 multi-item factors exhibited adequate internal reliability since the values of Cronbach's alpha coefficient exceeded the 0.70 criterion. Thus, the proposed model can be regarded as reliable.

For each of the 83 criteria the mean scores were calculated. These mean scores served as the basis for the calculation of weights of each item. Specifically, the weight for each criterion was calculated by dividing the mean score of the criterion by the sum of the mean scores from all criteria and multiplying it by 100. The factors of the model were also given weights based on the sum of the weights of the criteria that comprise them. The same was done for the model categories. As a consequence each local government website was rated on a total score that ranged from 0 to 100. Our weighting procedure differs from studies which first assign weights to the categories or factors of the model and then distribute the weights of the factor to the criteria/metric that comprise them [11, 16]. This way we avoided the pitfall of treating the attributes that comprise each factor equally since citizens assign different levels of importance to the different criteria even though they belong to the same factor.

3.3 Applying the Model

The above described model was then applied for the evaluation of local government websites in Greece via a quantitative website analysis. The sample for this study consisted of the 325 Greek municipalities. Thus, our analysis was based on the total population of the Greek municipalities. Data collection took place on June 2015. During data collection, researchers examined whether each municipality had a website. Inactive websites or websites under construction were excluded from the analysis. Then, each website was checked for the presence of the 83 evaluation criteria. If a criterion was found in a website then its importance weight was awarded to the website otherwise the value of 0 was given. For example, if a local government website published information about new jobs then researchers assigned the value of 1.514 on that criterion. As [11] suggest the use of binary values in the evaluation of governmental websites decreases the evaluator's subjectivity that would exist if other types of scales were used such as Likert.

All the values for the criteria that comprise a specific factor were then summed to a unique score for that factor. This score indicates how well the website performs on that factor. The total score for each factor of the model of a given website can be compared to its maximum value. The maximum values that each website could receive for each of the factors are shown in the Tables under the label Total. Next, for each website the scores of the factors that comprise each of the four main categories of the e-government model were summed up to create four category scores. The maximum scores that a website can receive across the four categories are the following: (a) information 62.67, (b) transactions 13.36, (c) interaction/participation 20.62, and (d) integration 3.35. Then all the category scores are summed up to create a total e-government score for the website. Moreover, the overall score of the website can be calculated and compared with the maximum value of 100. This way the level of e-government sophistication of each local government website can be assessed.

4   Results

Of the 325 municipalities 313 of them (96.3 %) had an active website, while 12 of them did not have a portal or had a website that was under construction. Subsequent analysis was based on the 313 local governments with an active website.

4.1   Information for Citizens Factor

Table 1 shows the importance weights for the criteria that comprise the information for citizens' factor as well as the percentage of the Greek local municipal websites that support information for citizens attributes. Based on the findings, the majority of Greek

Table 1. Importance weights and percentage of Greek local government websites that support information for citizens criteria

Information for citizens criteria		
Items	Weight	% of websites that support
Information about new jobs	1.514	78.3
Disabled persons accessibility	1.484	12.5
Explanations of requirements and documentation needed for applications	1.411	60.1
Downloadable documents and forms	1.394	67.4
Contact information (i.e., telephone numbers, addresses) of municipal agencies, departments, and employees	1.394	84.3
Instructions on how to complete forms	1.391	50.5
Information of the municipal agencies (i.e., "help at home" programme, open care center for eldery, citizen service centers)	1.354	72.8
Information about actions, events and priorities of municipality (i.e., society, education, environment, health, culture)	1.348	88.5
General information about the municipality	1.271	89.8
Information and links of local organizations, businesses, cultural and athletic organizations, media, non-governmental agencies	1.232	69.3
Frequently asked questions	1.218	24.3
Press releases	1.205	86.9
Downloadable publications and reports	1.198	44.1
Information about policies and regulations	1.195	59.1
Information about municipal organizations	1.195	69.3
Searchable databases	1.178	46.3
Mobile application for accessing the municipal website	1.155	9.3
Index for decisions made by municipal committees	1.135	43.8
Information about fuel prices	1.135	19.2
Information about the weather (weather predictions)	1.109	52.4
Information about elections	1.099	37.4
Registration to RSS feed, newsletter, newsgroups	1.082	45
Online radio	1.036	10.2
Web TV	0.996	8.3
Total	29.729	

local governments publish in their portals general information about the municipality (89.8 %) and the actions, events, and priorities of municipality towards society, education, environment, and health (88.5 %). Moreover, most of municipalities upload press releases in their websites (86.9 %) and disclose contact information (i.e., addresses, telephone numbers) about the agencies, departments, and employees (84.3 %). However, on criteria deemed important by citizens such as disabled persons accessibility most of Greek municipalities performed badly (12.5 %). At a factor level, findings suggest that websites of municipalities exhibited moderate scores on the information for citizens' factor, since the mean value for the 313 municipalities on this factor was 15.70. Only, 3 out of the 313 municipalities exhibited the maximum score of 29.73 pointing out that a mere 3 local government websites incorporate all the attributes that comprise the information for citizens' factor.

4.2   Information for Tourists Factor

Table 2 shows the importance weights for the items that are included in the information for tourists' factor as well as the percentage of the Greek local municipal websites that have adopted applications that provide information for tourists. Based on the findings, most of the Greek municipalities include in their portals information and multimedia about various attractions, museums, and local events (88.2 %). Moreover, almost half of the municipalities with an active portal contained attributes that were considered by citizens as important regarding information provision to tourists. The average score of the 313 municipalities on the information for tourists' factor was 4.90, which indicates that portals of Greek local governments are modestly supporting information and applications for tourists. From the evaluation of websites it was found that 49 out of the 313 Greek municipal portals (15.65 %) had the maximum score of the information for tourists' factor (9.22). A careful examination of the municipalities with the highest

Table 2. Importance weights and percentage of Greek local government websites that support information for tourists criteria

Information for tourists criteria		
Items	Weight	% of websites that support
Instructions on how to reach various places (i.e., museums, attractions)	1.364	56.5
Public transportation options and schedules (i.e., bus routes)	1.361	42.5
Versions of the site in other languages	1.348	53
Google maps with major locations (i.e., pharmacies, banks, doctors)	1.344	41.5
Operating hours of museums, attractions, etc.	1.321	32.3
Information, photos, videos about attractions, museums, local events, and activities	1.251	88.2
Information, photos, videos from accommodations, restaurants, entertainment venues	1.228	61.7
Total	9.218	

score indicates that the majority of them are places of tourism attractions (i.e. Athens, Rodos, Sithonia, Sifnos, Syros, Spetses, Tinos, and Chios).

4.3   Information About Mayor and Council Members Factor

Regarding the information about mayor and council member factor, Table 3 shows the importance weights for the metrics that evaluate this factor as well as the percentage of Greek municipalities that present in their websites information about the mayor and the council members. Based on the findings, the majority of local government portals publish information about their council members (i.e., list of members, duties of members, CV's) (88.8 %) and the mayor (i.e., CV, academic studies, political career, professional career, personal information, marital status, biography). Moreover, 81.5 % of municipalities present contact information of the mayor (i.e., telephone numbers, and office hours). On average, the 313 local government websites were evaluated on the information for mayor and council members' factor with a mean value of 5.43. This indicates that Greek municipalities performed moderately well on that factor. In addition, 76 out of 313 municipalities (24.2 %) exhibited the highest score on the information for mayor and council members' factor (maximum: 8.93).

Table 3. Importance weights and percentage of Greek local government websites that support information for mayor and council members criteria

Information for mayor and council members		
Items	Weight	% of websites that support
Information for council members (i.e., list of members, duties of members, CV's)	1.225	88.8
Current activities of the council	1.222	44.7
Information about internal regulations of the council	1.222	41.9
Contact information of council members (i.e., telephone numbers, office hours)	1.119	62
Information about the mayor (i.e., CV, studies, political career, professional career, personal information, marital status, biography)	1.085	86.6
Information about mayor's accomplishments to date	1.079	38.7
Mayor's financial statements	0.993	43.1
Contact information of mayor (telephone numbers, office hours)	0.989	81.5
Total	8.933	

4.4   Information About Municipal Projects Factor

Figure 1 illustrates the importance weights of the items that comprise information about municipal projects factor as well as the percentage of Greek municipalities that publish in their portals information about the projects of the municipality. As results suggest,

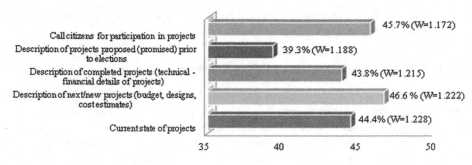

Fig. 1. Importance weights and percentage of Greek local government websites that support information for municipal projects criteria

almost half of the municipalities with a website inform citizens about their next/new projects (46.6 %) and encourage them for participation in the projects (45.7 %). The average score for the 313 municipalities on the information for municipal projects factor was 2.64, a value that is relatively low compared to the maximum score of that factor (maximum: 6.02). This finding indicates that municipalities on average did not perform well on this factor. It should be noted that 32.2 % of the municipalities (101 out of 313) received the maximum score on the information for municipal projects factor.

4.5   Information About Council Meetings and Decisions Factor

Table 4 shows the importance weights and the percentage of Greek municipalities' portals that incorporate the items that comprise the information about council meetings/decisions factor. Based on the results, the majority of local governments' portals publish information about the mayor/committees decisions (79.9 %), invite

Table 4. Importance weights and percentage of Greek local government websites that support information for council meetings and decisions criteria

Information for council meetings/decisions		
Items	Weight	% of websites that support
Publication of mayors/committees decisions	1.275	79.9
Publication of decisions of deliberations conducted about municipal issues	1.175	32.6
Publication of the proceedings of council meetings	1.145	53
Live broadcasting of council meetings/committees	1.089	13.4
Online announcement of the agenda for the upcoming council meetings	1.042	60.4
Videos of council meetings/committees	1.036	9.9
Online invitation of citizens for participation in upcoming council meetings	1.022	67.4
Audio recordings of council meetings/committees	0.983	4.8
Total	8.767	

citizens to participate in the forthcoming council meetings (67.4 %) and announce the agenda of the next council meetings (60.4 %). On the contrary, municipalities' portals do not disclose online the decisions of deliberations conducted around major local issues (32.6 %) and do not use applications such as live broadcasts (13.4 %), videos (9.9 %), and audio recordings (4.8 %) for the promotion of their council meetings. The mean score of the 313 municipalities on the information for council meetings/decisions factor was 3.622, which means that the portal of local governments in Greece performed moderately well on that factor. Moreover, only 14 municipalities exhibited the maximum score on the factor about the information for council meetings/decisions (maximum = 8.77).

4.6   Transaction for Citizens Factor

Table 5 shows the importance weights as well as the percentage of Greek municipalities that support online services for citizens via their websites. Findings suggest that a critical number of local government websites include online applications for licenses, permits and certifications (48.9 %) and support online issuing of certifications (40.9). On the contrary, only a small number of municipalities offer services like online payments of taxes and fines (20.8) and online tracking system of applications (23 %). On average, Greek municipal portals performed rather poorly on the transactions for citizens' factor (mean value: 2.58). Moreover, only 34 municipalities (10.86 %) can be regarded as top municipalities in the provision of online transactions to citizens and received the maximum score on that factor (maximum: 8.14).

Table 5. Importance weights and percentage of Greek local government websites that support transactions for citizens criteria

Transactions for citizens		
Items	Weight	% of websites that support
Online application for licenses, permits, certifications	1.407	48.9
Online issuing of certifications	1.398	40.9
Online registration for a job	1.378	26.5
Online tracking system of applications	1.358	23
Online request of information about online services	1.301	29.1
Online payments of taxes, fines, etc.	1.298	20.8
Total	8.139	

4.7   Transaction for Businesses Factor

Figure 2 shows the importance weights of as well as the percentage of local governments' websites that include the items that comprise the transactions for businesses factor. Results indicate that majority of the municipalities do not support online transactions for businesses. For example, only a small percentage of local governments

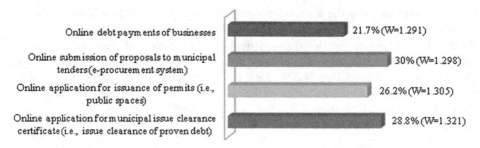

Fig. 2. Importance weights and percentage of Greek local government websites that support transactions for businesses criteria

enable business owners to submit proposals to municipal tenders (30 %) and apply for municipal issue clearance certificate (28.8 %). Overall, the 313 municipalities that have a website performed low on the transactions for businesses factor since the mean value on that factor was 1.39 considering that the maximum value of the factor that is 5.22. Furthermore, 56 out of the 313 local government websites (17.89 %) included all the four attributes that comprise the transaction for businesses factor; thus, receive the maximum score of 5.22.

4.8   E-Consultation Factor

Moving to citizens' evaluation of the interaction-participation category, Table 6 shows the importance weights of items that evaluate e-consultation factor as well as the

Table 6. Importance weights and percentage of Greek local government websites that support e-consultation criteria

E-consultation		
Items	Weight	% of websites that support
Online submission of complaints	1.324	45.4
Submission of online requests	1.305	50.8
Embed "contact" form	1.258	70.6
Suggestions or comments boxes	1.248	35.1
Embed "send an email" form	1.245	40.3
Contact email of mayor	1.178	77.6
Contact emails of municipal employees, agencies	1.172	61.3
Submission of questions/comments before council meetings	1.159	20.8
Contact emails of council members	1.129	54.6
Links to social media	1.102	27.5
Agenda comments form where citizens can submit comments regarding agenda items to be discussed for an upcoming city council	1.022	18.8
Total	13.142	

percentage of Greek municipalities that include in their websites applications which support e-consultation. A high percentage of municipalities publish the contact email of mayor (77.6 %) and employees or agencies (61.3 %) while they have an embed contact form in their websites (70.6 %), thus supporting mainly passive forms of e-consultation. In addition, half of the local governments enable via their portals the submission of online complaints (45.5 %) and requests (50.8), applications which were rated by respondents as highly important. On the contrary, only a small number of municipalities offer tools for more active forms of e-consultation such as submission of questions and comments before council meetings (20.8 %), and agenda comments forms where citizens could propose issues to be discussed for upcoming councils (20.8 %). The mean value for the 313 municipalities on the e-consultation factor was 6.07 (maximum: 13.14) suggesting that the Greek local governments' portals performed moderately well on that factor. Moreover, only 23 out of the 313 websites (7.3 %) received the maximum score on the e-consultation factor.

4.9   E-Deliberation Factor

Regarding the deliberative features of a municipal website, Fig. 3 shows the importance weights for the three items that comprise the e-deliberation factor as well as the percentage of Greek municipalities with a website that support these three deliberative features. Based on results, it can be argued that only a small percentage of the Greek municipal websites incorporate a discussion forum where citizens can deliberate on critical local issues (21.7 %), offer scheduled e-meetings for discussion (15.3 %), and hold videoconferences with municipal agencies or council members (7.7 %). On average, Greek local governments performed poorly on the e-deliberation factor based on the mean value (0.469). Moreover, only 22 websites out of the 313 municipalities (7 %) were found to incorporate all the three examined deliberative features; thus received the maximum value of 3.12.

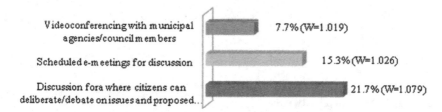

Fig. 3. Importance weights and percentage of Greek local government websites that support e-deliberation criteria

4.10   E-Discourse, E-Petitions, E-Voting, and E-Polling Factors

Table 7 presents the importance weights for the rest of the interaction-participation factors as well as and the percentage of Greek local governments who support applications for e-discourse, e-petitions, e-voting, and e-polling. Results indicate that Greek

Table 7. Importance weights and percentage of Greek local government websites that support e-discourse, e-petitions, e-voting, and e-polling criteria

Index	E-discourse, e-petitions, e-voting, and e-polling		
	Items	Weight	% of website that support
E-discourse	Chat capabilities where citizens can discuss with others municipal issues	1.012	18.8
E-petitions	E-petitions	1.079	10.9
E-voting	E-voting	1.115	32.9
E-polling	E-polling	1.149	28.8

municipalities do not adopt tools for active forms of citizens' participation since only a small percentage of them offer capabilities giving voice to citizens such as chat-rooms (18.8 %), e-petitioning (10.9 %), e-voting (32.9 %) and e-polling (28.8 %).

4.11   Integration Factor

Regarding the integration factor, Fig. 4 shows the importance weights for the three metrics that comprise the integration factor along with the percentage of Greek municipalities which use in their websites applications that support the integration category. Results indicate that the majority of municipalities enable user registration in their portals (62.6 %). However, only a small percentage of local governments' portals allow users to personalize the content of the site (35.5 %) and to customize the city homepage (19.2 %). On average, websites of local governments in Greece performed moderately well in regards to the integration factor since they exhibited a mean value of 1.349. Moreover, 60 municipalities (19.16 %) were evaluated with the maximum score on the level of online integration (maximum: 3.35).

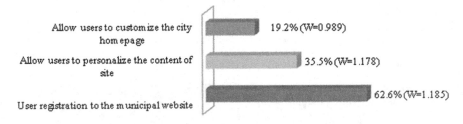

Fig. 4. Importance weights and percentage of Greek local government websites that support integration criteria

4.12   Evaluation of Greek Municipalities Across the Four Main Categories of E-Government Model

Greek municipalities were also evaluated across the four categories that comprise our e-government model, namely, information, transactions, interaction-participation, and integration. Looking at the mean category scores of the 313 municipalities it can be argued that Greek local government websites performed moderately well on the information (mean: 32.36, maximum: 62.67) as well as on the integration category (mean: 1.34, maximum: 3.35). However, municipalities were evaluated quite low on the transaction category (mean: 3.37, maximum: 13.36). As already noted the category of interaction-participation and the six indices that comprise it (i.e., e-consultation, e-deliberation, e-discourse, e-petitions, e-polling, and e-voting) measure the level of e-democracy sophistication of municipalities. It's worth mentioning that Greek local governments performed poorly in e-democracy (mean: 7.55, maximum: 20.62). Moreover, only 18 out of the 313 municipalities (5.7 %) can be regarded as top cities on the provision of e-democracy features since they received the maximum scores across all the six e-democracy indices. These municipalities are small and medium-sized cities characterized by high levels of voters' turnout. Based on the total e-government and e-democracy evaluation, Greek municipalities exhibited modest scores on average (mean: 45.28, maximum: 100.00). Hence, most of the portals of local governments in Greece are characterized by a moderate level in regards to the implementation of e-government and e-democracy initiatives. Top municipalities which received the highest e-government and e-democracy scores were Pylaia-Chortiati (score: 100.0), Soufli (score: 98.7), Prosotsani (score: 98.52), Chios (score: 98.52), Rafina-Pikermi (score: 97.41), Pineiou (score: 95.9), and Pylis (score: 91.53).

5 Conclusions

The purpose of this study is two-fold: first, to propose a framework for the evaluation of e-government initiatives at the municipal level, and second, to apply the proposed framework in the context of Greek local governments via a quantitative website analysis. The main contributions of the proposed model are the following: (1) it incorporates not only e-government features (i.e., information dissemination, online services provision) but also e-democracy aspects which enhance e-participation of citizens, (2) it treats e-participation as a multi-dimensional construct that moves from simple forms such as online consultation to more active forms of engagement like e-voting, (3) it adopts a citizen-centric approach since the evaluation of the metrics of the model is based on citizens' perceived importance of the metrics, (4) it reduces subjectivity of evaluators in rating the metrics, and (5) can be easily applied at the local government level and used to compare the websites across different municipalities.

Results suggest that Greek municipalities tend to provide mostly one-way information via their portals about the municipality, the main touristic attractions, the council members, and the mayor. Moreover, it can be argued that Greek local governments took a slow step towards increasing their transparency and citizens trust by disclosing information pertaining to the decisions made by the mayor and the committees. Another important finding is the fact that a large number of municipalities are trying to interact with their citizens by enabling mainly passive forms of participation through contact emails and forms.

The evaluation of Greek e-government initiatives at the local level revealed that municipalities in Greece are halfway through in providing complete information for citizens, tourists, mayors-council members, and council meetings, since they received moderate scores on those factors. The same can be argued for the adoption of applications and tools that allow citizens to communicate with their municipalities and submit online their proposals, complaints and opinions. On the contrary, Greek municipal websites still have a long way to go in regards to provision of (a) information about municipal projects, (b) services and transactions for citizens and businesses, and (c) opportunities for citizens to actively participate on issues that affect their municipalities. Arguably, local governments in Greece failed to advance their e-government technology by incorporating more e-democracy features such as discussion fora, scheduled e-meetings, videoconferences, chat-rooms, e-surveys, e-petitions, and e-voting.

Looking at the total e-government and e-democracy scores, it can be concluded that local governments in Greece are characterized by a moderate level in regards to the implementation of e-government and e-democracy initiatives with few municipalities receiving high scores. It seems that at the local level e-government in Greece has not changed much over the years, recalling that in 2006 the websites of the Greek prefectures provided mostly one-way information while they performed poorly at the transaction and interaction-participation level [16]. This poor advancement in local e-government is not suprising if one accounts for the inefficiencies as well as the lack of resources and personnel caused by the Greek financial crisis. Local e-government in Greece should start moving towards e-democracy. However, implementation of e-democracy initiatives by local municipal governments requires major transformations from the traditional bureaucratic models into more participatory and citizen-centric models.

The present study has several implications for e-government managers wishing to provide satisfactory e-services. Most of the times, there is a huge gap between what e-government services, governmental agencies think they could deliver to citizens and what meets the expectations of citizens. Thus, our model serves as a mapping tool that could be used by e-government managers to identify failure points as well as areas and opportunities for improvement based on what citizens demand. For example, when evaluating e-government projects via the proposed model managers could identify features that are regarded by citizens as important but they have not yet been incorporated in their e-government initiatives. Hence, managers can (1) re-engineer their e-government processes so as to fulfill citizens' e-government unfulfilled needs, and (2) maintain and consistently improve those e-government processes that are perceived by citizens as important. This way, citizens' satisfaction towards e-government projects could be enhanced.

The proposed model could provide important benefits and insights to future researchers as well. Specifically, the present study highlights the need for the development of e-government evaluation studies which adopt a citizen-centric orientation and combine aspects of e-government and e-democracy by treating these two concepts as different stages along the e-government development continuum. Since this study was context specific, future research could apply our proposed framework to other contexts in order to evaluate the level of e-government and e-democracy sophistication of local governments in other countries. This way, our model could be validated in other settings while fruitful comparisons could be made in regards to the level of local e-government and e-democracy readiness across countries with different cultures.

Acknowledgment. This research has been co-financed by the European Union (European Social Fund – ESF) and Greek national funds through the Operational Program "Education and Lifelong Learning" of the National Strategic Reference Framework (NSRF) - Research Funding Program: ARCHIMEDES III. Investing in knowledge society through the European Social Fund.

References

1. Shan, S., Wang, L., Wang, J., Hao, Y., Hua, F.: Research on e-government evaluation model based on the principal component analysis. Inf. Technol. Manag. **12**(2), 173–185 (2011)
2. Wang, L., Bretschneider, S., Gant, J.: Evaluating web-based e-government services with a citizen-centric approach. In: 38th Annual Hawaii International Conference on Systems Sciences, Big Island, Hawaii (2005)
3. Rowley, J.: E-government stakeholders—who are they and what do they want? Int. J. Inf. Manag. **31**(1), 53–62 (2011)
4. Karkin, N., Janssen, M.: Evaluating websites from a public value perspective: a review of Turkish local government websites. Int. J. Inf. Manag. **34**(3), 351–363 (2014)
5. Lee, C.P., Chang, K., Berry, F.S.: Testing the development and diffusion of e-government and e-democracy: a global perspective. Public Adm. Rev. **71**(3), 444–454 (2011)
6. Backus, M.: E-Governance and developing countries: introduction and examples. International Institute for Communication and Development. Research report no. 3 (2001)
7. Coursey, D., Norris, D.F.: Models of e-government: are they correct? Empirical Assess. Public Adm. Rev. **68**(3), 523–536 (2008)
8. Chatfield, A.T., Alhujran, O.: A cross-country comparative analysis of e-government service delivery among Arab countries. Inf. Technol. Dev. **15**(3), 151–170 (2009)
9. Siau, K., Long, Y.: Synthesizing e-government stage models-a meta-synthesis based on meta-ethnography approach. Ind. Manag. Data Syst. **105**(4), 443–458 (2005)
10. Alshawi, S., Alalwany, H.: E-government evaluation: citizen's perspective in developing countries. Inf. Technol. Dev. **15**(3), 193–208 (2009)
11. Panopoulou, E., Tambouris, E., Tarabanis, K.: A framework for evaluating web sites of public authorities. Aslib Proc. **60**(5), 517–546 (2008)
12. Holzer, M., Kim, S.T.: Digital Governance in Municipalities Worldwide. Rutgers University Campus, Newark (2005)
13. Sandoval-Almazan, R., Gil-Garcia, J.R.: Are government internet portals evolving towards more interaction, participation, and collaboration? Revisiting the rhetoric of e-government among municipalities. Gov. Inf. Q. **29**, S72–S81 (2012)
14. Cantijoch, M., Gibson, R.: Conceptualising and measuring e-participation. In: Internet, Voting, and Democracy Conference (II), Center for the Study of Democracy, University of California, Irvine (2011)
15. Pina, V., Torres, L., Royo, S.: E-government evolution in EU local governments: a comparative perspective. Online Inf. Rev. **33**(6), 1137–1168 (2009)
16. Yannas, P., Lappas, G.: Evaluating local e-government: an analysis of Greek prefecture websites. In: 2nd International Conference ICDIM 2007 on Digital Information Management, vol. 1, pp. 254–259. IEEE (2007)

17. Macintosh, A.: Using information and communication technologies to enhance citizen engagement in the policy process. Promise and Problems of E-Democracy Challenges of Online Citizen Engagement, pp. 19–142. OECD, Paris (2003)
18. Tambouris, E., Macintosh, A., Coleman, S., Wimmer, M., Vedel, T., Westholm, H., Lippa, B., Dalakiouridou, E., Parisopoulos, K., Rose, J.: Introducing eParticipation. University of Macedonia, Thessaloniki (2007)
19. Beckert, B., Lindner, R., Goos, K., Hennen, L., Aichholzer, G., Strauß, S.: E-democracy in Europe-prospects of internet-based political participation. Deliverable No. 2 of the STOA Project on E-democracy: Technical Possibilities of The Use of Electronic Voting and Other Internet Tools in European Elections, pp. 33–77 (2010, Unpublished)
20. Chandler, S., Emanuels, S.: Transformation not automation. In: 2nd European Conference on E-Government, Oxford, UK, pp. 91–102 (2002)
21. Moon, M.J.: The evolution of e-government among municipalities: rhetoric or reality? Public Adm. Rev. **62**(4), 424–433 (2002)
22. Baum, C., Di Maio, A.: Gartner's four phases of e-government model (2000). http://www.gartner.com

Smart Cross-Border e-Gov Systems and Applications

Alexander B. Sideridis[1(✉)], Loucas Protopappas[1], Stergios Tsiafoulis[2],
and Elias Pimenidis[3]

[1] Informatics Laboratory, Agricultural University of Athens, Athens, Greece
{as,loucas.protopappas}@aua.gr
[2] Greek Ministry of Interior-Administrative Reform and eGovernance, Athens, Greece
stetsiafoulis@gmail.com
[3] University of the West of England, Bristol, UK
Elias.Pimenidis@uwe.ac.uk

Abstract. Recent innovative developments in ICT like Internet of Things, Cloud Computing and Big Data encourage further the design and application of "Smart e-Government Systems and applications" for citizens and business. These smart systems are aiming to further improve everyday lives, expand business frontiers, and facilitate the movement of citizens by reducing the constraints imposed by existing borders between Member States of a federation like in cases of the European Union, USA and Eurasian Economic Union. Furthermore, these systems provide the means to combat international terrorism, fraud and crime more effectively. They could also have a positive impact in many other areas such as Banking, Health, Justice, Forensic and Crime sectors of bilateral or global inter-relations. Beyond the above important application areas, Smart e-Government Systems could have a considerable effect on the critically important areas of Life Sciences. Smart Cross-Border e-Government Systems will be characterized by their ability to be used by governmental organizations, citizens, business and any combination thereof independently of their location and nationality, in a cross border environment based on shared electronic authentication, identification and signature support services. Earlier on this year, common strategic policies and successfully implemented European Union projects have led to the availability of e-Authentication, e-Signature and e-Identification platforms. These latest technological advances dictate the redesign of existing and design of new Smart Cross-Border e-Government Services and Applications fully exploiting the ICT innovations.

Keywords: e-Government · Smart cross-border e-Government services · Life sciences · Internet of things · Cloud computing

1 Introduction

New models of e-Government systems have demonstrated the potential in meeting the needs for advanced e-Government services, in both enhancing citizen's daily activities and creating the appropriate basis in public administrations for the development of knowledge based economies. At present, Information and Communication Technologies (ICT) are

© Springer International Publishing Switzerland 2015
S.K. Katsikas and A.B. Sideridis (Eds.): E-Democracy 2015, CCIS 570, pp. 151–165, 2015.
DOI: 10.1007/978-3-319-27164-4_11

required to facilitate the appropriate structures of complex e-Government systems, in a very secure and authenticated global environment; further extending existing e-Government systems, or designing new ones, aiming to cover application areas beyond national borders and national economies in a global spectrum [1, 2].

The economic recession fears on a worldwide scale, combined with problems stemming from continued globalization, accentuate pressures on ICT. Demands to further secure and enrich with extra capabilities existing e-Government models, and to redesign well established ones are growing continuously. Furthermore, the need to design new ones capable of meeting complex requirements on e-Banking, e-Health, e-Justice, e-Forensic, e-Crime (combating international terrorism, fraud and crime) also increases. Nowadays, to the above important areas of global research activity new areas of primary concern have been added. These have until recently been considered to be as "mild" areas, from the secure government systems point of view. Such areas include Life Sciences and their practices; in particular, e-Agriculture, e-Forestry, e-Environment, e-Food Sciences and Technologies. To emphasize the added economic value of the above practices and due to limiting extent of the present paper, we refer to just three examples. One is that of primary agricultural production and the necessary export-import facilities for Small to Medium Enterprises (SMEs) in particular. In such cases the contribution of recent technological advances in areas such as e-Authentication (eAU), e-Signature (e-SIGN) and e-Identification (eID) is evident. These contribute in removing the administrative burden from Government to Citizens (G2C) and Citizens to Citizens (C2C) models as well the necessity of supporting administrative Government to Government (G2G) procedures to avoid cross border bureaucratic implications. As a second indicative example we refer to the necessity of e-Government systems for the appropriate weather prediction with accuracy reaching the locality of an agricultural farm. In such cases the reduction for the need of compensation due to lost production could reach a few billions of Euros, simply by accurate prediction of localized catastrophic meteorological phenomena. In designing the appropriate model in this example the contributions of Cloud Computing (CC), Big Data (BD) and Internet of Thinks (IoT) are evident. A third example is taken from the field of Forestry. The environmental and economic adverse effects caused by catastrophic fires and the significant contribution of ICT innovations (CC, BD and IoT) in avoiding them are extremely important. What was not evident so far, in justifying the immense research activity in the above mentioned areas, is the necessity of recent results in eAU, e-SIGN and eID mainly for cross border applications [2].

To effectively deal with complex cases in areas demanding global security for cross border applications, national Governments enthusiastically supported federal agencies and organizations to proceed with specific strategies in meeting such goals. International cooperation, as recession downturn in the economy from one hand and terrorism from the other, necessitate and press further intergovernmental Administration to Administration (A2A) and G2G models to be implemented and special eAU and eID platforms to be developed. To this end, the European Union (EU) has proposed to its Member States a convergence strategy of their national e-Government systems aiming to the creation of a Digital Single Market in Europe. Incentive programs and projects promoting interoperability had been announced and, by now, new eAU, e-sign and eID platforms are available to support Smart Cross Border e-Government Systems (SCBeG)

[3–6]. In particular, the EU has virtually created a secure workplace for Governments, citizens, enterprises and legal entities of any form [2]. Of course, it is up to the national Governments to adopt the results and platforms just announced by the successful outcome of the EU project STORK 2.0 [7]. Obviously it will take some time for the establishment of SCBeG systems and applications to embrace security sensitive "traditional" e-Banking, e-Health, e-Justice e-Education and e-Customs -already in existence- systems.

The proposed in this paper SCBeG systems on and beyond the above mentioned areas will benefit by the created interoperable environments which were key objectives of STORK 2 project. It is encouraging that in the final results of this project were included four cross-sectoral pilots satisfying requirements for Government (G2G), Government to Citizen (G2C), Government-to-Business (G2B) and/or Business-to-Business (B2B) modes of operation [8]. It is our belief that especially G2B and B2B models of SCBeG applications will mostly benefit Small Medium Enterprises (SME) and this will contribute to combat unemployment (free movement of young people without the burden of bureaucratic restrictions and full use of eID) and the present economic recession [2].

In the present paper an attempt is made to propose SCBeG models making full use of ICT innovations in CC, BD and IoT and combining these extra facilities with platforms available on eID (in conjunction with platforms on eAU and e-SIGN). The development of eAU and eID platforms will presented in Sect. 2, followed by Sect. 3 where these platforms will be used in structuring SCBeG systems. The wide new application areas of the proposed SCBeG will presented in Sect. 4 and finally discussed in Sect. 5.

2 Developments on e-Authentication and e-Identification

2.1 STORK 2.0 Authentication Platform – Overview

The European Digital Agenda, the European Action Plan on e-Government (2011–2015) and the European Directive on Electronic Services, underlined the importance of a pan-European interoperability framework for Electronic Identification (eID) for e-Government services [9–12]. The STORK 2.0 project (Secure idenTity acrOss boRders linKed 2.0) is a Pan European program that contributes for the establishment of a single Pan European interoperable platform for eID and authentication for European citizens. This project aimed to create a single operational framework and a common infrastructure for eID and authentication in the European Union (EU), which will be capable to provide information related to the characteristics of the users. The authorizations have to act on behalf of another natural or legal person in addition to information about the identity of users. The project contributed considerably to the creation of the Digital Single Market and mobility across the EU by enabling access to electronic services offered by Governments and Private Sectors of the Member States (MS). The results of the project have been tested through cross-border pilot services in four domain sectors of economy and business and in particular on (a) e-Learning and Academic Qualifications, (b) e-Banking, (c) Public Services for Business and (d) e-Health [13–16].

The consortium of the project is comprised by public administrations, non-profit organizations, private companies and academic institutions from 19 EU MS and associated countries. STORK 2.0 project builds on the success and results of STORK 1.0[1] which was achieved on the creation of an interoperability framework between the different approaches of electronic identification solutions among EU countries. STORK 1.0 exploited experiences from IDABC [17] and EU actions on electronic identification as MODINIS[2] (Study on Identity Management in eGovernment), project GUIDE[3] (Gentle User Interfaces for lDerly pEople) FIDIS[4] (Future of IDentity in the Information Society) and PRIME[5] (PRivacy and Identity Management for Europe), as well as the results of the work of the Porvoo Group[6].

A model proposed by IDABC and adopted by STORK, was the establishment of national nodes, named Pan-European Proxy Services (PEPS pan European service). The main objectives of these nodes were to conceal internal problems of the national systems of the other MS and to be a link of confidence for the creation of a circle of trust in Europe. Moreover, these nodes had to guarantee scalability, since any change within a MS should only affect its own portal. Another model for electronic authentication applicable to Germany and Austria is the MiddleWare (MW) model. In this user-centric architecture data are usually stored within identity tokens which are in the sole possession of the user, for example a smart card or a mobile phone. Communication with the token usually provided through a MW client that allows the user to confirm the authentication procedure with a personal identification number (PIN) or a transaction number (TAN) [18]. In MW service providers, in order to be able to support cross-border authentication, shall install a serverside - MW called VIDP in their environment, while a software component called client-MW has to be installed to user's PC. Client- MW handles the communication between user's token and V-IDP and the latter the transmission of the retrieved data from user's token to the Service Provider [19]. The two interoperability models, MW and Pan-European Proxy Service (PEPS), were explored and functioned through STORK pilot program, which combined these models in all possible ways. The common specifications of the proposed interoperability models have been designed in such a way that the underlying systems should operate with the same protocols, regardless of the model or the combinations.

The functionality of STORK is based on the establishment of a "Circle of Trust" between the MS nodes and the stakeholders, based on cryptographic keys. Each national node must carry out a number of essential functions; identify the domestic identity provider (IDP), retrieve user's identity characteristics (attributes) from the IDP and transfer these characteristics to a trusted service provider across borders. A PEPS can be viewed as a single getaway, which on one hand hides the complexities of national infrastructures and on the other hand implements a cross-border communication

---

[1] www.eid-stork.eu.
[2] https://www.cosic.esat.kuleuven.be/modinis-idm/twiki/bin/view.cgi.
[3] http://www.guide-project.eu/.
[4] http://www.fidis.net/.
[5] https://www.prime-project.eu/.
[6] http://www.fineid.fi/default.aspx?id=539.

protocol [20]. Figure 1 illustrates the logic of cross-border authentication procedure with PEPS architecture. The flow of data between the entities involved is implemented through the user's browser. Therefore, STORK authentication protocol is designed in such a way so that data between the different stakeholders to be shared and transferred using https posts carried out by user's browser.

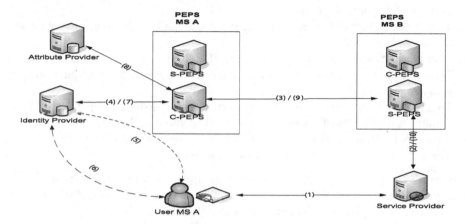

Fig. 1. PEPS model

STORK 2.0 project extends the functionality of the authentication platform established by STORK, by interconnecting to it Attributes Providers (AP) in order to enrich the provided electronic authentication services with information related to users (e.g. universities for academic qualifications) [21]. Moreover, STORK 2.0 supports data transfer related to authorizations and mandates from origin sources, i.e. Business Registries, in order to be proved that a person has the right to act on behalf of another person or a legal entity. In addition, e-SIGN functionalities are supported by the platform, enabling a user to sign any requested documents with his electronic identity.

Figure 1 demonstrates the scenario where the user from MS A needs to be authenticated to a service provider established in MS B. In this scenario, both the MS where the Service Provider (SP) is established and the MS of origin of the user, use PEPS architecture. In this scenario the PEPS's part of MS A is called Citizens PEPS (C-PEPS) referring to the country of origin of the citizen and the part of the PEPS in MS B (service provider) called S-PEPS referred to the country of origin of the service provider. The C-PEPS of MS A and the S-PEPS of MS B have a trusted relation by sharing their digital certificates. The same applies between S-PEPS and the SP. The service supports cross border authentication thought STORK 2.0 and provides the user with the ability to choose that authentication through STORK. The user authenticates himself through his national PEPS. PEPS always ask for the user's consent to provide his personal data to the SP. If more than the identity attributes are needed and STORK support them, the user will be asked to choose the source of the attributes, in some cases authenticate again to the source, and give his explicit permission to relay them to the service provider.

The authentication process is as follows:

- The user wishes to access a secure source of the service provider (1);
- The service provider forward the authentication process to the corresponding S-PEPS (2);
- The S-PEPS forwards the authentication procedure to the relevant C-PEPS (3) of the country of origin of the user;
- The authentication of the user is taking place through C-PEPS to a national identity provider (4,7);
- User is authenticates himself to the chosen IDP (5,6);
- The C-PEPS may retrieve also additional identification information from a attribute provider (8);
- User authentication and identification information is transferred from the C-PEPS of country A to S-PEPS of country B (9) with the consent of the user;
- Finally S-PEPS forward this information to the service provider (10);
- The user has now access to the requested resource;

It is worth noticing that privacy is an important aspect in both models. In order to be compatible the two models with the EU Directive on data protection (95/46/EC) [22], users must always give their consent for the use of their data abroad.

Figure 2 illustrates a scenario that combines MW and PEPS, assuming that the user's country uses architecture middleware (MW). The user interacts for the authentication with the V-IDP that is established in the SP country. This architecture has been adopted due to privacy restrictions in Austria that prohibit the exportation of citizen's personal data.

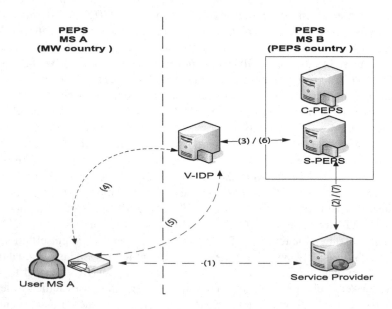

Fig. 2. MW to PEPS model

The authentication process is done in accordance with the standard SAML (Secure Assertion Markup Language). The OASIS [23] format (SAML) establishes a framework which is based on XML language describing and exchanging intelligence. Secure information is expressed in the form of SAML assertions that the applications can trust [24]. The OASIS SAML standard sets precisely rules for the preparation and submission of the requests, the generation, the communication and the use of these SAML assertions. One of the main advantages of the SAML standard is that is based on the XML language empowered the standard with scalability, which makes it very flexible. Two federation partners are able to exchange any identity characteristic they want through the payload of the assertions SAML, provided that those characteristics can be represented in XML language [24].

Different authentication schemes and tokens do not provide the same level of quality of authentication. Some of the existing schemes simply authenticate the users by the couple of credentials username/password, while others use the same but strengthened with a One-Time Password (OTP) that is produced by specific devices or is sent to a mobile device of a user, e.g. SMS (see banking sector — two factor authentication). In a number of cases, Public Key Infrastructure (PKI) is used for producing - PKI digital certificates and storing it in computer systems or to secure cryptographic chips e.g. a smart card or an electronic identity citizen card.

As a consequence, some electronic portals and service providers could not allow access to users using low assurance means of authentication, as the quality of reliability of the authentication provided would be insufficient for the risks associated with the access to the service offered. The quality of authentication is affected not only by the different authentication schemes and tokens but also by the administration procedures, as the administrative procedures vary in each country. Different usage scenarios have different requirements on the quality of electronic authentication. For these reasons STORK, defines a scale from 1 to 4 on the Quality Assurance of Authentication (QAA), as shown in Table 1. For the determination of the QAA of an electronic authentication, organisational and technical aspects of the authentication procedure are taken into account [25]. These concern both the phases of registration and of the online authentication process that compose the authentication scheme. Every eID Provider (IDP) shall make available, on request, the user's level of quality of the authentication in order to enable each Service Provider (SP) to decide whether the conditions are met so as to provide the electronic service. STORK 2.0 goes further by defining a scale on the quality assurance level of the provided attribute and a QAA that in general is a result of the validation of the link between the eID and the attribute, the quality of the attribute and the quality of the attribute provider [26].

Table 1. STORK QAA

STORK QAA levels	Description
1	No or little credibility
2	Low reliability
3	An important credibility
4	High reliability

STORK 2.0 platforms empower users with the capability to authenticate themselves through a simple and common way to a variety of services that are provided from service providers along Europe, by the use of their national means of electronic authentication. Nineteen countries of the European Economic Area are interconnected to the STORK eID interoperable platform and support the authentication methods of the origin country of the user. The Regulation (EU) No 910/2014 on "Electronic identification and trust services for electronic transactions in the internal market (eIDAS Regulation)" that repeals the Directive 1999/93/EC (Signature Directive) and has been adopted in July 2014 by the European Parliament and the Council of the EU promotes and strengthens cross border authentication [27]. The Regulation provides the legislative and the regulatory framework for the creation of an appropriate environment in which citizens, businesses and public administrations can interact securely. Key points of the Regulation is the mandatory cross-border recognition of the authentication schemes of all the MS in public administration services, the provision of such services without cost and the association of the individual authentication schemes with pre-established assurance Levels of Authentication (LoA). The Regulation takes into account STORK results especially regarding the established cross border authentication platform and the major in importance scale of the quality assurance levels of the authentication.

Cross border authentication is expected to increase the effectiveness of public and private online services, e-business and electronic commerce in the EU.

3   Structure of Smart Cross-Border e-Gov Systems

Cross-Border e-Gov Systems (CBeG), as previously mentioned, can act beneficially upon every domain (e-Banking, e-Health, e-Justice e-Education, e-Customs) through the use of innovative applications. STORK 2.0 that recently completed, and launched by the European Commission, established a European eID Interoperability Platform that allows citizens and SMEs to establish new e-relations across borders [7]. The deliverables of STORK 2.0 project [7] have shown that its goals have been achieved and the participating countries improve now their competitiveness and interoperability at various levels. The possibilities that provided by CBeG help significantly the countries that suffer from economic recession, in order to combat lots of their chronic problems such as, unemployment and bureaucracy. Indicatively, the ministry of Interior and Administrative Reconstruction of Greece incorporated the cross-border service login into their national e-Gov Portal ERMIS.GOV.GR and National Bank of Greece implemented an interconnected pilot online service for electronic e-banking.

Security and privacy are key enablers of CBeG systems especially in EU. During the early years, the European Union has implemented a multi-level security framework (Fig. 3), in order to ensure its secure and trustworthy services [28]. The above framework concludes lots of standards, tools and models that deliver a predictable regulatory environment related to electronic identification and trust services. An important dimension in "digitization" and interoperability is the "Digital Agenda for Europe" (presented by the European Commission) forms one of the seven pillars of the Europe 2020 Strategy which sets objectives for growth of the European Union (EU) by 2020 [29, 30]. Furthermore, strong liaisons are being established among other platforms and development programs (Connecting Europe Facility (CEF), electronic IDentification And trust Services (IDAS), Interoperability Solution for European Public Administrations (ISA) [31–34], the thematic network SSEDIC [35], as well as ISA's STORK sustainability action, closely following and relating to other international efforts in eID. Two prominent examples are the Joint Up platform [36] that shares and reuses interoperability solutions for public administrations and the CEF platform that provides 'out of the box' capabilities to enable interoperability between administrations, businesses and citizens.

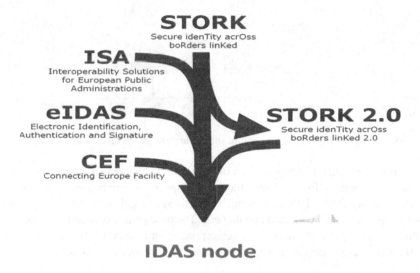

Fig. 3. IDAS node. Source: https://www.eid-stork2.eu

The building blocks of the above platforms make a full use of digital technologies, but the new emerging technologies (CC, BD and IoT) can shield and transform the existing cross-border e-Gov systems in SCBeG, as new eAU, e-SIGN and eID platforms are available to support them. The above technologies could update the proposed systems, as they will be faster, safer, more transparent and more reliable.

Cloud service providers have adopted different models, e.g. Infrastructure, Platform, or Software as a Service model (IaaS, PaaS, SaaS [37]), offering cloud secure services for citizens and SMEs. Plus, eID, eAU and e-SIGN are some of the very major issues that afflicting the security of system. Hence, several identity models have already emerged [38], building an appropriate interoperability layer on top of those individual national solutions, using cloud computing. Cloud computing at the forefront of the digital economy as, in conjunction with the rolled-out national eID that it is provided by STORK 2.0 interoperability platform, it could provide in SMEs a series of new potential cloud benefits, such as, deploying applications faster, establishing standard processes and cost efficiency.

As mentioned in Sect. 2, STORK 2.0 project's architecture is based on established international standards (OASIS web SSO, ISO/IEC 27001, OASIS DSS [28]) and it consists of a combination of two distinct identity models (Pan-European Proxy Services

(PEPS) and Middleware Model (MW) [39]). All these, in conjunction with the CC, compose the edifice of extended the STORK VIDP architecture [40] (Fig. 4), which supports external eID authentication at different cloud service providers.

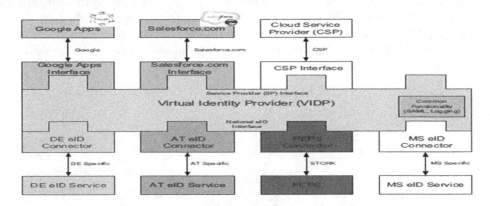

Fig. 4. Extended VIDP architecture supporting eID based cloud authentication

Additionally, Big Data (BD) and Internet of Things (IoT) are the new promising technologies that can support SMEs to enhance their performance and competitiveness in the wider European Digital Market. BD have been characterized as a goldmine because of the huge amounts of personal data collected and that could be used by any procedure. Also, BD and IoT can help spherically any domain via enterprise optimization risk management, operational flexibility and streamlining of time-consuming, bureaucratic procedures.

4   Application Areas of Smart Cross-Border e-Gov Systems

The SCBeG, in conjunction with the latest evolving technologies (CC, BD and IoT) and ICT innovations are adding extra advanced capabilities on many domains. The main scope of SCBeG has been expanded significantly, as they have been involved in and continue to richly seed several Life Science disciplines (e-Agriculture, e-Forestry, e-Environment, e-Food Sciences). Also, using the available platforms on eID and eAU, which STORK 2.0 has implemented successfully, the proposed systems could solve functional, financial and bureaucratic problems for citizens and SMEs, throughout the European borders. The G2G and G2C models of SCBeG applications that we suggest above, can help public administrations and local authorities of every country to manage better their fiscal and domestic issues, taking advantage of the statistical, geological and geographical data, which are provided by the new technologies.

Nowadays, SCBeG, in parallel with eID and eAU can be easily utilized to put in order various financial activities of citizens and SMEs that they are financially activated in many countries of the European Union. STORK 2.0 structured a well-organised framework for a uniform taxation control system placing emphasis on legitimacy, tax coordination and tax compliance in the EU [41]. During the recent past, many models [41–45] have been implemented in order to establish a commonly agreed European tax collection System. Therefore, the new very promising technologies (CC, BD and IoT) enforce significantly the authorities, utilizing the national eID to monitor all transactions of any citizen or any SMEs.

Meanwhile, the members-states of the EU make continuous efforts to improve their national and local e-gov services. According to a recent e-government survey conducted by the UN, Europe (0.6936) continues to lead having the highest regional e-Government Development Index (EGDI), followed by the Americas (0.5074), Asia (0.4951), Oceania (0.4086) and finally Africa (0.2661). The existing ranking indicates that the large majority of countries, following the EU ICT policies and e-government strategies, improved their maturity level of e-services at all levels of government whether cross-border, national or local [46].

The proposed SCBeG could enhance support of economic and social development, particularly in empowering official and local authority representatives to ensure link-ages, networking, and efficient, transparent, timely services, especially across EU borders [47]. At present though, not all public e-services function well across borders reducing the mobility of citizens and businesses and this is where the proposed Smart Cross Border e-Services could see their biggest contribution. The full use of eID, eAU and e-SIGN platforms that launched by STORK 2.0 could also work beneficially in every domain in Public Administration. The migration of the inhabitants of the countries that are suffering from economic recession further increases the need of fully functional national and local cross-border e-services. The A2A and G2G models could simplify the procedures for citizens and SMEs in order to be accessed in local e-government services, such as Personal Documents, Health Services and Public Supplies [47].

Greece has progressed satisfactorily during the two year period 2012–2014, reaching the 34th position in 2014 for e-government development index, going up three positions compared to 2012. The cross-border mobility of Greece lags behind its EU partners but the efforts of national and local authorities are constant and unremitting in order to reach the EU average level.

As Greece is trying to get back on to a growth path, improving its e-governmental services on national level, there is an urgent need for the e-services of Central Admin-istration and Local Administration to be adjusted according to new challenges. Despite the recession it has managed to improve the sophistication level of its 20 e-gov services (12 services for citizens and 8 services for businesses) and since recently the majority of these services are fully completed electronically. In a recent EU survey the 20 local e-government services offered by Greece have demonstrated performance improvement of 83 % compared to only 13 % in 2013.

At present many e-services offered in Greece are still facing functional and compati-bility issues at "cross-border" level. Key to improving the competitiveness and reliability of services is the interaction and the cross-functional cooperation with the Large Scale Pilot (LSPs) projects, which are used widely by most of the EU countries. In order to improve Greek e-services need to embrace multi-language functionality and to develop the infra-structure to integrate the widely-used new technologies such as IoT, CC, and BD. The SCBeG can be a driving force for efficient and innovative Public and Central Administra-tion, aiming to a more functional, friendly and citizen and business-centric delivery of public services. The new emerging technologies, combined with neural networks could endow the new or existing e-services with a series of innovative capabilities such as inter-operability, advanced search and retrieval procedures, powerful pattern recognition, without electronic and geographical barriers.

5   Smart Cross Border Systems – The Way Forward

The development and integration of cross-border applications across the European Union is a continuously evolving concept that is already delivering benefits across users. New technical developments and emerging standards will allow the full benefits of such applications to be enjoyed by individual users, organizations and government agencies.

Authentication and privacy issues will continue to dominate the agenda as user bodies and the volume of data processed and gathered through services will be increasing in considerable volumes in the next few years. This collection of data will raise new opportunities for added value creation by private and government organizations and enterprises that would like to explore such data, link it with other sizable data banks created by different transactional services and combined with data gathered from social media. When combined with technologies relevant to the concepts of Big Data and Internet of Things, the opportunities will be virtually unlimited. This is where the challenges of ensuring adequate authentication that would not limit the performance and efficiency of services and at the same time preserve the integrity of the data and the privacy of the users that create and/or supply it [48].

Ubiquitous systems that support applications such as recommender systems for transactional services can be utilized to strengthen the privacy features of cross-border systems. Guaranteeing the privacy of data for such services will enhance demand of such services as the benefits will be multiple for both users (individual and organizations) and the various government agencies. The latter could see rapid progress in supporting and achieving long term strategic objectives such as battling tax evasion, corruption and cross-border crime. The only drawback in such systems and services is the need for continuous evolution and support, of particular importance in the case of emerging technologies and the lack of agreed standards between developers and large service providers. This in turn makes it difficult to design and implement systems that would allow for the evaluation and the support of integration of such diverse technologies and services to the core of cross-border services provided by government agencies [49]. To continue to provide such benefits governments across the European Union and possibly beyond, need to agree and practically support continuous development and evolution programmes that will allow the services to stay in pace with technological developments.

The economic uncertainty of present times challenges such plans and development programmes in a variety of ways. The integration of cross-border services has become a much needed priority to support reforms that are urgently required as in the case of Greece. At the same time the expenditure required to keep up the pace might prove a budgetary challenge considering the cost cutting practices across the EU and in Greece in particular. The austerity measures that dictate public policy may appear as a drawback but could turn into an opportunity. An EU wide initiative, centrally budgeted and managed, may provide a better and a more secure answer to the challenges facing the European Union and its cross-border functionality.

References

1. Sideridis, A.B.: Present and future e-Government advances at the service of rural area citizens. In: International Conference on Agricultural Informatics 2013: The past, the present and future of Agricultural Informatics, Debrecen (2013)
2. Sideridis, A.B., Protopappas L.: Recent ICT advances applied to smart e-government systems in Life Sciences. In: Information and Communication Technologies in Agriculture, Food and Environment. 7th HAICTA 2015 International Conference, Kavala (2015)
3. European Commission: The European eGovernment Action Plan 2011–2015-Harnessing ICT to promote smart, sustainable and innovative Government in ICT for Goverment and Public Services 2010. EC Publications, Brussels (2010)
4. European Commission: Towards interoperability for European public services. Brussels: T.C. Communication from the Commission to the European Parliament, the European Economic and Social Committee and the Committee of the Regions (2010)
5. European Commission. http://ec.europa.eu/information_society/apps/projects
6. European Commission. http://ec.europa.eu/digital-agenda/en/ict-policy-support-programme
7. STORK 2.0. https://www.eid-stork2.eu
8. Protopappas, L., Sideridis, A.B.: The strategy and the progress made on e-Government services in the EU. In: Sideridis, A.B., Yialouris, C.P., Kardasiadou, Z., Zorkadis, V. (eds.) E-Democracy 2013. CCIS, vol. 441, pp. 192–201. Springer, Heidelberg (2014)
9. European Commission: The European eGovernment Action Plan 2011–2015-Harnessing ICT to promote smart, sustainable & innovative Government in ICT for Goverment and Public Services, Brussels (2010)
10. European Commission: European Interoperability Framework for Pan-European eGovernment Services, Belgium (2004)
11. Commission Staff Working Document, Linking up Europe: the Importance of Inter operability for eGovernment Service, Brussels (2003)
12. European Public Administrations (ISA), European Interoperability Framework for European Public Services. European Commission (2010)
13. STORK 2.0 eID Consortium, D5.1.1 eLearning Pilot Technical Business Objectives and Specifications (2013). www.eid-stork2.eu
14. STORK 2.0 eID Consortium, D5.2.1 eBanking Pilot Technical Business Objectives and Specifications (2013). www.eid-stork2.eu
15. STORK 2.0 eID Consortium, D5.3.1 eGov4Business Pilot Technical Business Objectives and Specifications (2013). www.eid-stork2.eu
16. STORK 2.0 eID Consortium, D5.4.1 eHealth Pilot Technical Business Objectives and Specifications (2013). www.eid-stork2.eu
17. IDABC, Common specifications for eID interoperability in the eGovernment context in eID, Interoperability for PEGS (2007)
18. Leitold, H., Zwattendorfer, B.: STORK: architecture, implementation and pilots. In: ISSE 2010 Securing Electronic Business Processes, pp 131–142 (2010)
19. Tauber, A., et al.: Approaching the challenge of eID interoperability: an austrian perspective. Eur. J. ePract. **14**, 22–39 (2012)
20. STORK eID Consortium, D5.8.1.c Software Design (2007)
21. STORK 2.0 eID Consortium, D4.3 First Version of Technical Design (2015). www.eidstork2.eu

22. The European Parliament and the Council of the European Union, Directive 95/46/EC of the European Parliament and of the Council of 24 October 1995 on the protection of individuals with regard to the processing of personal data and on the free movement of such data, Official Journal L 281 (1995)
23. OASIS, Security Assertion Markup Language (SAML) V2.0 Technical Overview (2008)
24. STORK eID Consortium, D 3.2.1 SAML (2010). www.eid-stork.eu
25. STORK eID Consortium, D2.3 Quality authenticator schem (2009). www.eid-stork.eu
26. STORK eID Consortium, D3.2 Addendum. AQAA Guidelines (2015). www.eid-stork2.eu
27. European Parliament and the Council of the European Union, Regulation (EU) No 910/2014 of the European Parliament and of the Council of 23 July 2014 on electronic identification and trust services for electronic transactions in the internal market and repealing Directive 1999/93/EC 27, Official Journal of the European Union, L 257/73 (2014)
28. STORK   2.0.   https://www.eid-stork2.eu/images/stories/documents/ETSI%202015% 20presentation%20-STORK%202.0.pdf
29. Euroactiv. http://www.euroactiv.com/infosociety/digital-agenda-put-eu-back-gear-news-286500
30. http://ec.europa.eu/digital-agenda/en/digital-agenda-europe-2020-strategy
31. European Commission. http://ec.europa.eu/digital-agenda/en/connecting-europe-facility
32. European   Commission.   http://ec.europa.eu/digital-agenda/en/connecting-europe-facility# services-already-available
33. European Commission. https://ec.europa.eu/dgs/connect/en/content/electronic-identification-and-trust-services-eidas-regulatory-environment-and-beyond
34. European Commission. http://ec.europa.eu/isa
35. SSEDIC Memorandum, http://www.eid-ssedic.eu/images/stories/pdf/presentation/SSEDIC %20Memorandum.pdf
36. European Commission. https://joinup.ec.europa.eu/
37. Zhang, Q., Cheng, L., Boutaba, R.: Cloud computing: state-of-the-art and research challenges. J. Internet Serv. Appl. 1(1), 7–18 (2010)
38. Bauer, M., Meints, M., Hansen, M.: D3.1: Structured Overview on Prototypes and Concepts of Identity Management System, FIDIS (2005)
39. Leitold, H.: STORK Overview (2009). https://online.tugraz.at/tug_online/voe_main2. getvolltext?pCurrPk=44744
40. Zwattendorfer, B., Tauber, A.: Secure cloud authentication using eids. In: Proceedings of IEEE CCIS 2012 (2012)
41. European Commission: Taxation paper - Behavioural Economics and Taxation, EU (2014)
42. European Commission: Group Taxation within the European Union: Did Papillon and Art. 24(5) of the OECD Model Tax Convention Create a Butterfly Effect? European Taxation, 2011, vol. 51, issue 5 (2011)
43. Nielsen, S.: A simple model of commodity taxation and cross-border shopping. Scand J. Econom. 103, 599–623 (2001)
44. Sutherland, H., Figari, F.: EUROMOD: the European Union tax-benefit microsimulation model. Int. J. Microsimul. 6, 4–26 (2013)
45. Bargain, O., et al.: Tax-Benefit Systems in Europe and the US: Between Equity and Efficiency. IZA Discussion Paper 5440 (2011)
46. United Nations: United Nations e-Government Survey 2014 - e-Government for the Future We Want (2014). http://www.un.org/desa
47. Asgarkhani, M.: The effectiveness of e-Service in local government: a case study. Electron. J. e-Gov. 3(4), 157–166 (2005)

48. Pimenidis, E., Georgiadis, C.K.: Can e-Government applications contribute to performance improvement in public administration? Int. J. Oper. Res. Inf. Syst. **5**(1), 48–57 (2014)
49. Pimenidis, E., Iliadis, L.S., Georgiadis, C.K.: Can e-Government systems bridge the digital divide? In: Proceedings of the 5th European Conference on Information Management and Evaluation (ECIME 2011), Dipartimento di Informatica e Comunicazione, Università dell'Insubria, Como, Italy, 8-9 September 2011, pp. 403–411 (2011)

Legal Issues

How Open Data Become Proprietary
in the Court of Justice of the European Union

Maria Bottis[✉]

Department of Archives, Library Science and Museology,
School of Information Science and Informatics, Ionian University, Corfu, Greece
botti@otenet.gr

Abstract. Database protection has become a seriously debated issue in Europe
and the United States since the 1990s. In Europe, the Database Directive of 1996
offered two-tiered protection, for original and non-original databases, instituting
the database maker's *sui generis* right; the United States declined to change its
steady position against protecting non-original databases. The Court of Justice of
the European Union, interpreting the Directive, carved a narrow database right.
While these decisions enjoyed universal acclaim from many theorists, suddenly in
the 2015 *Ryanair* decision, the CJEU subtly blasted its prior database jurisprudence, highlighting contract as a means to enclose data into absolute proprietary
models in a way completely unforeseeable until then. We are left behind to watch
the enclosing of open data acquire a legitimization never before possible.

Keywords: Database right · Open data · European court of justice · *Contract
v. copyright*

1 Introduction

Databases are omnipresent and valuable. They represent the tools without which a
series of economy sectors and other fields, like research and education, are totally
unable to function with any degree of credibility [1]. Their progeny was collections of
facts, or lists with numbers or other data; the collector, and in the modern times, the
maker of the database has always sought protection from copying [2]. The structuring
of a functional and complete database is, indeed, a formidable achievement and the law
should not, in general, leave it free for copying.

On the other hand, as the American jurisprudence has shown, it is crucial to
examine the true nature of the contents of a database. One cannot collect data, facts e.tc.
of an open and public nature, like telephone numbers, enclose them in a database
available to the public and then, claim copyright, as if he was the author of Anna
Karenina [3]. Copyright protects originality, not effort [4].

It seems, therefore, that database protection stood at the crossroads between
copyright, unfair competition and contract from the beginning. Database makers have
used a series of legal bases to claim protection for their databases, not always successfully [5]. In Europe, an important step to resolve this matter was the European
Directive 96/9/EC on the protection of databases. In the United States, *Feist Publications v. Rural* [4] of the Supreme Court fully clarified in 1991 that non-original

© Springer International Publishing Switzerland 2015
S.K. Katsikas and A.B. Sideridis (Eds.): E-Democracy 2015, CCIS 570, pp. 169–174, 2015.
DOI: 10.1007/978-3-319-27164-4_12

databases were and are still not entitled to any copyright protection at all. In this paper, we will examine these two different approaches and the 2015 judgment of the Court of Justice of the European Union which came to alter the picture dramatically.

2   The 96/9/EC Directive of the Protection of Databases

The model of protection initially examined by the European authorities for databases was a clear unfair competition model, disallowing significant copying of another's database for commercial purposes by a competitor [2]. However, as the works towards the Directive were proceeding, the model changed thoroughly and abruptly became an almost pure copyright model. Original databases, meaning databases original in the structuring, design and presentation of their content acquired copyright protection - a protection though certainly not extending to the content of the database, if this as not original in itself [6].

The jewel of the Directive was the protection of non-original databases, where content, design, structure, presentation etc. did not show any creative effort but which were the result of substantial investment of time, effort and capital (the most expensive legal, medical, economic and other databases fall into this class) [11, 12]. The Directive offered a sui generis right to the maker of the database (a new term, necessary as there is no author, no creator of a non-original database), lasting 15 years from the creation of the database or from any real update of the database (if a database is, as they usually are, constantly updated, the right lasts forever). All EU member states (very few on time, though) implemented the Directive, albeit in an almost provocatively non-uniform way [7, 9]. It seems, though, that database makers were content with the new rules; in their responses to the EU questionnaire to formally evaluate the Directive, as dictated by law, all database makers asked stated that they wanted the sui generis database right to remain for their benefit, even if most of them, five years after the Directive had never heard of it [8].

The obvious result was that database makers had the power to enclose data of a public nature (for example, courts' judgments and statutes) into protected databases, if they could prove that they had devoted substantial investment into the creation and presentation of these data [9]. In this case, and if the database was available to the public (digital or analogue, this was unimportant), lawful users (another new term in the intellectual property lexicon) of the database could not be contractually deprived of their right to extract and reutilize insubstantial parts of the database for any reason. This freedom was safeguarded by the Directive, as exceptions to the rule, so that no contract whatever could be valid between the database maker and the lawful user, if it disallowed this freedom of extraction and reutilization of insubstantial parts of the database [2]. This was the exception/limitation of the right, by analogy to the known exceptions/limitations to the copyright holder's rights, exceptions and limitations that aim to protect the public interest, and to calibrate the respective rights and interests of creators, users and the general public. As much as this little freedom was preserved in favor of the lawful user of a database and as much as this freedom may or may not be exercised when a database is technologically protected by Digital Rights Management schemes, this freedom did exist in the Directive and gave the impression that the public interest and the lawful user were not absent from the mind of the European legislator [9].

3 The 1991 US Supreme Court Decision *Feist Publications v. Rural Ltd. Co*

Database protection has its little history also in the United States. From the beginnings of the 20th century, the American courts had heard cases of illegitimate copying of another's lists of horses, or images of flowers' collections etc. and the like [2, 8]. They did offer some protection to these collections under the "sweat of the brow" doctrine, which recognized skill and labor as legitimate basis for copyright protection. However, in 1991, with *Feist Publications v. Rural* [4], the Supreme Court famously decided that copyright protects originality, not effort; and the total copying of the telephone directory of the defendant was deemed unprotected by copyright laws. Many other possible legal foundations remained open, of course, for the plaintiff, such as unfair competition (if the defendant was a competitor), contract (if there was one), tort (misappropriation) and so on [3]. But copyright was left to the protection of original works of the mind and a telephone directory was simply not amongst them. Actually, the 1991 decision of the US Supreme Court led to the intense pressures to the European legislator to enact a Directive on database protection, so that in his turn, the American legislator would be seemingly pressured to also offer similar statutory safeguards for the American database makers [8].

4 CJEU Jurisprudence of Database Protection Before 2015

The 1996 database Directive and especially, the *sui generis* right attracted adverse criticism [10]. The mandatory evaluation of the Directive by the European Commission even proposed banning, if not of the whole Directive, of the *sui generis* right, in the sense that it did not seem to have offered anything important to the European map of copyright protection. The propositions were left as such; probably, there is no power greater than inertia in these cases. The few cases that reached the European Court of Justice before 2015 had carved a limited database protection right for the authors and makers. In the *William Hill/British Horseracing Board* line of cases [15], the Court denied protection for databases with the *sui generis* right when these databases were not the immediate result of the substantial investment the Directive demands, but they were a by-product, a 'spin-off' [13], whereas the investment was directed towards a different main activity (such as organizing football games).

Taking one more step towards "domestication", with the *Football Dataco* case [16], the Court demanded an important element of creativity in the structure and presentation of a database, so that it could be held original and give rise to the (pure) copyright protection for databases of the Directive. And still, of course, this protection did not extend to the databases' contents, when they were not original in themselves (example: telephone numbers, lists of restaurants, real estate lists etc.). So, as it was successfully commented in the literature, the Court had "domesticated" the hotly debated *sui generis* right of the database maker to her database: any substantial investment had to do not with creating the data ("synthetic" data [18] in this case) but with obtaining them. Also, significant originality should be shown in the design, structure and presentation of the database, if the database "author" sought the other route, of protection due to originality.

5   The 2015 Ryanair CJEU Decision

In 2015, all this subtly but decisively changed. In *Ryanair* [19], the database in question was again a database with "synthetic" data [18], meaning data *made* by the database maker and not obtained: data about the airlines routes, timetables, tickets' prices etc. This is a database in the same line as the database of the *British Horseracing Board* [15] or the *Football Dataco* [16]. Ryanair sued PR Aviation for using these data for its own database, which offered comparisons of tickets' prices and the possibility to buy a ticket. The main argument of Ryanair was that the database was a. original, triggering copyright database protection and b. if not original, the database was the result of substantial investment, hence deserving the *sui generis* right protection. Almost as an afterthought, the company also claimed that PR Aviation was also contractually bound not to use any of Ryanair's data into her database, as Ryanair had inserted in its site specific clauses prohibiting this use by third parties.

PR Aviation naturally claimed that Ryanair's database was a. not original in the design etc. of its contents b. not deserving the *sui generis* right, as the data it contained was the spin-off [13] of the main activity of the company (to organize air flights and sell air tickets). As the Database Directive expressly prohibits any contractual clause which would preclude a lawful user of the database from extracting and reusing insubstantial parts of the database, PR Aviation felt pretty safe that its behavior, certainly enhancing free competition between competitors for tickets' sales, was perfectly legal – especially since Ryanair was a "sole-source" database, available to the public [12].

Finally, an "afterthought" argument was added by Ryanair: that if the database was (diametrically appositively from its own arguments just above this one) not original, nor non-original in the Directive's sense, so this had to mean that the lawful user's rights were also irrelevant, therefore the Directive itself was totally irrelevant in this case. So any contractual clause could and would stand, if permitted by the Member State's statutes protecting consumers. There was no "database", no "lawful user", no substantial etc. investment; the whole case was quite surprisingly not a database maker's rights case at all: it was a contracts' case. And the Court of Justice of the European Union agreed: as if *William Hill/British Horseracing Board* and *Football DataCo* had never existed, it "threw" the whole case out of the intellectual property rules of databases and confined it into another field: contract.

6   The Sovereignty of Contract

Was this correct? There is indeed a seductive pure-logic argument: if we have a database which simultaneously is: (a) not original and (b) not non-original, both in the Directive's sense, then the Directive does not apply to it. The Court, let's say lacks jurisdiction. The Directive is not applicable. But the majestic failure or denial of the Court to take a step behind and explore what exactly *is* a database that is not original nor non-original in the Directive's sense, is extremely disappointing. It is almost provocative. Does the fact of being both not original and not non-original, in the Directive's sense, dictate automatically that the database is a work able to be protected stronger than any other database falling into one of these two classes, or appositively, that it is not a database *at all*, that it deserves no protection of any kind at all-contract included? Why does the Court use the words "author" and "database" to describe this class of "databases" [19]? Do these datasets [20] have an "author"?

A simple examination of the data within this database would lead us to the inescapable result that they are the epitome of "synthetic data"; nothing could be further from an original work of our intellect than this. Moreover, these are data open to the public; one has unlimited access to the details of Ryanair's flights through Ryanair's own database. It is only when the same information, "flight Athens-Rome on 15.00 pm, 22/11/2015" becomes part of another website that Ryanair demands the enclosure of it. Open data, via contract, become proprietary, in the most strict sense, as contract, when freed from any consumers protection law there may be, can be tailored exactly as the "owner" of the data wishes: unlimitedly. And here, consumers' protection simply cannot "return" these data to their original situation, that is their complete freedom and openness, as they indeed should and had been, free and open to all.

7   Open Data no More

It is difficult to imagine a harder blow to the Database Directive than Ryanair, nor a more subtle one. It carries the innocent façade of a ruling leaving the Directive just "out of the matter", whereas it effectively negates its whole existence and subtracts from it any meaning at all. All "synthetic data" producers now can simply claim that their databases, full with previously thought as open and public data, are not original, nor non-original; they are further than this, albeit towards the wrong end: they are something one can contract in, or out, at the wish of the initial data "producer". And contract, once accepted as possible, carries within it the heavy justification of the empowerment of freedom-of the free will to dictate terms to the other side, as this side is supposedly free not to enter into the contract in the first place. Contract also is inherently mostly a private matter, one that the State should better leave intact to develop, so as not to hamper the sacred principle of economic freedom. All this, applied to enclose data previously open to all, seem (to the careful, behind-the-lines reader) contradictory, perverse, incapable of suffering the test of intellectual property's wisdom as it was been delivered to us since the Statute of Anne.

Not all commentators agree with this criticism of the decision [21]. But when we are outside the domain of copyright, but on the wrong side of the "outside", we lose in an instant the protection of fair use principles, or exceptions and limitations for the civil law world. We also lose the sense of what it really is that you are claiming exclusiveness to. We start to believe that indeed, the world of the protection of intangible goods has simply collapsed under the weight of a two-party private agreement, rendering this whole world evanescent. The same rule here applied with (previously) open data in databases could apply, in the future, in trademark or patent disputes. As long as we have in our hands something that could be seen as not an invention (not a new, useful etc. technical solution to a problem) or not a trademark (not a sign carrying distinctiveness etc.), but still *something* which can be contracted out, then we are free from any patent and trademark law limitations and we are left with contract. We need to think very carefully whether this is a legal result that will be, in the end, beneficial to society [10].

References

1. Bits of Power. Issues of Global Access to Scientific data, Committee on issues on the transborder flow of scientific data,USA National Committee for CODATA, Commission on Physical Sciences, Mathematics and Applications, National Research Council, National, Academy Press, Washington (1997)
2. Davison, M.: The Legal Protection of Databases. Cambridge University Press, Cambridge (2003)
3. Reichman, J., Samuelson, P.: Intellectual property rights to data? Vander. L. Rev. **50**, 49 (1997)
4. Feist Publications v. Rural Tel. Ser. Co. Inc., 499 US 340 (1991)
5. Shields, P., Racina, R.: What's all that fuss about *Feist*? The sky is not falling on the intellectual property rights of online database proprietors. U. Dayton L. Rev. **17**, 563 (1992)
6. Smith S.: Legal protection of factual compilations and databases in England: how will the database directive change the law in this area, IPQR 2001, 100
7. Hugenholtz, B.: The new database right: early case law from Europe (2001). www.ivir.nl
8. Bottis, M.: Legal protection of databases, Nomiki Vivliothiki (2004). (in Greek)
9. Hugenholtz, B.: Implementing the database directive. In: Kabel, M. (ed.) Intellectual Property and Information Law, Essays in Honor of Herman Cohen Jehoram, pp. 187–200. Kluwer Law International, The Hague (1998)
10. Benkler, Y.: Constitutional bounds of database protection: the role of the judicial review in the creation and definition in private rights in information. Berkeley L. Tech. J. **15**, 535 (2000)
11. Grosheide, F.W.: Database protection: the European way. Wash. U.L.J Pol'y **8**, 39 (2002)
12. Hugenholtz, B.: Abuse of database right. Sole source information banks under the EU Database Doctrine. In: Leveque, F., Shelanski, H. (eds.) Antitrust, Patents and Copyright: EU and US Perspectives, pp. 203–219. Edward Elgar, Cheltenmam (2005)
13. Hugenholtz, B.: Program schedules, event data and telephone subscriber listings under the database directive-the "spin-off" doctrine in The Netherlands and elsewhere in Europe. Paper Presented at Eleventh Annual Conference on International IP law and Policy, Fordham University School of Law, New York (14–25 April 2005). www.ivir.nl

DNA Analysis and Criminal Proceedings: The Greek Legal Paradigm

Konstantia-Christine Lachana[✉]

Faculty of Law, Department of Criminal and Criminological Sciences,
Aristotle University of Thessaloniki, Thessaloniki, Greece
chr.lachana@gmail.com

Abstract. With the advent of DNA technology and the revolutionization it entails for the administration of criminal justice, the forensic use of DNA analysis as a key crime-fighting tool has gained a prominent role in the enforcement of penal repression, both domestically as well as transnationally; albeit amidst escalating concerns from a fundamental rights standpoint. The present contribution focuses on the (reformed) Greek DNA sampling and databasing penal policy as codified in article 200A CPC, adumbrates its general outline, offers a critical overview of its problematic parameters, highlights the ensuing rule of law deficiencies and forwards *de lege ferenda* ameliorative suggestions.

Keywords: DNA analysis · Measures of procedural coercion · Article 200A CPC · Fundamental principles of investigation · Data protection principles

1 Introduction

Over recent years the scientific progress in modern genetic technology has contributed to a worldwide consensus over the preponderance and immeasurable value of genetic data in criminal investigations (owing mainly to their unique qualities *vis-à-vis* other human biometric features) on the one hand and to a growing receptiveness of DNA analysis as a major bio-identifier of possible perpetrators and thus a *relatively* reliable means of forensic evidence, on the other. Novel traits displayed by the DNA-related data, such as the uniqueness, individuality and inalterability of the human genome, the treasure trove of the information distilled from the DNA sequences, even from an infinitesimal quantity of tissue sample, and portraying the past, present and future not only of the person involved but also of his/her family relations in the same genetic line or the inability of their bearer to control their diffusion in the environment, account for genetic data's distinctiveness and the law enforcement agencies' preference to resort to their

© Springer International Publishing Switzerland 2015
S.K. Katsikas and A.B. Sideridis (Eds.): E-Democracy 2015, CCIS 570, pp. 175–189, 2015.
DOI: 10.1007/978-3-319-27164-4_13

processing in the course of their activities[1]. Yet, it is precisely due to these particularities that the proliferation of national and supranational DNA retrieval, storage and exchange regulative schemes poses equally unprecedented challenges from a human rights' perspective, testing in this respect the endurance of our civil libertarian criminal law traditions.

The Greek criminal procedural system welcomed the genetic revolution's break-through officially back in 2001, with the insertion of an express statutory basis in the Criminal Procedure Code (art.200A[2]) authorizing –under a set of prerequisites whose strictness has been gradually waning- the performance of DNA analysis as a *special form of expert opinion* and a *serious measure of procedural coercion*, orderable *initially* during the *intermediary proceedings* via an indictment of the Judicial Council but *currently* at *all stages of pre-trial proceedings*, including the *preliminary inquiry* (art. 31 par.1a' CPC) or even –up until last April- in the absence of a prosecutorial order if a *summary investigation* is being conducted pursuant to art.243 par.2 CPC[3]. Following its introduction, art.200A CPC underwent a series of subsequent revisions, the antepenultimate and most sweeping one being with L.3783/2009 (art.12 par.3)[4]; the country's purported response to the mandates of Council Decision 2008/615/JHA (otherwise

---

[1] On the unique features of genetic data and their ability to reveal what has been aptly named as an individual's "genetic diary" [cf. Market M., Genetic Diaries: An Analysis of Privacy Protections in DNA Databanks, Suffolk U. L. Rev., vol.30, 185ff. (1996)], see Opinion 2/2009 of the Hellenic DPA (HDPA) on DNA Analysis and the Creation of a Database of DNA Profiles, 29.7.2009, item 2.1., and Shapiro D./Weinberg M., DNA Data Banking: The Dangerous Erosion of Privacy, Clev. St. L. Rev., vol.38, 455 ff. (469ff.) (1990). On the relative probative value of DNA analysis, see Decisions of the National Commission for Human Rights (NCHR), The Operation of Video Cameras in Public Places and the Sound or Image Recording, the DNA Analysis during Criminal Proceedings and the Files of Genetic Prints (Art.12 par.3 L.3783 / 2009), 18.2.2010, p.7 and of the National Bioethics Commission (NBC) on the Use of Genetic Prints in Criminal Proceedings, 23.3.2001, pt. 3.

[2] Said provision was added by art.5 L.2928/2001, Government Gazette (GG) 141A'/27.6.2001 and was modified also in 2004 (art.42 par.3 L.3251/2004, GG 129A'/9.7.2004) and in 2008 (art. 6 par.3 L.3728/2008, GG 257A'/18.12.2008) prior to the amendments analyzed in text. For a presentation of the legal issues associated with art.200A CPC in its previous form, see among others Mallios E., The Use of DNA in Criminal Proceedings, Nomiko Vima, 1749–1772, (2001), Siaperas G., The Consent of the Individual to the Taking of his Genetic Material (DNA), Poiniki Dikaiosyni, 1451ff., (2005), Symeonidou-Kastanidou E., Law 2928/ 2001 on the "Protection of the Citizen from Illicit Acts and Offences by Criminal Organizations"-Basic Features and a First Interpretative Approach, Poiniki Dikaiosyni, 694–699(696), (2001).

[3] Subsequent to the latest normative revise (see art.19 L.4322/2015, GG 42 A'/27.4.2015), this possibility is now ruled out as it is explicitly stipulated in art.200A par.1b' CPC that the removal of genetic material can only be authorized by the competent Public Prosecutor or the Investigating Judge.

[4] GG 138A/7.8.2009.

known as the *Prüm Decision*[5]), calling for the establishment of national automated DNA analysis files in order to combat transnational criminality through the enhancement of cross-border information exchanges. Outflanking the European normative requirements, the outcome of the Greek transposition venture induced far-reaching modifications in the structure of art.200A CPC covering *both* stages of the said *composite processual act*, namely: (*a*) the initial phase of collection and analysis of cellular material in the framework of a *present*, ongoing investigation, and (*b*) the regulation of the obtained sample's fate, specifically the retention and filing of the retrieved DNA profiles for the purpose of their *future* evidentiary utilization in *posterior* criminal proceedings[6].

Placed in a rather unpromising historic conjuncture, these amendments add up to a string of recent legislative interventions whose enactment has generated a serious debilitating effect on the national data protection level in the field of justice and police affairs. Suffice it to mention the -constitutionally debatable- exemption of judicial and public prosecution authorities as well as all agencies acting under their supervision from the scope of the data protection statute (L.2472/1997[7]), in the interest of detecting and persecuting a long list of felonies or even misdemeanors committed with intent[8]. That being noted, art.200A CPC *does* operate as *dual function* rule (procedural *and*

---

[5] OJ L 210/1, 6.8.2008. On the Prüm Decision and the homonym Treaty whose content was thereby integrated into the European institutional framework, see *generally* UK Parliament, House of Lords (HoL), Prüm: An Effective Weapon Against Terrorism and Crime?, 18th Report of Session 2006–07, Stationary Office Ltd.: London (2007) and *specifically* Kierkegaard S., Security and DNA Transfer Within the EU. The Prüm Decision- An Uncontrolled Fishing Expedition in "Big Brother" Europe, CLSR, vol.24, 243–252, (2008), McCartney C. et als, Transnational Exchange of Forensic DNA: Viability, Legitimacy and Acceptability, Eur. J. Crim. Policy Res, vol.17, 305–322, (2011). For an overview of the EU security-enhancing legislative initiatives propelled by the introduction of the availability principle, see Lachana K.-Ch., Recent Developments in the Transnational Information Exchange Between Law-enforcement Authorities in the EU: The Introduction and Implementation of the Principle of Availability, in Bottis M. et als. (eds.), Values and Freedoms in Modern Information Law and Ethics, pp. 1175–1179, Nomiki Bibliothiki, (2012).

[6] On the conceptual disparities between the notions of *genetic material* (=*cellular sample*) and *DNA profile* (=*genetic print*), see instead of others the definitions provided in ECtHR, *S. and Marper v. UK*, nos.30562/04 and 30566/04, 4.12.2008, paras. 70 *et seq.*, and, from the theory, Lachana K.-Ch., Genetic Material, in Androulakis N./Margaritis L./Farsedakis I.(eds.), Dictionary of Legal Terminology, III, Criminal Law and Criminology, Nomiki Bibliothiki, forthcoming. Hereinafter the first, broader term is employed to denote any material of a biological origin, e.g. blood, saliva, sperm etc., whose analysis enables access to the human DNA, namely the, replete with valuable genetic information, chemical substance contained in the 23 chromosomes of every bodily cell, while the second term refers to the outcome of the analysis of the non-nuclear (=non-codified) DNA sequences. *Genetic data* signifies "all data, of whatever type, concerning the characteristics of an individual which are inherited or acquired during early prenatal development", see likewise arts. 4(10), COM (2012)11 final, 25.1.2012, and 3(10), COM (2012)10 final, 25.1.2012, respectively.

[7] GG 50A/10.4.1997 (as amended).

[8] See art.3 par.2 point b) of L.2472/1997, added by art.8 par.1 of L.3625/2007, GG 290A/24.12.2007.

substantive, in that it serves as the exclusive legal foundation for the permissibility of state intrusions into the informational and other legally protected interests of the alleged offender, through the institution of a standalone *special ground of justification* negating the unlawfulness of genetic data processing) and it is in light of this *two-pronged jurid-ical identity* that the amplitude of its reform should be assessed. In other words, as a result of the said functional dualism, when implementing the restrictive measure under discussion, the need to abide by the *fundamental (procedural) principles of investiga-tion*[9] including the *nemo tenetur se ipsum prodere/accusare* principle and the *presumptio innocentiae* intersects with the obligation to respect the *(substantive) general and special data protection guarantee principles* set forth in L.2472/1997 but also enjoying a supra-national entrenchment[10]. Institutionally-wise this need remains sadly unaccomplished as it is argued below.

Bearing in mind that the European legislation, against whose standards the Greek norm's legality is measured up, is hardly a guarantor itself of a satisfying and uniform level of protection for the citizens' right to genetic informational privacy[11], the contours of DNA analysis' *status quo* in the Greek legal order are demarcated in the following lines and the problematic areas associated with its standardization and enforcement pinpointed.

2   The Standardization of Genetic Material Sampling and Analysis: Problematic Aspects with Regards to Art.200A(1) CPC

As far as the *initial* stage of the specific investigative measure is concerned, *de lege lata* the lawfulness of *compulsory (=even in the absence of the examinee's consent)* extrac-tion and analysis of genetic material by the *law enforcement authorities (=the general and special investigating officers laid down in arts. 33 and 34 CPC)* is conditioned upon the *cumulative* fulfillment of the following mandatory stipulations: (*i*) substantiation of *serious indications of guilt* against someone for the commitment of a felony or misde-meanor punishable by imprisonment of *at least one year*, (*ii*) issuance of a relevant (*written* and *well-founded*) *order by the competent Public Prosecutor or the Investi-gating Judge* ahead of the defendant's submission, *in a manner utterly respectful of his/*

---

[9] I.e. the principles of necessity, necessary proportion, prohibition of excessiveness and of unfav-orable treatment. On their function, see Androulakis N., The Limits of Investigative Action and the Principle of Necessity, Poinika Chronika, 3–15, (1975), Dalakouras Th., Criminal Proce-dural Law, pp. 99ff., Law & Economy, P.N. Sakkoulas, (2012).

[10] Arts.8 ECHR, 8 ECFR, 16 TFEU, Framework Decision 2008/977/JHA (OJ L 350/60, 30.12.2008), CoE Convention 108 and its Additional Protocol, as well as Recommendations No. R (87)15 and No. R (92)1.

[11] On the deficiencies of the European legislation, see esp. Symeonidou-Kastanidou E., DNA Analysis and Criminal Proceedings: The European Institutional Framework, EJCCLCJ, 139–160, (2011), (=Poinika Chronika, 3–12, 2011). On CoE Recommendation No. R. (92)1, which is of direct relevance, see Spinelli K., The Recommendation No. R. (92)1 for the Use of DNA Analysis Within the System of Criminal Justice- Uses Without Abuses, Poinika Chronika, 287 *et seq.*, (2001).

her dignity, to DNA sampling, (*iii*) indispensable presence of a prosecuting official in cases cell tissue is to be removed from the *intimate parts* of the human body, (*iv*) finding of human tissue (=unknown, unidentified sample) at the crime scene or on the victim, subjectable to a cross-examination with the alleged perpetrator's sample, (*v*) restriction of the analysis solely onto the data that are absolutely necessary for determining the offender (as opposed to those revealing facets of his/her personality)[12], (*vi*) performance of the examination at a state or university laboratory and (*vii*) immediate destruction of the cellular sample upon the testing's completion[13].

2.1 Objective Scope of Application

A first pivotal issue emanating from the current *status* of art.200A par.1a' CPC and signifying a rule of law retreat relates to the remarkable enlargement of the *catalogue of offences* whose investigation justifies the measure's application, through the inclusion of nearly *any* criminally proscribed behavior. Sure enough, no incumbency of this kind derives with sufficient precision either from the silent thereon Recommendation No. R (87) 15 or from the vague wording of Recommendation No. R (92)1, Principle 5, on "*appropriate cases*" capable of validating DNA analysis irrespective of the offence's gravity. Nevertheless and undoubtedly so, the latter constitutes a decisive indicator for establishing compliance with the *principle of proportionality*, which further implies that the *twelve-month* penalty threshold[14] continues to be far too low for the harm inflicted by such an invasive affront on the alleged culprit's genetic informational privacy, phys- ical integrity and so on, leaving the expansion of the norm's objective regulative purview to such a degree non-legitimized[15]. In addition to its disproportionateness, the standing authorization of DNA sampling for the purpose of verifying crimes *of lesser or at least not increased seriousness* -such as a basic perjury pursuant to art.224 PC or an admin- istrative road traffic violation punishable with a custodial sentence of over a year incar- ceration-, *absent any personalized requirements pertaining to the offence per se, the*

---

[12] As a result, the sample's obtainment is only authorized for *investigative* purposes (i.e. for solving the crime for which the alleged perpetrator was arrested) and *not* for *database* ends (i.e. with the sole intention of including it in the DNA databank). On this distinction see e.g. Taylor N., Privacy and the DNA Database, EHRLR, vol.4, 373–392 (375ff.) (2005). It bears reminding that the execution of DNA analysis on convicts for offences "of a certain gravity" for *purely preventive* crime-fighting ends has been ruled compatible with art.8 ECHR by the Strasbourg judicature, see ECtHR, *Van der Velden v. The Netherlands*, no. 29514/05, 7.12.2006, par. 2, ECtHR, *W. v. The Netherlands*, no. 20689/08, 20.1.2009, ECtHR, *S. and Marper v. UK*, *ibid*, par.104.

[13] At any rate, with or without these terms, the accused's right to request the performance of DNA analysis in his/her defense is co-recognized along with his/her power to petition the former's iteration from the same sample and appoint, optionally, a technical advisor of his choosing (see art.200A par.1 c' and par.2 a', b' CPC).

[14] Having recently replaced the former *three-month* one, see art.19 par.1 L.4322/2015.

[15] Cf. HDPA, Opinion 15/2001- Analysis of Genetic Material for the Purposes of Crime Detection and Penal Pursuit, 15.2.2001, item. 8, NBC, Decision of 23.3.2001, *op. cit.*, pt. 6, proposing, in the *ancien régime,* the measure's constriction to "*particularly serious crimes*".

circumstances of its perpetration or the offender's personality, appears further: (*a*) problematic in view of the subsequent storage of *all* these DNA profiles in the national database, (*b*) intersystemically discrepant compared to arts. 253A CPC, 253B CPC, 4 L.2225/1994[16] and 28 par.3 L.4139/2013[17], which render the lawfulness of the special investigative methods inscribed in them contingent upon the severity of the offences under detection, and (*c*) incongruous with the vast majority of the corresponding European national provisions which apply much stricter standards, necessitating the assertion of *bigger* or *particular gravity* in the criminal conduct in question, for the sample's acquisition to ensue[18].

This stigma of unconstitutionality can only be healed through a rectifying normative insertion of an *exhaustive itemization of the (serious) crimes which are amenable to the enforcement of DNA collection* –preferably combined with their re-confinement to those against sexual freedom or relating to the economic exploitation of sexual life, as was the case before- and a statutory prohibition to activate the said identity verification method, save in cases of *proven absolute necessity for lack of less intrusive and onerous evidentiary means.* With regards to the subsequent filing of genetic prints for the benefit of *future* criminal proceedings (=when persecuting different offences but *qualitatively tantamount* to the aforementioned ones), on top of every other criterion hitherto propounded[19], it would be expedient to employ, by virtue of hermeneutical analogy, the criterion of *"committing new criminal acts"*, as it is already envisaged in art.282 par.4 CPC and required for the imposition of the weightiest measure of procedural coercion, i.e. *pre-trial detention (argumentum a maiore ad minus).* Indeed, this recently *objectified* probabilistic model of risk assessment calculations on the defendant's future relapsing to delinquency, offers a secure basis for *negative prognostication*, premised not on arbitrary, subjective factors *comme auparavant* but on *"prior irreversible convictions for equivalent punishable acts"*. Plus, the issuance of a *written* and *well-reasoned* order is demanded (by the Investigating Judge in the case of pre-trial detention).

2.2   Range of Affected People

Ratione personae, as the reference to "serious indications of guilt" denotes, the acquisition of *at least* a *suspect's* procedural capacity by the undergoer of his/her biological sample's removal is reiterated in art.200A par.1 CPC as an imperative proviso of substantive legality for the effectuation of DNA analysis. Consequently, insofar as the examinee's formal designation as a suspect (or defendant) for the perpetration of one or

---

[16] GG 121A/20.7.1994.

[17] GG 74A/20.3.2013.

[18] The notional clarification of "particular or distinguishable gravity" is usually specified through a designating catalogue of the offences covered (France, Belgium, Spain) and/or a *minimum* delimitation of the threatened criminal sanctions (Luxembourg, Italy, Finland, Sweden, the Netherlands, Ireland, Belgium etc.).

[19] Cf. Aggelis S., The Filing of Genetic Prints for the Investigation of Crimes in Accordance with Art.12 par.3 L.3783/2009, Poinika Chronika, 945–948 (947), (2009), HDPA, Opinion 2/2009, *op. cit.*, item.3.1, NCHR, Decision of 18.2.2010, *ibid*, p.20.

more offences among the previously described ones is requested, other uninvolved or suspicionless third people are ruled out from the norm's subjective ambit. In this regard, art.200A CPC's formulation: (*a*) surpasses the (either way lowered) protective bar set by Recommendation No. R(92) 1, Principle 2 and allowing for the inclusion of e.g. by-passers, (*b*) aligns with the other EU Member States' statutory choices which, in their majority, extend the measure's realm to suspects or even mere arrestees while often co-provide for kinship or large-scale DNA investigations[20] and (*c*) adheres to the *principle of suitable degree of suspicions in criminal proceedings* by asking for the institution of the highest level of suspicions (and thereby the strongest evidence of the suspect's culpability) for such an intrusive means of procedural coercion to be carried out (similarly to art. 282 par.1 CPC)[21].

Still, notwithstanding such ostensible normative "assets", the rule of law eroding ramifications of the juridico-technical malformation in art.200A par.1 CPC, prior at least to its 2015 reform, should not be overlooked. As it was alluded to earlier, in abrogating the Judicial Council's commissioning and overall supervisory competence and in substituting it with the law enforcement authorities' empowerment to obtain cellular sample upon a suspect's apprehension, the Greek legislature deprived DNA analysis of its former robust *judicial* safeguards against abuse or arbitrariness and downgraded it to a *simple investigative act*, performable *inter alia*, up until of late, during a *summary investigation* on flagrant offences or in other emergency cases where any delay runs the risk of losing evidence etc., *under the sole responsibility of the investigating officers enumerated in arts.33 and 34 CPC*[22]. Although by definition non-equipped with the essential legal expertise, the latter, when executing their call of duty dictated by art.243 par.2 CPC, were summoned to engage in complex evaluative considerations and individualize inherently *vague* juridical concepts (i.e. serious indications of guilt, risk of committing wrongdoings in the future- recidivism), causing *legal uncertainty* as to which empirical factors were to be subsumed under these abstract terms by each officer's discretionary and thus highly haphazard interpretation. Not only did this *deficit in foreseeability* run counter to arts.8 par.2 ECHR and 8 ECFR in conjunction with art.52 par. 1 ECFR, but it also led to a constitutionally unacceptable *overstepping of the necessary proportion* when combined with the immoderate enlargement of offences for whose inspection the *automatized*, by and large, conduct of DNA testing ensued, according to arts.243 and 251 CPC, exempt from any judicial filter.

---

[20] Familial genetic searching as well as mass DNA screenings are standardized *inter alia* in the Dutch and the British legal orders, see Vervaele J.A.E. et als., The Dutch Focus on DNA in the Criminal Justice System: Net-Widening of Judicial Data, IRDP, vol.83, 459ff.(465) (2012) and Maquire C.N. et als., Familial Searching: A Specialist Forensic DNA Profiling Service Utilising the National DNA Database to Identify Unknown Offenders via Their Relatives- the U.K. Experience, Forensic Sci. Int. Genet., vol. 8, n.1, 1–9, (2014), respectively.

[21] On said principle, see e.g. Dalakouras Th., The Principle of Suitable Degree of Suspicions or Power of Indices, Poinikos Logos, 1793 ff.(2003) (=Essays in Honor of Androulakis N., pp. 851ff., Ant.Sakkoulas, 2003).

[22] For a similar criticism against said downgrade cf. HDPA, Opinion 2/2009, *op. cit*, item 3.2., Kotsalis L., DNA Bank, Security and Human Rights, Nomiko Vima, 1881ff. (1882), (2009), NCHR, Decision of 18.2.2010, *op. cit*, pp.9–10.

Contrary to any inferences which might be drawn out of the lax phrasing espoused by the framers of Recommendation No. R(92)1 on the matter at hand, only through an in-depth *judicial* review can the *ultimum refugium* character of DNA analysis be secured and its implementation strictly in lack of alternative, *less meddlesome* means, ascertained[23]. On that account, it has been highly recommendable to re-entrust the measure's ordering authority upon the issuance of either a Judicial Council's *well-reasoned* indictment or a *written* and *firmly corroborated* decision by the Public Prosecutor of the Misdemeanor Court, at the very least (see arts. 139 CPC, 93 par.3 Const.[24]). Meanwhile, the deprecated and undefined *per se* by the CPC term "law enforcement authorities" should have been equated hermeneutically with "prosecutorial agencies", on the supportive grounds of arts. 31, 35 and 243 CPC[25]. The freshly legislated placement of DNA sampling under the auspices of the Public Prosecutor or the Investigating Judge has gone some way to redressing the hitherto absence of judicial control. Yet, a *restrictive* interpretation of art.200A par.1 CPC's regulative purview is *still* exigent so as to limit its application *only* to the procedural stage *after* the initiation of prosecution and the pressing of felony or misdemeanor charges against a *defendant* in the course of an *ordinary* (arts. 246ff. CPC) or *summary* (arts. 243 ff. CPC) *investigation*, barring the *preliminary inquiry* (art.31 par.1a' and par.2, 3 CPC in conjunction with art. 43 par.1b' CPC).

2.3   Coercive DNA Sampling: A Perpetual Tug-of-War

Last but not least, another contentious development all along the radical reconfiguration of art.200A par.1a' CPC involves the introduction of a *compulsory clause* whereby the investigating authorities' *absolute* (=non-optional) statutory commitment to collect genetic material for the purposes of DNA analysis, even against the opposite will of the person concerned or in spite of his refusal, was *formally* institutionalized (while *de facto* activated upon the satisfaction of *all* the prescribed legality conditions[26]). Despite the antecedent grammatical proclamation of the measure's *potential* enforceability, its *binding* nature has been fully resolved ever since the provision's drafting, in the sense that *no previous*, *informed* and *valid consent* was sought after the alleged offender; ergo his denial to cooperate for DNA testing was freely evaluated by the Trial Court without

---

[23] Cf. likewise Symeonidou-Kastanidou, *op. cit*, 146.

[24] Stipulating the imperative principle for controlling judicial power, namely that all court rulings, indictments, prosecutorial orders, decisions etc. must be fully justified. Proponents of the suggestion put forth in text include HDPA, Opinion 2/2009, *ibid*, item 3.2., and Kotsalis, *op.cit*.

[25] Cf. Conclusive Report of the Public Prosecutor of the Court of Second Instance of Thessaloniki (Seferidis I.) of 14th.10.2013, Poiniki Dikaiosyni, 903ff. (2013), (espousing a correspondent in result construal).

[26] According to the most correct opinion, see *infra* in text.

bearing any incriminating probative value whatsoever[27]. Unsurprisingly then, granted this widely recognized mandatory character of DNA sampling in the past regulative regime and the prevailing, clear-cut distinction between compulsoriness and coercion, the aforementioned normative addition *gave a fresh, invigorating impetus* to the protracted, thorny *controversy* over the permissibility of employing *coercive means* for the sample's removal, in case of the accused's unwillingness to consent. Considering the unvaryingly tacit letter of the law hereupon, technically speaking, such a legitimizing prospect *-consonant, in principle, with the European juridical corpus[28]-*, still remains open.

In a nutshell, at the heart of the said doctrinal dispute lay the following, ruggedly sketched, dilemma: whether the violent sample's retrieval contravenes *eo ipso* and *in any event* the overarching principle of *human dignity* (art.2 par.1 Const., art.3 ECHR) and is therefore constitutionally untenable, *or* whether the use of force for the harvesting of cell tissue does not *a priori* bring forth the instrumentalization of the human body, echoing the means-end reasoning of the Kantian maxim, nor does it encroach *at all times* upon the *presumption of innocence* (arts.6 par.2 ECHR, 14 par. 2 ICPR) and the *privilege against self-incrimination* (arts.273 par.2 CPC, 6 par.1a' ECHR and 14 par.3 g' ICPR), *unless* it objectifies the person *in concreto* for the sake of rendering criminal justice[29]. The materialization of such a reduction of the human to a mere end in himself is a question of fact; examples would include, *inter alia*, inhuman or degrading treatment, exceedance of the necessary measure, breach of the fundamental principles of interrogation, "experiencing of serious pain or suffering as a result of the forcible medical intervention" by the person concerned, to put it in the Strasbourg judges' parlance[30], and so on. Between these two poles (rejecting the use of coercion as altogether incongruent with human dignity and countenancing it under stringent requirements) oscillated the large stream of divergent academic and jurisprudential thinking in Greece heretofore.

Against this backdrop, the underlying meaning of the newly standardized clause lends itself to two different interpretations: *either* it is denounced as superfluous and bereft of substance, since the sample's obtainment is only mandatory when all prerequisites articulated in art.200A par.1a' CPC are met- along the lines of HDPA's approach rightly suggesting in her Opinion 2/2009 the relevant adverb's striking off from the norm,

---

[27] Pursuant to the principle of free evaluation of evidence enshrined in art.177 CPC. See esp. the Minutes of the Greek Parliament, 5.6.2001, p.9064, where, during the parliamentary discussion of the draft law (2928/2001), the acting at the time Minister of Justice stressed precisely the distinction between the, governed by the statute, "mandatory DNA retrieval" and "the exercise of violence upon the human body", which is "something different". Cf. also Manoledakis I., Security and Freedom: Interpretation of L.2928/2001 on Organized Crime and Relative Texts, pp.157-158, Sakkoulas publ. (2002).

[28] Cf. Recommendation No. R (92)1, Principle 4, as well as Universal Declaration on the Human Genome and Human Rights of 11.11.1997, art.9 and CoE Oviedo Convention of 4.4.1997, art. 26.

[29] For a detailed presentation of the various stances voiced, see Siaperas, *op.cit.*, 1454ff.

[30] ECtHR, *Jalloh v. Germany*, no. 54810/00, 11.7.2006, par.72 with further references. Cf. also ECtHR, *Tirado Ortiz and Lozano Martin v. Spain*, no.43486/98, 22.6.1999, par.1.

for its preservation may well prove to be misleading apart from unnecessary[31]-, *or* it can be (mis)construed as implicitly embodying a police entitlement to resort to physical force, in cases such a recourse appears the sole effective means warranting the measure's obligatory imposition. The latter conceptualization was sustained by the Hellenic Supreme Court's Prosecution Office in her Opinion 15/2011[32], where *Areios Pagos'* Vice Public Prosecutor Mr. Kontaxis championed in favor of the notional identification of the two terms at issue and drew corroborating parallels with instances where bodily duress is (or seems to be) condoned, short of a concrete legal authorization.

Each of the arguments underpinning Opinion 15/2011 has been criticized and rebutted in detail[33]. By virtue of the reasons indicated, *no* legitimizing influence can be exerted on the subject matter out of the current verbiage of art.200A par.1 CPC, in the ongoing absence of an *expressis verbis* statutory basis authorizing the use of coercion and properly delimiting state power to a conformable with the principle of proportionality degree. A *generalized, unconstrained* and *destitute of special, rigid legal requirements* establishment of a ditto right can neither be tolerated, in light of arts. 2 par.1, 5 par.3 and 5a', 7 par.2 Const. and 3 ECHR -as it would transgress their protective nucleus-, nor is it enjoined by the Prüm Decision's rules. The same holds steadily true in the aftermath of the 2015 reform, since, indicative though it might be of the legislative intent to outlaw any sort of inordinate physical compulsion, the *abstract* normative stipulation of the need to conduct DNA analysis "with the utmost respect of the individual's human dignity" seems more to dwell in the sphere of wishful thinking than to provide for a solid framework of permissible state action[34].

If ever enacted, a qualifying normative basis on coercion's allowability should *at minimum* encompass *all evaluative indicators of proportionality* set by the Strasbourg case law for the justification of state interferences with the rights enshrined in arts.8 and 3 ECHR[35]; namely increased gravity of the persecuted offence, exercising no more than the strictly necessary and sensible amount of force in a way that does not engender any risk of

---

[31] *Op. cit.*, item 3.1.

[32] Poiniki Dikaiosyni, 1299 (2011) = Poinika Chronika, 68 (2012) = Nomiko Vima, 703 (2012).

[33] See Lachana K.-Ch., Compulsoriness and Coercion for the Extraction of DNA Sample in the Framework of the Revised Provision of Art.200A of the Greek Criminal Procedure Code (Occasioned by the Opinion n.15/2011 of the Hellenic Supreme Court's Prosecution Office), Poiniki Dikaiosyni, 1168–1179, (2012).

[34] See art.200A par.1 b' CPC as amended by art.19 par.1 L.4322/2015.

[35] On the criteria see e.g. ECtHR, *Jalloh v. Germany, op.cit*, par.117, ECtHR, *O'Halloran and Francis v. UK*, nos.15809/02, 25624/02, 29.6.2007, paras.55ff. As regards the *normative interrelation* between arts.8 and 3 ECHR, whereas the Strasbourg Court used to distinguish the two provisions' scope of application on the basis of the physical assault's intensity, stressing art. 8 ECHR's wider yet subsidiary protective role which was to be activated in cases the bodily maltreatment failed to attain the "*minimum level of severity*" required under art.3 ECHR (: "*the first point of reference*"), the recent jurisprudential trend leans towards the *joint* examination of their applicability terms, cf. ECtHR, *Costello-Roberts v. UK*, no. 13134/87, 25.3.1993, paras. 34, 36 and ECtHR, *M.C. v. Bulgaria* no. 39272/98, 4.12.2003, par.166, respectively. On the said jurisprudential turnaround, see Karavias M., Article 8, in Sicilianos L.-A.(ed.), ECHR- Article By Article Interpretation, at 318, Nomiki Bibliothiki, (2013).

a lasting detriment to the individual's health or swing into humiliating or degrading treatment, unavailability or exhaustion of more lenient investigative means appropriate to unravel the crime, circumscription of the forcibly retrievable biological material to certain types of bodily tissue excluding e.g. blood, banning of coercive DNA sampling on minors, as well as firm processual bulwarks against abuses (prior notification of the interested party on his/her rights, reinstating of Judicial Council's ordering authority etc.). Good cases in point fulfilling some of the above suggested legality criteria are *expressly* put into effect in Luxembourg (art.48-5 par.3 CPC), Belgium (art.90*undecies* par.1, par.2c' and d', par.3 CPC), Italy (art.224*bis* CPC) and the Netherlands (art.151*b* par.1 and 2 CPC)[36].

3   The Broadening of Genetic Prints' Filing: Subsisting Rule of Law Deficiencies in Art.200A (2) d, e, f CPC

Equally problematic from a rule of law vantage appears the successively amended standardization of the *subsequent* stage of retaining *DNA profiles* for their *future* exploitation in posterior criminal proceedings. To begin with, under the guise of harmonizing the Greek legal order with the Prüm Decision's incumbencies, L.3783/2009: (*i*) reversed the originally legislated immediate destruction rule which called for direct erasure of genetic prints once proceedings having given rise to their generation were irrevocably concluded[37], (*ii*) mandated, for future evidentiary purposes not restrained to the investigation of offences equivalent to those whose inspection triggered the sample's obtainment[38], the *blanket* and *indiscriminate* inclusion of DNA profiles of *all* people who were once labelled as suspects in the national database *until their death*, on condition that DNA analysis resulted in their *positive* identification even if no charges were pressed against them or if they were later exonerated, and (*iii*) allocated the supervision of the forensic DNA databank, which is operated by the Criminal Investigation Department at the Hellenic Police Headquarters, to a Public Prosecutor or a Deputy Public Prosecutor of the Court of Second Instance appointed by the Supreme Judicial Council for a two-year term of office.

Five years later, art.7 par.1 of L.4274/2014 added to the filing procedure the monitoring role of the Public Prosecutor of the Court of First Instance envisaged in art.4 L. 2265 /1994[39] and repealed the prompt removal clause with regards to the *negative* (i.e. producing no match) genetic prints. Henceforth, the latter are to remain registered in the DNA databank *until the issuance of a final acquittal indictment or a ditto ruling or the*

---

[36] Generally speaking, as it has been noted, "in Southern European countries, when an individual refuses to submit to DNA testing, the taking of a sample by force is not permitted, while in North European countries the sample cannot be withheld", see Guillén M. et als, Ethical-legal Problems of DNA Databases in Criminal Investigation, J. Med. Ethics, vol.26, 266–271 (266), (2000).

[37] Save in exceptional cases rendering their preservation necessary for the solving of other offences laid down in art.200A par.1 CPC, upon the issuance of a written and well-reasoned indictment by the Judicial Council of the Court of Second Instance. The immediate destruction rule *does* apply however with respect to the cell sample, according to art.200A par.2 d' CPC, as it was previously pointed out.

[38] Said restraining sameness of the offences covered was reinstated by art.19 par.3 L.4322/2015.

[39] GG 209A'/5.12.1994.

dropping of the case (pursuant to art.43 paras.2–3 CPC), *unless* "their comparison with unidentified identical prints maintained in the same file turns out *positive*, in which case their retention is prolonged *till the irrevocable acquittal* of the individuals concerned" (art. 200A par.2d' CPC). All in all, the Greek DNA databasing policy continues to fall under the rubric of the so-called *expansive* countries, characterized by their "comparatively lower thresholds for inclusion and lengthier retention periods for profiles which may allow for a faster expansion in the number of profiles in the DNA database"[40]. In point of fact, even if designed with the aspiration to increase crime detection rates, yield a deterrence effect and bring art.200A CPC into closer alignment with the other European national regulations[41], extending the life of the *negative*, after their testing, genetic prints equates *in practice* with the abolition of the *sole* proviso of substantive legality for the measure's authorization and portends inclusion of a wider section of Greek citizenry in the national repository of genetic prints. At the same time, the setting of *temporal* boundaries in the hitherto unlimited retention period on the basis of the irrevocable acquittal or conviction of the profile's subject goes to some length to address a host of previously raised objections; yet it is hardly sufficient for transcending the enduring normative dysplasia.

Greek doctrinal opinion, sided with HDPA and NCHR, has been outspokenly critical of the 2009 reforms and the ensuing validation of a *particularly vague, generalized and defective in its formulation* provision which failed to meet *all qualitative features* necessitated by the ECtHR jurisprudence for the compatibility of restrictive measures with art.8 ECHR[42]. Regrettably, the non-incorporation of all the remedial suggestions postulated did not allow for the confinement of state's intervention to a level consonant with the fundamental investigative and data protection principles. To be more specific, as far as the *subjective profile entry criteria* are concerned, akin to genetic material's collection, the DNA profiles' storage in the special automatized file is currently carried out by the law enforcement authorities under the supervision of the Public Prosecutor referred to in art.4 L.2265/1994, immediately after the *positive or negative* identification of a person against whom *serious indications of guilt* are substantiated for the perpetration of a felony or misdemeanor punishable by imprisonment *of at least twelve months*[43]. The newly standardized expungement from the database of DNA profiles pertaining to the *irrevocably acquitted* ones or *those against whom proceedings were discontinued* adheres to the

---

[40] As opposed to the *restricted* ones, see on this distinction Santos et als., Forensic DNA Databases in European Countries: Is Size Linked to Performance?, Life Sciences, Society and Policy, vol.9, n.12, (2013), http://www.lsspjournal.com/content/9/1/12 For an interesting compilation of national legal essays, see Hindmarsh R./ Prainsack B. (eds.), Genetic Suspects- Global Governance of Forensic DNA Profiling and Databasing, Cambridge: Cambridge University Press, (2010).

[41] The rationale underlying the preservation of "negative" DNA profiles is attributed by the Explanatory Report of L.4274/2014 to the need to contrast them with other data banked unidentified/ orphan profiles with a view to ascertaining the suspect's involvement in unsolved offences.

[42] Apart from the authors mentioned in the previous references, see additionally Voultsos P. et als, Launching the Greek Forensic DNA Database- The Legal Framework and Arising Ethical Issues, Forensic Sci. Int. Genet., vol.5, n.5, 407–410, (2011).

[43] Hence, the measure's subjective ambit covers the same pool of people who are subjected to DNA sampling.

minimum European legal and jurisprudential standards applicable hereon[44], signaling thus an improvement. Even so, instead of the partly unfavorable solution promulgated with respect to the negative genetic prints, it would have been preferable to condition the measure's imposition upon *the irreversible conviction* of perpetrators *for grave malfeasances* of a deeper dye as well as upon *their granting their prior, valid and informed consent*, all through paying due regard to the criterion of *"reoffending"* described above.

Another step in the right direction consists, as previously mentioned, in the *curtailment of the storage period* for genetic prints belonging to the *irreversibly acquitted* people and its differentiation from the spanning *till death* profile retention which at present concerns *only* the convicts. The concrete delimitation of the filing's time horizon could be applauded as a first, *minimum* legislative improvement, respectful of the *principle of limited duration of data keeping* as well as of the *presumption of innocence*, while the designation of the *convict's death* as the ultimum eradication point withstands the running-the-gauntlet of its juris-comparative cross-examination with other expansive foreign provisions, which significantly elongate the retention period's end even beyond death and often provide for a specific age limit to be reached by the convict as an alternative terminal boundary[45]. That being noted, however, art.200A par.2 CPC's compliance with the principle of proportionality is not fully restored, insofar as *no* institutional assurances are furnished for: (*i*) the *in concreto*, actual justification of the dire need to keep profiles for the investigative end sought on the basis of *precise, empirical terms* vouching for the rational nexus between the measure's duration and the crime-fighting pursuit, (*ii*) the realization of *objective* criteria, besides the subjective ones, for the individualized enforcement of DNA databasing, (*iii*) the compulsory, immediate destruction of profiles following the storage period's lapse, (*iv*) the regulation –even under more lenient terms- of the maintenance of *unidentified* genetic prints, and of course, (*v*) the establishment of the preferential, more favorable penal treatment of *underage delinquents*, through the submittal of their DNA profiles to shorter retention periods than those of adult offenders, in fulfillment of the positive state obligation for augmented youth care, flowing from the Constitution (art.21 par. 1), the ECFR (art.24) as well as a wealth of other international and European conventional documents[46].

Lastly, art.200A par.2 CPC fails to encapsulate *well-fortified guarantee buttresses against potential abuses or arbitrariness* linked to the DNA databank's function on the one hand and codify *normative specializations of the data protection principles* on the other, falling, by the same token, short of the concomitant, binding requirements embedded in the constitutional charter as well as the European institutional and jurisprudential *acquis*. In particular, absent from the norm are: the analytical specification of the conditions for lawful processing of genetic prints after their filing; the nominative stipulation of the agencies vested with access rights; the delineation of invigorated

---

[44] Cf. Symeonidou-Kastanidou, *op. cit.*, 150ff.

[45] Cf. Santos et als, *ibid*.

[46] Such as the UN Convention on the Rights of the Child (20.11.1989), art.40, the UN Standard Minimum Rules for the Administration of Juvenile Justice ("Beijing Rules"- 29.11.1985), or the CoE European Convention on the exercise of Children's Rights (25.1.1996), arts.1 and 3–9. On the last two points described in text, cf. also critically HDPA, Opinion 2/2009, *op. cit*, item 3.1, NCHR, Decision of 18.2.2010, *ibid*, p.16, Aggelis, *ibid*, 947, Symeonidou-Kastanidou, *op. cit*, 155–156.

organizational and technical security measures for the retained profiles warranting the prevention of unauthorized third party access; the clear-cut prohibition to dispose of the registered prints for purposes other than the predefined, counter-crime policy related ones[47]; the fully-fledged delimitation of data suitability, usefulness and quantitative symmetry as well as of the overall necessity of their filing for accomplishing the intended repressive goal; the uninhibited enunciation of the rights of notification, correction and objection conferred upon the aggrieved individuals; and the submittal of the special archive's review to the control of the independent DPA[48].

Admittedly, in the assignment of the DNA databank's monitoring power to the *exclusive* (*not conjoint*[49]) competence of prosecutorial authorities, one can easily trace the Greek legislature's much criticized predilection to barter away HDPA's supervisory role in furtherance of investigative efficiency; a predilection finding supportive grounds in the case at issue upon the equivocal wording of art.30 par.5 of the Prüm Decision. Still, the absolute exclusion of HDPA's review from such a sensitive field of state action sits oddly with the Constitution (art.9A), the Additional Protocol of CoE Convention 108 (181 of the 8th.11.2001), Recommendation No. R(87)15 (Principle 1.1), Framework-Decision 2008/977/JHA (art.25), TFEU (art.16 par.2) and ECFR (art.8 par.3), where the obligation to entrust data processing's supervision to independent administrative authorities, equipped with the apposite expertise of their members, is entrenched.

4 Conclusion

The foregoing observations attest to the necessity of a major overhaul in the way the poorly shielded, for the greater part, Greek genetic citizens are treated by the domestic lawmaker. It is incumbent upon the latter to demonstrate by concrete evidence that the iterated invocation of constitutional rights' guarantees is more than a mere lip service, void of meaningful content. Until the imperative adoption of a *special* statute defining with extensive precision all conditions for the DNA databank's legitimate function on

---

[47] So as to prevent the so-called *"function creep"*, see Dahl J.-Y./ Sætnan A. R.(2009), "It All Happened so Slowly"- On Controlling Function Creep in Forensic DNA Databases, Int. J. Law, Crime & Justice, vol.37, n.3, 83–103, (2009).

[48] Given that "every usage of DNA information- every search run against a DNA record- is an intrusive act", said prerequisites should be met *each time* a citizen's DNA profile is accessed in order to ascertain that the "benefits outweigh the intrusion", see Mayer-Schönberger V., Strands of Privacy: DNA Databases and Informational Privacy and the OECD Guidelines, in Lazer D. (ed.), DNA and the Criminal Justice System: The Technology of Justice, 225–246 (233), Cambridge Mass: The MIT Press, (2004).

[49] Despite the ambivalent interpretation advanced hereupon by HDPA (Opinion 2/2009, *ibid*, item 3.2.), an *exclusive* competence is standardized –*illegitimately* as it is correctly pointed out by NCHR, Decision of 18.2.2010, *ibid*, p.18-19, Kotsalis, *ibid* and Symeonidou-Kastanidou, *ibid*, 158, on the basis of a reasoning akin to the one elaborated in text. *Contra* Aggelis, *op.cit*, 947, subscribing to the current normative exclusion. In the same direction Tsiftsoglou A., Public Security and Privacy, pp.151ff, 153, 155, Sakkoulas publ., (2015), arguing in favor of the Public Prosecution Office's custodial role as an adequate institutional guarantee.

the one hand and governing efficiently the individuals' substantive and procedural safeguards on the other, the potency of their protection will continue to ebb and flow in a piecemeal fashion and the Greek penal procedural system to be burdened with a contentious provision, which remains riddled with gaps, pitfalls and inconsistencies, adulterates its liberal nature, belittles fundamental rule of law conquests so ingrained into our collective understandings and upends much treasured, value-based balances in the name of strengthening penal repression. Interesting European exemplifications of such national *special* statutes with the ability to serve as blueprints have been brought into effect in: Italy[50], Spain[51], Denmark[52], Latvia[53], Luxembourg[54] etc.

---

[50] Legge 30 giugno 2009, n° 85, istituzione della banca dati nazionale del DNA e del laboratorio centrale per la banca dati nazionale del DNA. Adesione della Repubblica italiana al Trattato concluso il 27 maggio 2005 relativo all'approfondimento della cooperazione transfrontaliera, in particolare allo scopo di contrastare il terrorismo, la criminalità transfrontaliera e la migrazione illegale (Trattato di Prum), GU n.160 del 13 luglio 2009 - Supplemento ordinario n. 108.

[51] Ley Orgànica 10/2007, de 8 de octubre, reguladora de la base de datos policial sobre identificadores obtenidos a partir del AND, BOE núm. 242, 9.10.2007, p.40969.

[52] Lov om oprettelse af et centralt dna-profilregister, n.434 af 31.5.2000, as amended.

[53] DNS nacionālās datu bāzes izveidošanas un izmantošanas likums 17.6.2004, Latvijas Vēstnesis, 106 (3054), 7.7.2004., Ziņotājs, 14, 29.7.2004, as modified.

[54] Loi du 25 août 2006 relative aux procédures d'identification par empreintes génétiques en matière pénale et portant modification du Code d'instruction criminelle, MEM-A No.163, 8.9.2006, p.2984.

Security and Privacy in the Cloud

TREDISEC: Trust-Aware REliable and Distributed Information SEcurity in the Cloud

Julien Bringer[1], Beatriz Gallego[2], Ghassan Karame[3], Mathias Kohler[4], Panos Louridas[5], Melek Önen[6]([✉]), Hubert Ritzdorf[7], Alessandro Sorniotti[8], and David Vallejo[9]

[1] MORPHO, Paris, France
julien.bringer@morpho.com
[2] ATOS, Bezons, France
beatriz.gallego-nicasio@atos.net
[3] NEC, Heidelberg, Germany
Ghassan.Karame@neclab.eu
[4] SAP, Weinheim, Germany
mathias.kohler@sap.com
[5] GRNET, Athina, Greece
louridas@grnet.gr
[6] EURECOM, Biot, France
melek.onen@eurecom.fr
[7] ETHZ, Zurich, Switzerland
rihubert@inf.ethz.ch
[8] IBM, New York City, USA
aso@zurich.ibm.com
[9] ARSYS, Logrono, Spain
dvallejo@arsys.es

Abstract. While the revolutionary cloud computing paradigm offers substantial benefits to businesses, recent data breaches and the lack of dedicated end-to-end security solutions refrain the rapid adoption of this technology. The TREDISEC project aims at increasing trust in cloud computing by designing new security primitives ensuring data security and user privacy and supporting the underlying storage and computation technology at the same time.

Keywords: Cloud security · Data reduction · Privacy · Verifiability · Multi-tenancy · Access-control

1 Introduction

Cloud computing services are increasingly being adopted by individuals and companies thanks to their various advantages such as high storage and computation capacities, reliability and low maintenance costs. Yet, data security and user privacy remain the major concern for cloud customers since by moving their

© Springer International Publishing Switzerland 2015
S.K. Katsikas and A.B. Sideridis (Eds.): E-Democracy 2015, CCIS 570, pp. 193–197, 2015.
DOI: 10.1007/978-3-319-27164-4_14

data and their computing tasks into the cloud they inherently lend the control to cloud service providers. Therefore, customers nowadays call for end-to-end security solutions in order to retain full control over their data.

Implementing existing end-to-end security solutions unfortunately cancels out the advantages of the cloud technology such as cost effective storage. For example, cloud storage providers constantly look for techniques aimed to maximize space savings. One of the most popular techniques that has been adopted by many major providers to minimize redundant data is data deduplication. Unfortunately, deduplication and encryption are two conflicting technologies. Two identical data segments become indistinguishable after being encrypted. This means that if data are encrypted by users in a standard way, the cloud storage provider cannot apply deduplication.

In TREDISEC[1], we aim at designing new security primitives that not only ensure data protection and user privacy but also maintain the cost effectiveness of cloud systems. With this goal, we will first identify the functional requirements that are crucial to the cloud business and explore non-functional requirements such as storage efficiency and multi-tenancy. We will further analyze the conflicts between these requirements and security needs in order to develop new solutions that address these shortcomings and enhance security.

2   TREDISEC Challenges

The main challenges resulting from the combination of security, functional and non functional requirements, and which TREDISEC aims at resolving thanks to the newly designed primitives, are the following:

2.1   Data Confidentiality with Data Reduction

As already mentioned in the introduction, storage efficiency functions such as deduplication or compression become ineffective when data is encrypted. A technique which has been initially proposed in convergent encryption [7] which derives the data encryption key from the data itself, namely by computing the hash of the data segment: whenever a user wishes to encrypt a data segment, it first hashes the data to obtain the encryption key and further encrypts the data with this computed key. Although convergent encryption seems to be a promising solution to achieve deduplication and confidentiality at the same time, existing solutions based on this technique either do not achieve acceptable levels of security [10,18] or rely on the existence of a fully trusted third party [3,14,16]. TREDISEC's new primitives will provide stronger data confidentiality guarantees while benefiting from the various advantages of data reduction techniques in the cloud.

2.2   Secure Data Processing with Multi-tenancy

In order not to cancel out the performance advantages of the cloud, there is a strong need for privacy preserving data processing solutions. Among data processing primitives, word search is one of the most fundamental operation. Classical

---
[1] http://www.tredisec.eu.

encryption solutions prevent the cloud from operating over encrypted data. Recent privacy preserving word search solutions such as [5,6,13,15] ensure both the privacy of the data and the query for a user querying her personal data. These solutions are not yet directly applicable in real industrial strength use cases. TREDISEC will extend current solutions with advanced features such as the optimization of the encryption operation or the ability to delegate search operations to authorized third parties and consider the multi-tenant environment whereby a large number of tenants outsource their data and computation to the cloud.

2.3 Verifiability with Data Reduction and Multi-tenancy

Since data storage and processing operations are performed remotely by potentially malicious clouds, end-users should receive some guarantees on both the storage and processing of data. Existing storage integrity solutions rely on Proofs of Retrievability (PoR) [1,2,8,12,17] which provide the end-user with the assurance that a data segment is actually stored in the remote storage; these solutions still induce high computational costs and cannot be combined with data reduction techniques. TREDISEC will enable the verification of data retrievability while data is deduplicated or compressed. Furthermore, data reduction techniques usually imply the storage of a single copy of data for several users; in this case, users having already outsourced data should prove their actual ownership. Existing Proof of Ownership (PoW) [4,9] solutions are unfortunately not yet mature enough in terms of both performance and security. TREDISEC will design efficient and secure PoW schemes where deduplication takes place among multiple tenants and over encrypted data. Additionally, TREDISEC will also investigate existing processing verifiability solutions such as probabilistically checkable proofs in order to provide end-users with some cryptographic tools that efficiently verify the correctness of some dedicated functions.

2.4 Distributed Enforcement of Access Control Policies for Multi-tenancy Settings

The security of a multi-tenant system require reliable access control polices and enforcement mechanisms. Current Attribute Based Access Control (ABAC) models such as the one in [11] fall short in the multi-tenancy settings since users' attributes can be distributed across different trust domains. TREDISEC will extend current ABAC models to govern access control in multi-tenant cloud storage systems. Furthermore, current cloud platforms are agnostic to the concept of shared ownership. TREDISEC will design new cryptographic primitives to enforce distributed usage of data while preventing malicious tenants from combining their credentials and escalating their access rights. TREDISEC will also investigate the problem of secure data deletion: end-users will have cryptographic guarantees on the timely deletion of their data and the back-up copies.

3   Conclusion

The ultimate goal of TREDISEC is to converge to a unified framework where these primitives are integrated and where all objectives are satisfied to the highest extent possible. With this goal, we will explore different architectural models while following the end-to-end security principle as closely as allowed by functional and non-functional requirements. The resulting TREDISEC framework will be evaluated across several different use cases.

Acknowledgments. This work was supported by the TREDISEC project (G.A. no 644412), funded by the European Union (EU) under the Information and Communication Technologies (ICT) theme of the Horizon 2020 (H2020) research and innovation programme.

References

1. Ateniese, G., Burns, R.C., Curtmola, R., Herring, J., Kissner, L., Peterson, Z.N.J., Song, D.: Provable data possession at untrusted stores. In: ACM Conference on Computer and Communications Security, pp. 598–609. ACM (2008)
2. Azraoui, M., Elkhiyaoui, K., Molva, R., Önen, M.: StealthGuard: proofs of retrievability with hidden watchdogs. In: Proceedings of 19th European Symposium on Research in Computer Security (ESORICS), pp. 239–256 (2014)
3. Bellare, M., Keelveedhi, S., Ristenpart, T.: Dupless: server-aided encryption for deduplicated storage. In: Proceedings of the 22nd USENIX Conference on Security, pp. 179–194 (2013)
4. Blasco, J., Di Pietro, R., Orfila, A., Sorniotti, A.: A tunable proof of ownership scheme for deduplication using bloom filters. In: Proceedings of IEEE Conference on Communications and Network Security (CNS), pp. 481–489 (2014)
5. Blass, E.-O., Di Pietro, R., Molva, R., Önen, M.: PRISM – privacy-preserving search in mapreduce. In: Fischer-Hübner, S., Wright, M. (eds.) PETS 2012. LNCS, vol. 7384, pp. 180–200. Springer, Heidelberg (2012)
6. Curtmola, R., Garay, J., Kamara, S., Ostrovsky, R.: Searchable symmetric encryption: improved definitions and efficient constructions. In: Proceedings of the 13th ACM Conference on Computer and Communications Security, CCS 2006, pp. 79–88. ACM (2006). ISBN 1-59593-518-5
7. Douceur, J.R., Adya, A., Bolosky, W.J., Simon, P., Theimer, M.: Reclaiming space from duplicate files in a serverless distributed file system. In: 22nd International Conference on Distributed Computing Systems, pp. 617–624. IEEE (2002)
8. Erway, C., Küpçü, A., Papamanthou, C., Tamassia, R.: Dynamic provable data possession. In Proceedings of the 16th ACM Conference on Computer and Communications Security, CCS 2009, pp. 213–222 (2009)
9. Halevi, S., Harnik, D., Pinkas, B., Shulman-Peleg, A.: Proofs of ownership in remote storage systems. In: Proceedings of the 18th ACM Conference on Computer and Communications Security, (CCS), pp. 491–500 (2011)
10. Harnik, D., Pinkas, B., Shulman-Peleg, A.: Side channels in cloud services: deduplication in cloud storage. In: IEEE Security and Privacy, pp. 40–47 (2010)
11. Jin, X., Krishnan, R., Sandhu, R.S.: A unified attribute-based access control model covering DAC, MAC and BAC. In: DBSec (2012)

12. Juels, A., Kaliski Jr., B.S.: Pors: proofs of retrievability for large files. In: Ning, P., De Capitani di Vimercati, S., Syverson, P.F. (eds.) ACM Conference on Computer and Communications Security, pp. 584–597. ACM (2007). http://dblp.uni-trier. de/db/conf/ccs/ccs2007.html. ISBN 978-1-59593-703-2

13. Kerschbaum, F., Härterich, M., Grofig, P., Kohler, M., Schaad, A., Schröpfer, A., Tighzert, W.: Optimal re-encryption strategy for joins in encrypted databases. In: Wang, L., Shafiq, B. (eds.) DBSec 2013. LNCS, vol. 7964, pp. 195–210. Springer, Heidelberg (2013)

14. Liu, J., Asokan, N., Pinkas, B.: Secure deduplication of encrypted data without additional independent servers. In: Proceedings of IEEE Conference on Communications Security (CCS) (2015)

15. Popa, R.A., Redfield, C.S., Zeldovich, N., Balakrishnan, H., Catherine, M.: Cryptdb: protecting confidentiality with encrypted query processing. In: Symposium on Operating Systems Principles (SOSP) (2011)

16. Puzio, P., Molva, R., Önen, M., Loureiro, S.: Cloudedup: secure deduplication with encrypted data for cloud storage. In: Proceedings of the IEEE 5th International Conference on Cloud Computing Technology and Science (CloudCom), pp. 363–370 (2013)

17. Shacham, H., Waters, B.: Compact proofs of retrievability. In: Pieprzyk, J. (ed.) ASIACRYPT 2008. LNCS, vol. 5350, pp. 90–107. Springer, Heidelberg (2008)

18. Storer, M.W., Greenan, K., DE Long, D., Miller, E.L.: Secure data deduplication. In: Proceedings of the 4th ACM International Workshop on Storage Security and Survivability, pp. 1–10 (2008)

Towards User-Centric Management of Security and Dependability in Clouds of Clouds

Marc Lacoste[1]([✉]) and Fabien Charmet[2]

[1] Orange Labs, Issy-les-Moulineaux, France
marc.lacoste@orange.com
[2] Télécom SudParis, CNRS Samovar UMR 5157, Évry, France

Abstract. SUPERCLOUD aims to fulfill the vision of user-centric secure and dependable clouds of clouds through a new security management architecture and infrastructure. It will support user-centric deployments across multi-clouds enabling composition of innovative trustworthy services, thus uplifting Europe innovation capacity and competitiveness.

Keywords: Clouds-of-clouds security · User-centric security · Self-service security · Self-managed security · End-to-end security · Resilience

1 Introduction

Today, the cloud is moving distributed. However, the overall distributed cloud paradigm still remains highly provider-centric. Several major security and dependability challenges are ahead. First, *cloud infrastructures are extremely vulnerable to attacks spanning several layers* (e.g., customer VMs, cloud provider services, provider hypervisor). The hypervisor is notably a target of choice due to its complexity. Hence the difficulty of an integrated protection. Second, *security management lacks flexibility and control*. The problem comes from heterogeneity of security components and policies between cloud providers. This has a strong security impact by introducing more vulnerabilities due to mismatching APIs and workflows. And third, *security administration challenges* remain. Manual administration of protection of such infrastructures is clearly out of reach because of the complexity and heterogeneity of their components. Automation of security management is clearly necessary but lacking today.

2 The SUPERCLOUD Project

The SUPERCLOUD project [1] proposes new security and dependability infrastructure management paradigms for clouds of clouds. The security architecture will be *user-centric*: self-service clouds of clouds enable customers to define their own protection requirements and avoid provider lock-ins. Security will also be *self-managed*: self-protecting multi-clouds facilitate security administration thanks to automation.

© Springer International Publishing Switzerland 2015
S.K. Katsikas and A.B. Sideridis (Eds.): E-Democracy 2015, CCIS 570, pp. 198–201, 2015.
DOI: 10.1007/978-3-319-27164-4_15

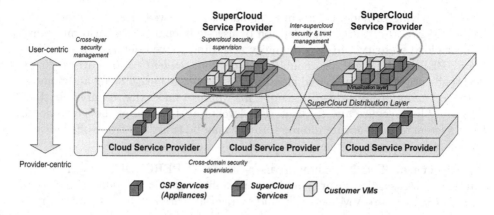

Fig. 1. Super-cloud architecture.

3   Approach

The project will build on the concept of *super-cloud* [2] as new architectural abstraction for distributed cloud security management. The super-cloud is a distributed management plane providing an end-to-end interface between user-centric and provider-centric views of multiple clouds (see Fig. 1). It captures both distributed resource abstraction, and flexible but unified control for security and resilience across different clouds. The super-cloud is essentially a logically-centralized control plane for security, not only for computation and storage, in line with recent advances in cloud computing, but also for the network, with many simplicity, interoperability, and flexibility benefits.

4   Objectives

SUPERCLOUD aims to achieve four key properties. First, *self-service security* through a cloud architecture giving users the flexibility to define their own protection requirements and instantiate policies accordingly. Second, *self-managed security* through an autonomic security management framework that operates seamlessly over compute, storage and network layers, and across provider domains to ensure compliance with security policies. Third, *end-to-end security* by proposing trust models and security mechanisms that enable composition of services and trust statements across provider domains. Finally, *resilience* through a resource management framework safely composing provider-agnostic resources using primitives from different providers.

5   Architecture and Key Enabling Technologies

SUPERCLOUD will enable *user-centric security and dependability* through a unified distribution layer for cloud resources, independently from their type and from underlying providers. This intermediate layer between resource production by providers and resource consumption by users will enable high customizability of user cloud security and dependability according to well-defined SLAs.

SUPERCLOUD will also enable *provider-independent control* over security and resilience of the distributed cloud infrastructure, security being autonomous managed and guaranteed end-to-end. This will also make the resource distribution layer both secure and resilient. The level of abstraction of the super-cloud, from system to middleware interoperability may be tuned for trade-offs between user-centric and provider-centric control for security services.

Architecture. The Northbound, user-centric SUPERCLOUD interface will implement self-service security and dependability, allowing to build *Self-Service Clouds* (SSC) where VM, network, and storage security can be customized independently from the underlying provider. Such clouds may be defined from the service level to the full IaaS, with also complex trust relationships between resources and SSCs, according to ecosystem relationships between SUPERCLOUD providers. The Southbound, provider-centric SUPERCLOUD interface will define a unified security and dependability management plane of compute, data, and network resources independently from providers.

SUPERCLOUD will fulfill that vision with a two-level infrastructure. The Northbound interface will be captured by a *distributed infrastructure* federating multiple cloud resources to build SSCs, and to implement self-service security. The Southbound interface will be captured by a monitoring infrastructure providing *a set of security and resilience services* to guarantee security of the overall SUPERCLOUD architecture. It will realize self-managed security, end-to-end security, and resilience. Thus, the super-cloud will allow both user-controlled management of security of SSCs and unified control of security of resources of the underlying cloud providers.

Key Enabling Technologies. For *computation*, the super-cloud will provide both a distributed abstraction layer for computational resources (VMs) independently from the provider, and an automated security monitoring infrastructure, enabling to supervise security both across cloud domains and throughout layers. It will also allow two-dimensional management of trust, by composing chains of trust, both vertically across layers, and horizontally across domains, relying on hardware-enabled security mechanisms as trust anchors. Nested virtualization will be investigated as a core technology for implementing such security management paradigms.

For *data management*, the super-cloud will provide a uniform abstraction to manage stored data in a multi-provider context for security services that rely on access control policies and cryptographic protection. It will offer a careful balance between user- and provider-control over such security services and guarantee data resilience through redundancy over multiple providers.

For *network management*, the super-cloud will use virtual networks spanning multiple cloud providers that can be easily managed using expressive security policies. It will notably guarantee security and resilience, both of the data plane (network interconnection within and between cloud platforms), and of the control plane. The super-cloud will also perform two-dimensional network monitoring and forensics to guarantee a sanitized and auditable network environment, both at the cloud and super-cloud levels. SUPERCLOUD will leverage the benefits of *Software-Defined Networking* (SDN), through the development of a platform creating a common virtual network abstraction to SUPERCLOUD users, and which spans multiple heterogeneous cloud providers.

6   Expected Results

SUPERCLOUD will build a self-management infrastructure for security and dependability of heterogeneous resources across federated clouds. Customers will be provided with self-service environments enabling adaptive, customizable security for their cloud applications and services. SUPERCLOUD will also provide innovative cryptographic methods and tools for protecting data across distributed clouds through on-demand data security services, such as access control, blind computation, and data availability. Finally, SUPERCLOUD will enable resilient network-as-a-service, leveraging software-defined networking paradigms. It will provide strong guarantees for end-to-end security and integrated trust management across multiple infrastructure layers and cloud domains. The SUPERCLOUD core technology will be validated through testbed integration for real-world use cases in the healthcare domain.

Acknowledgments. This paper is based on contributions from the entire SUPERCLOUD consortium. The project leading to this application received funding from the European Union Horizon 2020 Research and Innovation Program under grant agreement no. 643964. This work is supported (in part) by the Swiss State Secretariat for Education Research and Innovation (SERI) under contract number 15.0091

References

1. SUPERCLOUD H2020 project. http://www.supercloud-project.eu/
2. Williams, D., Jamjoom, H., Weatherspoon, H.: Plug into the supercloud. IEEE Internet Comput. **17**(2), 28–34 (2013)

Cloud Security and Privacy by Design

Thomas Lorünser[1]([✉]), Thomas Länger[2], and Daniel Slamanig[3]

[1] AIT Austrian Institute of Technology, Vienna, Austria
thomas.loruenser@ait.ac.at
[2] University of Lausanne, Lausanne, Switzerland
thomas.laenger@unil.ch
[3] Graz University of Technology, Graz, Austria
daniel.slamanig@iaik.tugraz.at

Abstract. In current cloud paradigms and models, security and privacy are typically treated as add-ons and are not adequately integrated as functions of the cloud systems. The EU Project PRISMACLOUD (Horizon 2020 programme; duration 2/2015–7/2018) sets out to address this challenge and yields a portfolio of novel technologies to build security enabled cloud services, guaranteeing the required security by built-in strong cryptography.

Keywords: Secure cloud computing · Cryptography · Privacy · Information theoretic security · Usability · Security by design

1 Motivation and Objectives

With an annual turnover in the region of USD 150 billion, and with huge growing rates, the market for cloud computing can be considered as a major growth area in ICT [14]. Several technology research and advisory firms attribute a bright economic future, e.g., the management consulter Accenture states that 46 % of all IT spending by 2016 will be for cloud-related platforms and applications [10]. The European Commission promotes in its "European Cloud Computing Strategy" of 2012 [4] the rapid adoption of cloud computing in all sectors of the economy to boost productivity. The Commission concludes that "cloud computing has the potential to slash users' IT expenditure and to enable many new services to be developed. Using the cloud, even the smallest firms shall be able to reach out to ever larger markets, while it will enable governments to make their services more attractive and efficient while at the same time cueven while reining in spending."

Cloud computing is a new delivery model of processing, storage and communication resources and will be at the heart of future ICT applications. In combination with other IT mega-trends like Big Data and the Internet of Things, it will give rise to many new smart applications in numerous domains. However, besides the benefits of cloud computing, new problems are arising. Many are not yet sufficiently solved, especially information security and privacy problems. The fundamental concept of the cloud is storage and processing by a third party (the

S.K. Katsikas and A.B. Sideridis (Eds.): E-Democracy 2015, CCIS 570, pp. 202–206, 2015.
DOI: 10.1007/978-3-319-27164-4_16

cloud service provider) which is no longer comparable to traditional outsourc-ing, especially when a public cloud service is used. The intrinsic multi-tenancy of cloud computing and the broad connectivity introduces new security threats, leading to tremendous risk for personal and sensitive data. Organizational and legal tools have been introduced to increase trust in the cloud provider, but recent incidents show that these measures are by far not sufficient to guard personal data and trade secrets against illegal interceptions, insider threats, or vulnerabilities.

The PRISMACLOUD consortium aims at a new approach towards cloud secu-rity within the EU Horizon 2020 research framework. For us, the only reason-able way to achieve the required security properties for outsourced data is by adopting suitable cryptographic mechanisms. Thus, the goal of PRISMACLOUD is to develop the next-generation of cryptographically secured cloud services with security and privacy built in by design and from end-to-end. The main objectives of PRISMACLOUD are:

- Development of cryptographic tools to protect the security of data during its lifecycle in the cloud.
- Development of cryptographic tools and methods to protect privacy of users.
- Creation of enabling technologies for cloud infrastructures.
- Development of a methodology for secure service composition.
- Experimental evaluation and validation of project results.

The outcome of the project will contribute to enable trustworthy and privacy preserving services to be deployed in only partially trusted cloud infrastructures, i.e. in the public cloud setting.

2 Concept and Approach

The concept underlying PRISMACLOUD is to develop and improve novel crypto-graphic technologies and to study how they can be integrated in a user-friendly way for improving the security of services for both businesses and individuals. Ideally data in the cloud shall be protected from end-to-end with strong crypto-graphic guarantees and users shall remain in full control over their data. At the same time, privacy enhancing technologies shall be applied to minimize the infor-mation a client involuntarily discloses while using a cloud service. The project will present new secure cloud technologies for European citizens, administra-tion, and industries, with strong security guarantees capable of increasing trust in outsourcing storage and computation to the cloud.

The PRISMACLOUD approach is centred around research and development activities for bringing recent and novel cryptographic tools to practical applica-tion. Innovations for trustworthy cloud computing shall be created to the benefit of European industry and society [4]. The main pillars in PRISMACLOUD enable *verifiability of the cloud*, improve *privacy enhancing technologies* and develop methods for protecting *confidentiality and integrity for data at rest*. Further-more, a broad set of accompanying measures will be carried out for assisting the introduction of the new technologies to the market and thus to the user.

To enable **verifiability**, we develop *verifiable and authenticity preserving data processing tools*. The correctness of outsourced computations (e.g., by means of [2,15]) will be verified, and malleable as well as functional signatures (cf. [3]) will secure the authenticity and verifiability of processes and workflows. These cryptographic primitives allow for controlled modification of authenticated data. Every modification beyond what is allowed renders the authentication tag (i.e., signature or tag of a message authentication code) invalid. Although currently only linear functions (like counting and summation) and polynomial functions of bounded degree (like variance) are practically usable from a performance point of view, we have identified applications, e.g. in our eHealth pilot, where such tools allow to greatly improve the security of services, i.e., the leakage of sensitive data can be effectively reduced when processing data in the cloud.

Another technology in the field of verifiability provides means to digitally sign graph representations of virtualised infrastructures [6]. Basically, such a signature binds the verification of a (human) cloud auditor to an actual infrastructure and it enables the infrastructure provider to prove topology properties of the virtualised infrastructure (like connectivity isolation) to customers without revealing too much details of the topology (e.g., information about configurations of other tenants also using the infrastructure). In PRISMACLOUD we will develop the necessary tools to verify and certify the *integrity of virtualized infrastructures*.

Research in data minimization technologies for *privacy preserving service usage* will increase the **privacy of users**. It is usually not necessary for users to reveal more than very little information when needing to prove an authorisation or the possession of a right. Still, the cloud provider must be cryptographically reassured of the user's authorization. We will use technology related to *attribute-based anonymous credentials* (Privacy ABCs) [1] and related concepts to enable the implementation of privacy protecting and data minimising authentication and authorisation systems for cloud applications and services. Such primitives allow to encode attributes into digital credentials in a way, that attributes can be selectively disclosed (or statements about the encoded attributes can be proven without revealing their effective values) in an anonymous and unlinkable way. Privacy ABCs will enable users to prove to services that they are authorized while respecting data minimization and without having to reveal their identity.

We will also improve methods for the *anonymization of big data* and demonstrate its' applicability in the healthcare domain, i.e. for the purpose of medical research. Thereby, algorithmic approaches such as *k-anonymity* [13] provide a tool for preventing subjects of the data to be identified, while leaving the data practically useful for analysis. As, however, achieving optimal *k*-anonymity is **NP**-hard [8], these approaches are currently only suitable for relatively small data set. Our goal is to improve the effectively of these approaches for the anonymization of very large data sets.

For **protecting data at rest**, we support novel concepts, which will at the same time enable dynamic collaboration, as well controlled sharing of information. Currently, most available cloud storage services store the data either unencrypted or apply encryption which remains under complete control of the cloud service provider; some cloud users wrap a layer of cryptography around their data before they store it in the cloud. In the first case, the cloud provider has to be trusted to provide effective protection of the data as regards confidentiality and integrity. This includes all copies and replications of the data which are created for availability purposes in all layers of the storage architecture. Users also have to consider, that the cloud provider is capable of reading all the data in plain and has to be trusted not to exploit that knowledge. In the second case, collaboration on the data is severely impeded, and availability of the data is threatened if the user loses its cryptographic keys.

For *unstructured data*, we will develop a new distributed system approach by applying the cloud-of-clouds paradigm. The cryptographic storage network for the secure, distributed storage of data uses an information-dispersal algorithm, based on secret sharing mechanisms [11]. The information is split into a number of shares, of which any subset of a fixed number allows the reconstruction of the original data. This approach is capable of *long-term security and everlasting privacy* [9]. We will investigate methods to efficiently realize such systems with improved practical usability [7,12]. In the case of structured data or legacy applications, we will supply *cryptography for seamless service integration*, and in particular format- as well as order-preserving encryption and tokenization [17].

The cryptography research and implementation in PRISMACLOUD is accompanied by **methodology, guidelines, and evaluation** activities, supporting the diffusion of the results to the users. A *standards action plan* containing a set of recommendations and recommended actions to ensure an optimized impact of PRISMACLOUD results for qualified practical application will be developed in accordance with the European Cloud Computing Strategy's goals to "help cloud take off" [4]. We will present a *holistic security model* and methods to compose security and privacy preserving services in a convenient way. *Usability concepts and end-user aspects* are taken seriously and will guide all technical aspects in the project [16]. Besides licit use, we will assess the impact of potential criminal uses and misuses of the secure cloud infrastructures to foster, enhance, and promote cybercrime [5].

The PRISMACLOUD results shall be practically *demonstrated and validated* by demonstrating implementations of three industry contributed use cases in the domains of eHealth, eGovernment, and smart city, where personal and other data of highest sensitivity is involved.

References

1. Camenisch, J., Lehmann, A., Neven, G.: Electronic identities need private credentials. IEEE Sec. Priv. **10**(1), 80–83 (2012). http://doi.ieeecomputersociety.org/10.1109/MSP.2012.7
2. Catalano, D.: Homomorphic signatures and message authentication codes. In: Abdalla, M., De Prisco, R. (eds.) SCN 2014. LNCS, vol. 8642, pp. 514–519. Springer, Heidelberg (2014)
3. Demirel, D., Derler, D., Hanser, C., Pöhls, H.C., Slamanig, D., Traverso, G.: PRISMACLOUD D4.4: overview of functional and malleable signature schemes. Technical report, H2020 Prismacloud (2015). www.prismacloud.eu

4. European commission: European cloud computing strategy "unleashing the potential of cloud computing in Europe" (2012). http://ec.europa.eu/digital-agenda/en/european-cloud-computing-strategy. Accessed 31 March 2015

5. Ghernaouti, S.: Cyber Power - Crime, Conflict and Security in Cyberspace. EPFL Press, Burlington (2013)

6. Groß, T.: Signatures and efficient proofs on committed graphs and NP-statements. In: Böhme, R., Okamoto, T. (eds.) FC 2015. LNCS, vol. 8975, pp. 293–314. Springer, Heidelberg (2015)

7. Lorünser, T., Happe, A., Slamanig, D.: ARCHISTAR: towards secure and robust cloud based data sharing. In: IEEE 7th International Conference on Cloud Computing Technology and Science, CloudCom 2015, Vancouver, 30 November–3 December 2015. IEEE (2015)

8. Meyerson, A., Williams, R.: On the complexity of optimal k-anonymity. In: Symposium on Principles of Database Systems, PODS 2004, New York, USA (2004)

9. Müller-Quade, J., Unruh, D.: Long-term security and universal composability. J. Crypt. **23**(4), 594–671 (2010)

10. PRWeb: a cloud computing forecast summary for 2013–2017 from IDC, gartner and KPMG, citing a study by accenture (2013). http://www.prweb.com/releases/2013/11/prweb11341594.htm. Accessed 31 March 2015

11. Shamir, A.: How to share a secret. Commun. ACM **22**(11), 612–613 (1979)

12. Slamanig, D., Hanser, C.: On cloud storage and the cloud of clouds approach. In: ICITST-2012, pp. 649–655. IEEE Press (2012)

13. Sweeney, L.: k-anonymity: a model for protecting privacy. Int. J. Uncertainty Fuzziness Knowl.-Based Syst. **10**(5), 557–570 (2002)

14. Transparency market research: cloud computing services market - global industry size, share, trends, analysis and forecasts 2012–2018 (2012). http://www.transparencymarketresearch.com/cloud-computing-services-market.html. Accessed 31 March 2015

15. Walfish, M., Blumberg, A.J.: Verifying computations without reexecuting them. Commun. ACM **58**(2), 74–84 (2015)

16. Wästlund, E., Angulo, J., Fischer-Hübner, S.: Evoking comprehensive mental models of anonymous credentials. In: iNetSeC, pp. 1–14 (2011)

17. Weiss, M., Rozenberg, B., Barham, M.: Practical solutions for format-preserving encryption. CoRR abs/1506.04113 (2015). http://arxiv.org/abs/1506.04113

Secure Architectures and Applications

Secure Hardware-Software Architectures for Robust Computing Systems

Elias Athanasopoulos[1], Martin Boehner[2], Sotiris Ioannidis[1],
Cristiano Giuffrida[3], Dmitry Pidan[4], Vassilis Prevelakis[5(✉)], Ioannis Sourdis[6],
Christos Strydis[7], and John Thomson[8]

[1] Foundation for Research and Technology – Hellas, Heraklion, Greece
[2] Elektrobit Automotive GMBH, Stuttgart, Germany
[3] Vrije Universiteit Amsterdam, Amsterdam, The Netherlands
[4] IBM – Science and Technology LTD, Haifa, Israel
[5] Technische Universität Braunschweig, Braunschweig, Germany
prevelakis@ida.ing.tu-bs.de
[6] Chalmers Tekniska Högskola, Gothenburg, Sweden
[7] Neurasmus BV, Rotterdam, The Netherlands
[8] OnApp Limited, Cambridge, UK

Abstract. The Horizon 2020 SHARCS project is a framework for designing, building and demonstrating secure-by-design applications and services, that achieve end-to-end security for their users. In this paper we present the basic elements of SHARCS that will provide a powerful foundation for designing and developing trustworthy, secure-by-design applications and services for the Future Internet.

Keywords: Embedded systems · Security-by-design · SHARCS

1 Introduction

The Horizon 2020 SHARCS project aims at designing, building and demonstrating secure-by-design system architectures that deliver end-to-end security for their users. The new technologies developed will be directly utilizable by applications and services that require end-to-end security.

Tremendous technological achievements such as Medical IoT, Smart Cars, Smarter Cities, Smarter Grids etc. have led society as a whole and individual citizens to rely ever more on critical systems which sense and control the physical environment. Such "Cyber Physical Systems" (CPS) use a blend of embedded devices and traditional computing systems, and a variety of communication channels. The adoption of CPS necessitates the revisiting the security stack to ensure that the new generation of devices and services encompass lessons learned as part of the ICT cyber-security battles of the last decades.

This work is supported by the H2020 ICT-32-2014 project SHARCS under Grant greement number 644571.

S.K. Katsikas and A.B. Sideridis (Eds.): E-Democracy 2015, CCIS 570, pp. 209–212, 2015.
DOI: 10.1007/978-3-319-27164-4_17

To address the pervasive security problems, the SHARCS project will push security mechanisms down the system stack, from software to hardware.

Hardware security mechanisms, in most cases, have the advantage of being more efficient in terms of performance, simplicity, and power usage. SHARCS will also implement a series of bottom-up design and implementation concepts to explore the entire system stack, and the interactions between the various components. Some of the challenges that will be addressed by SHARCS include: how to utilize the new functionality, how maintain backwards compatibility with legacy applications, and how to handle the interactions between different administrative domains (e.g., one that has high security requirements and one with low security expectations). SHARCS also investigates how to dynamically recover from errors and how to minimize the burden on software developers and users.

The main objectives of the SHARCS project are the following:

1. Extend existing hardware and software platforms towards developing secure-by-design enabling technologies. .
2. Leverage hardware technology features present in today's processors and embedded devices to facilitate software-layer security.
3. Build methods and tools for providing maximum possible security-by-design guarantees for legacy systems.
4. Evaluate acceptance, effectiveness and platform independence of SHARCS technologies and processes.
5. Create high impact in the security and trustworthiness of ICT systems.

2   Concept and Approach

Ideally when designing a secure system, one would like to take a clean-slate approach. That is, start from the assumption that existing hardware, operating systems, programming languages, software applications and services, are all sharing vulnerabilities and bad design choices in terms of security properties and guarantees that one must start from scratch. Such an approach has its merits, as long-term security in a computing system is not viable when one has to continuously patch and repair newly surfacing vulnerabilities. However, obviously starting from zero and re-building everything securely is not *always* realistic. To stress this, we give two real-world examples from different application domains which demonstrate that there are cases where a *clean-slate* approach makes perfect sense, and cases where rebuilding everything from scratch is clearly not an option. Later in this part we discuss a *third* example, which manifests that there are also in-the-middle options, where a clean-slate approach may be possible, as well as a relaxed version where some hardware parts have been replaced with software ones (e.g., hypervisor).

Consider a medical implant designed and implemented for a very particular reason: for the treatment of seizures. This device must meet very precise security constraints and it cannot afford failures (e.g., human life in jeopardy). Moreover, this device has to operate using low power consumption. Nevertheless, the most important properties of this device are: (a) it is custom made, not generic-purpose, (b) *all* layers, hardware and software, are typically controlled or assembled by one manufacturer, therefore security can be incorporated holistically, and (c) there is strict regulation control over the requirements of the device. In this case a clean-slate approach is the ideal strategy, since the device can and should be secure-by-design for meeting the advanced security expectations.

Now, let us consider the opposite extreme, an application running on an untrusted cloud infrastructure. In this case, the application is not as security critical as the medical implant, however, we need to enforce security guarantees for its secure operation. The properties of this setup are completely opposite with those of a medical implant: (a) the cloud is a generic infrastructure, where applications with different profiles execute, (b) layers are typically controlled by different entities, and (c) no security related regulations control the requirements of the cloud. In this setup a clean-slate approach is not an option, however enhancements may be incorporated to the hypervisor to emulate parts of the hardware that are not available. Where changes to the hypervisor are not feasible, more relaxed security may still be offered by software means. For example, we can link the running application with code, which monitors the execution and can infer – using existing features in unmodified hardware – possible violations at run-time.

Finally, as a third example, consider a smart car. This case falls in between the use-cases previously discussed, namely the medical implant and the application running in the public cloud. Depending on the function being automated, it may or may not use generic hardware, it may or may not be completely controlled by the manufacturer and the level of regulation may vary accordingly. Under the SHARCS framework, a smart car device may rely either on hardware security or hypervisor enhancements for emulating parts of the hardware that are not available.

Clearly, there is no *single solution-for-everything*. In SHARCS we propose to fill security gaps, by offering a set of *different models* that are viable in *different application domains*. In Fig. 1 we present the different SHARCS framework operational models. We start from the left by introducing a full-featured SHARCS stack, which incorporates security changes in all layers. This model offers security guarantees for critical applications, such as a medical implant, control over critical infrastructure, and smart cars applications (for example, computer-controlled safety devices that take over driving duties, such as braking or steering, in emergencies), and follows a clean-slate approach. Obviously, as we have already analyzed, a clean-slate approach is not always feasible. Therefore, we also propose a more relaxed model utilizing standard hardware and where the hardware modifications have been replaced with hypervisor modifications. This relaxed model, may be suitable for applications such as secure cloud, critical infrastructure and smart car applications where enhanced hardware cannot be used. An advantage of this model is that in some cases it may be applied as a software upgrade to existing hardware. Last, we propose a model incorporating software only changes, where we seek to contribute lessons learned in SHARCS in cases where neither the hardware nor hypervisor may be enhanced.

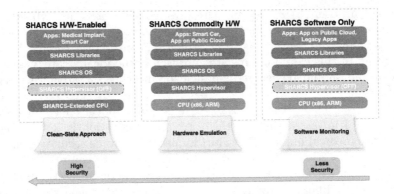

Fig. 1. Examples of different SHARCS framework operational models. Ideally, SHARCS pushes new functionality to the hardware level, and provides all necessary software-stack changes for producing and running hardened applications. However, modifying all levels is not always possible, therefore we provide two more *relaxed* SHARCS-supported models. First, one that incorporates zero hardware changes. For realizing this model all SHARCS features are communicated to a commodity processor (x86 or ARM) using a hypervisor. Second, one that incorporates zero SHARCS features implemented at the CPU, and there is no hypervisor available. For realizing this model, we link the application with SHARCS libraries and add kernel modules at the OS, which embed code for reliably and securely monitoring the application at run-time.

SHARCS incorporates new security features in hardware, leverages existing hardware features for building defense mechanisms, and propagates all needed changes to the software stack for supporting new hardened applications and old legacy ones with increased security guarantees. SHARCS employs novel architectural concepts such as Instruction Set Randomization (ISR) [1] and Control-Flow Integrity (CFI) [2], and the design and implementation of a new policy, which can be applied to legacy applications, where software re-compilation is not possible. This new policy is enforced using an existing hardware feature, available in the x86 platform, which is not designed primarily for security. SHARCS, also, takes advantage of additional techniques, such as information flow tracking, secure H/W memory, fine-grained memory protection, and type safety.

References

1. Kc, G.S., Keromytis, A.D., Prevelakis, V.: Countering code-injection attacks with instruction-set randomization. In: ACM Conference on Computer and Communications Security (CCS) (2003)
2. Zhang, C., Wei, T., Chen, Z., Duan, L., Szekeres, L., McCamant, S., Song, D., Zou, W.: Practical control flow integrity and randomization for binary executables. In: Security and Privacy Symposium, pp. 559–573 (2013)

TAPPS - Trusted Apps for Open Cyber-Physical Systems

Christian Prehofer[1]([⊠]), George Kornaros[2], and Michele Paolino[3]

[1] fortiss, An-Institut Technische Universität München, Munich, Germany
prehofer@fortiss.org
[2] Informatics Engineering Department, TEI Crete, Heraklion, Greece
kornaros@ie.teicrete.gr
[3] Virtual Open Systems SAS, Grenoble, France
m.paolino@virtualopensystems.com

Abstract. Cyber-physical systems (CPS) are devices with sensors and actuators which link the physical with the virtual world. For CPS there is a strong trend towards open systems, which can be extended during operation by instantly adding functionalities on demand. The main goal of the TAPPS (Trusted Apps for open CPS) project is the development of a platform for CPS apps which can also access and modify safety critical device internals. As current, rich execution platforms for apps are limited in security, TAPPS will provide and validate an end-to-end solution for development and deployment of trusted apps. The project will develop a dedicated, real-time Trusted Execution Environment (TEE) for highly-trusted CPS apps. Additionally, TAPPS also includes an App Store and a model-based tool chain for trusted application development including verification tools. The multi-level trusted apps platform and tool chain are matured and validated in health and automotive application domains using industrial, realistic use cases paving the way for future exploitation in further demanding application domains.

1 Motivation and Approach

Cyber-physical systems (CPS) are devices with sensors and actuators which provide the link between the physical and the virtual world. An example is a connected vehicle able to read information from the road and combine it with cloud computing to provide new services to the driver. CPS are considered to be the next revolution in ICT with enormous economic potential enabling novel integrated services and products. In many areas of CPS devices, there is a strong trend towards open systems, which can be extended during operation by instantly adding functionalities on demand. In this area, the Trusted Apps for Open Cyber-Physical Systems (TAPPS) project focuses on the functional extension provided by apps, as it is already common for mobile and other consumer devices. However, there are considerable security issues for such devices. For example, a recent research work [2] reveals worrying results on this: in a

© Springer International Publishing Switzerland 2015
S.K. Katsikas and A.B. Sideridis (Eds.): E-Democracy 2015, CCIS 570, pp. 213–216, 2015.
DOI: 10.1007/978-3-319-27164-4_18

dataset of 22500+ Android apps, 26 % of their samples are identified as malicious. Considering now the sensitive interactions of CPS systems, including security, safety and privacy aspects, we see trust for such devices as a major societal challenge, which goes beyond the current role of computing in society [6].

The main goal of the TAPPS project is to extend and customize CPS devices with new 3rd party services and features in an efficient, secure and trusted apps platform. This extensibility is an important differentiator that enables new market extensions to keep pace with user expectations and latest technology. For instance, current apps for automotive vehicles provide infotainment functionality or control basic settings, both of which are not safety critical. As the next steps, apps targeting CPS devices can also use and adapt safety-sensitive functions, a concept which we call CPS apps. For instance, a sports upgrade package may change the driving behaviour of an automotive car, while another app may adapt the vehicle stability control according to road conditions. Similarly, in the health domain, we typically have vertical solutions for specific treatments. Here, we aim to open these towards multi-purpose devices, where apps may be installed for specific diagnosis or treatments. While such apps provide extra user value, there are considerable challenges for connected CPS devices regarding safety of the controlled system as well as safety and privacy of the user.

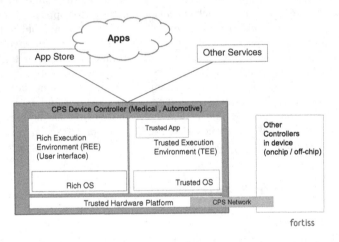

Fig. 1. Modern CPSs hosting both Rich and Trusted Execution Environments can provide services through an App Store without compromising platform security

As shown in Fig. 1 in both automotive and medical domains, modern system architectures are open and distributed. While deploying corporate or 3rd party software through an App store provides simpler CPSs management and reduced system costs, adverse effects can be caused by direct interaction with safety critical settings, access to configuration APIs and misuse of system resources. As more sophisticated services and communication features are incorporated into CPSs any intentional or unintentional misuse that could compromise the platform should be prevented.

2   Research Challenges and Approach

To address the above, the TAPPS project goes beyond traditional solutions for safety, security and reliability in the CPS domain and offers a new approach towards extensibility of CPS platforms. TAPPS is based on a dedicated, Trusted Execution Environment (TEE) [1] for distributed, safety-critical CPS applications. This is in addition to common rich execution environments (REE), which benefit from virtualization technologies and are oriented towards rich feature for applications. An overview of the TAPPS architecture and research challenges is shown in Fig. 2. TAPPS offers multiple layers of security and an open end-to-end tool chain for developing and deploying trusted CPS apps.

TAPPS provides the following independent layers of security: First, computing and network virtualization based on novel, flexible hardware security mechanism, while maintaining stringent real time constraints in CPS devices and their internal networks. Secondly, fine-grained access control to resources of the smart cyber-physical device to ensure safety and privacy. Third, formally verified apps to ensure correct and secure behavior.

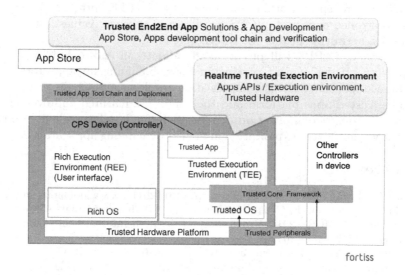

Fig. 2. TAPPS overview and research challenges

The TAPPS TEE will be largely based on open source technologies, as pursued in the Automotive Grade Linux alliance (AGL) (www.automotivelinux.org), interacting with the open source community [3]. In parallel to the TEE, a Rich Execution Environment (REE) will be offered to execute the less critical parts of apps, e.g., the user interface of external interfaces. Only the small core of the critical functions is run in the new TEE, leveraging its native safety and security features.

The second main objective of the project is an end-to-end solution for development and deployment of trusted apps. This includes an application store for management of CPS apps and for deployment, supporting both the REE and the separate TEE. Furthermore, a model-based development tool chain for designing and implementing trusted apps including APIs and verification tools. Integration and active contribution to related open source model-based development and verification tools is planned accordingly. The assumption is that we can check against unwanted behavior on the model level [5]. Using the deployment tool chain and App store, we ensure that only such checked code is running on the CPS device.

Finally, among the objectives is the creation of a realtime TEE for CPSs able to dynamically manage the various CPS partitions having mixed criticality requirements and supporting a trusted partition where different services can be securely executed. By using hardware enhancements for securing both on-chip [4] and off chip CPS networks, these can be mapped to the stacked layered network conceptual model. At the same time, in trusted Apps deterministic networks will be used to connect the distributed CPS with guaranteed behaviors such as a real-time communication possibility and guaranteed data exchange. Extensions to proven networking technologies (i.e., TTEthernet, CANbus) will ease the controlled exposure of CPS details such as sensor values towards non-trusted open networks such as the Internet/IoT.

In summary, TAPPS will provide and validate an end-to-end solution for development and deployment of trusted apps, including an app store and a model-based tool chain for trusted application development including verification tools. The trusted apps platform and tool chain are matured and evaluated in health and automotive application domains using industrial, realistic use cases paving the way for future exploitation in further demanding application domains.

References

1. GlobalPlatform. TEE system architecture v1.0 (2011). www.globalplatform.org
2. Gorla, A., Tavecchia, I., Gross, F., Zeller, A.: Checking app behavior against app descriptions. In: ICSE 2014: Proceedings of the 36th International Conference on Software Engineering (2014)
3. Paolino, M.: ARM Trustzone and KVM coexistence with RTOS for automotive, June 2015. http://events.linuxfoundation.org/sites/events/files/slides/als15_paolino.pdf
4. Kornaros, G., Christoforakis, I., Tomoutzoglou, O., Bakoyiannis, D., Vazakopoulou, K., Grammatikakis, M., Papagrigoriou, A.: Hardware support for cost-effective system-level protection in multi-core SoCs. In: Euromicro Conference on Digital System Design (DSD), August 2015, to appear
5. Prehofer, C.: From the internet of things to trusted apps for things. In: Green Computing and Communications (GreenCom), 2013 IEEE and Internet of Things (iThings/CPSCom), IEEE International Conference on and IEEE Cyber, Physical and Social Computing, pp. 2037–2042, August 2013
6. Tsiakis, T.: The role of information security and cryptography in digital democracy: (human) rights and freedom. In: Digital Democracy and the Impact of Technology on Governance and Politics: New Globalized Practices, p. 160 (2013)

Enabling Citizen-to-Government Communication

ROUTE-TO-PA H2020 Project: *Raising Open and User-Friendly Transparency-Enabling Technologies for Public Administrations*

Vittorio Scarano[1](✉), Delfina Malandrino[1], Michael Baker[2],
Françoise Détienne[2], Jerry Andriessen[3], Mirjam Pardijs[3], Adegboyega Ojo[4],
Lukasz Porwol[4], Przemyslaw Szufel[5], Bogumil Kamiński[5], Albert Meijer[6],
Erna Ruijer[6], John Forrester[7], Giuseppe Clementino[7], Ilias Trochidis[8],
Vangelis Banos[8], Martin Andriessen[9], Jan Pieter van de Klashorst[9],
Pauline Riordan[10], Ronan Farrell[10], Paolo Boscolo[11], Elena Palmisano[11],
Sander van der Waal[12], Jonathan Gray[12], Matteo Satta[13], and Eric Legale[13]

[1] University of Salerno, Fisciano (Salerno), Italy
{vitsca,dmalandrino}@unisa.it
[2] CNRS - Telecom ParisTech, Paris, France
{michael.baker,francoise.detienne}@telecom-paristech.fr
[3] Wise and Munro Learning Research, Den Haag, The Netherlands
jerry@wisenmunro.org, m.pardijs@fsw.leidenuniv.nl
[4] Insight Centre for Data Analytics, National University of Ireland, Galway, Ireland
{adegboyega.ojo,lukasz.porwol}@deri.org
[5] Division of Decision Support and Analysis, Warsaw School of Economics,
Warsaw, Poland
{pszufe,bkamins}@sgh.waw.pl
[6] School of Governance, Utrecht University, Utrecht, The Netherlands
{A.J.Meijer,H.J.M.Ruijer}@uu.nl
[7] ANCITEL S.p.A., Rome, Italy
{forrester,clementino}@ancitel.it
[8] Ortelio Ltd, Coventry, UK
it@ortelio.co.uk, vbanos@gmail.com
[9] Gemeente Den Haag, Den Haag, The Netherlands
martin.andriessen@denhaag.nl, jpvdklashorst@kbm-alliances.nl
[10] Dublin City Council and Dublinked, Dublin, Ireland
pauline.riordan@dublincity.ie, rfarrell@eeng.nuim.ie
[11] Comune di Prato, Prato, Italy
p.boscolo@comune.prato.it, elena.palmisano@pin.unifi.it
[12] Open Knowledge Foundation, Cambridge, UK
{sander.vanderwaal,jonathan.gray}@okfn.org
[13] Issy-Média and Ville d'Issy-les-Moulineaux, Issy-les-Moulineaux, France
{Matteo.Satta,Eric.Legale}@ville-issy.fr

Abstract. In this short paper, we introduce ROUTE-TO-PA project, funded by European Union under the Horizon 2020 program, whose aim is to improve the transparency of Public Administration, by allowing citizens to make better use of Open Data, through collaboration and personalization.

© Springer International Publishing Switzerland 2015
S.K. Katsikas and A.B. Sideridis (Eds.): E-Democracy 2015, CCIS 570, pp. 219–222, 2015.
DOI: 10.1007/978-3-319-27164-4_19

Keywords: Open data · Transparency · Social network · Transparency-enhancing tools · Horizon 2020 project

1   Main Motivations

ROUTE-TO-PA is a Horizon 2020 European funded innovation project that combines expertise in the fields of e-government, computer science, learning science and economy, to improve the impact of ICT-based technology platforms for transparency. As stated in the "Digital Agenda for Europe", in order to provide better public services to citizens and businesses, new opportunities for Public Administrations (PAs) to become more efficient and effective, provide user-friendly services, while reducing costs and administrative burden, are grounded on open government, i.e., increasing information and knowledge exchange, enhanced connectivity, openness and transparency.

In ROUTE-TO-PA we address the issue of transparency, i.e., opening up public data and services and facilitating citizen participation and engagement, with the result of making government processes and decision open. In terms of international practices in transparency, widespread access to the Internet has greatly reduced the cost of collecting, distributing, and accessing government information. But an important effect of the diffusion of networks in the population is that ICT, by promoting good governance, strengthening reform-oriented initiatives, reducing potential for corrupt behaviours, enhancing relationships between government employees and citizens, allowing for citizen tracking of activities, and by monitoring and controlling behaviours of government employees, is able to effectively reduce corruption [1].

Our focus is in contrasting the potential barriers to using ICT for transparency, that we identify in the complexity of the information provided, the lack of tools to facilitate the comprehension and the limited acceptance of ICTs for transparency among citizens.

The ROUTE-TO-PA team is strongly heterogeneous and multidisciplinary. It mixes up research, innovation and stakeholders, by encompassing research partners, small and large companies, pilot Public Administrations (from 4 different countries) and one non-profit foundation. Research is by itself multidisciplinary, as there are partners with expertise in e-government, computer science, psychology and economy. In a sense, our team has been designed to tackle the challenges of transparency with a trans-disciplinary approach.

2   ROUTE-TO-PA Vision and Objectives

ROUTE-TO-PA vision is to improve the engagement of citizens *(a)* by making them able to socially interact over open data, by forming or joining existing online communities that share common interest and discuss common issues of relevance to local policy, service delivery, and regulation; *(b)* by providing a robust and more holistic understanding of transparency, by underpinning the next generation open-data based transparency initiatives, ensuring that published data are those of value to citizens, with a personalized view in different forms to different segments of the citizens and public based on their profiles for facilitate better understanding.

Our main purpose here is to engage citizens through a "purposeful and personalized relationship" between citizens and open data, not only on a personal basis, but between government and networks of citizens that collectively attribute meanings to this information. The information by ROUTE-TO-PA is shared, interpreted, personalized, made easier to understand and discussed, to assess its meanings.

Concretely, the project is aiming to *(a)* develop a Social Platform for Open Data (SPOD) enabling social interactions among open data users and between open data users and government data; *(b)* build Transparency-Enhancing Toolset (TET) as extensions for existing major Open Data Platforms; and *(c)* develop a set of recommendations (GUIDE) as good practice guide for open data publishers for achieving higher quality transparency through open data.

ROUTE-TO-PA objectives are concrete since we will experiment in practice the innovation proposed by conducting 5 pilot studies in Prato Town Council (Italy), The Hague Town Council and Groningen Town Council (The Netherlands), Dublin Town Council (Ireland) and Issy-les-Moulineaux (France).

Our project will produce software by using open-source licensing model, and the platform will be given to the community of PAs and developers that, after the end of the project, will ensure further development and widespread, sustainable and scalable exploitation of the results achieved. The results of the project (both software and guidelines) will allow PAs to follow the economic and budgetary pressures that force administration to be more efficient and to reduce cost [2] by adhering to the philosophy of "Doing more with less".

The software and the experiences will be highly reusable, given that they will be piloted in different contexts, in different countries, whose results will be elaborated in guidelines and recommendations at the end of the project. "Reuse rather than reinvent" is one of the guidelines to long-term success of ICTs in Transparency [1] that we adopt as project "mantra" both from technological point of view (i.e., integration of existing popular open source products) and from the PA point of view (plug ROUTE-TO-PA onto existing experiences and needs by involving the Pilots).

3   The Ongoing Work and Further Directions

The team is currently working toward the first prototypes of SPOD and TET. The first year, in fact, will terminate its activities, in January 2016, with the two alpha versions of the software, that will be tested (in a first round) in the 5 pilots for the year 2016. In 2017 a new version, beta, will be submitted to another round of testing from the pilots, leading to the release of a highly tested and jointly designed software.

In our project, we adopted a collective intelligence and scenario-based design approach. The initial scenarios developed for each Pilot (during the workshop sessions and interviews on Open Data and transparency we conducted in the first 6 months of the project) highlighted information, social and collaborative, and understandability, usability and decision-making needs and requirements that are important for the development of the SPOD, TET and GUIDE. We, later, analysed the scenarios and mapped them into the most suitable user stories based on TET and SPOD objectives. Then we updated the user stories by incorporating contextual information delivered by project stakeholders and provided the analysis of the users stories, with use case models followed by detailed use case descriptions and requirements specification. Then we provided the breakdown of the specific and unique functionalities and capabilities that the system must provide to the user when engaged in various activities and exploring the enhanced platform.

From the technological point of view, the collective intelligence approach is followed by the application of agile methodologies, allowing citizens to participate already into the early development of the software: we strongly believe that our approach that involves stakeholders since the very beginning of the design and development will be one of the key factors to the success of our software.

The project will finish its activities on January 2018, with two rounds of pilot studies (February 2016 and February 2017) of SPOD and TET in the five pilots (see www.routetopa.eu for updates on the status of the activities).

Our team is strongly committed to ideate, design, develop, deploy and validate innovative and engaging ICT platforms to ensure citizen-friendly, conscious and effective access to open-data, by offering easy understanding of, and social collaboration on, open data offered by PAs.

Acknowledgments. This project has received funding from the European Unions Horizon 2020 research and innovation programme under grant agreement No 645860.

References

1. Bertot, J.C., Jaeger, P.T., Grimes, J.M.: Using ICTs to create a culture of transparency: e-government and social media as openness and anti-corruption tools for societies. Gov. Inf. Q. **27**(3), 264–271 (2010)
2. EU DG-CONNECT.: A vision for public services. In: European Commission, "Public Services" Unit of Directorate-General for Communications Networks, Content and Technology (DG-CONNECT), 13 June 2013

On the Use of a Secure and Privacy-Aware eGovernment Infrastructure: The SPAGOS Framework

Maria-Eleftheria Ch. Papadopoulou[1(✉)], Charalampos Z. Patrikakis[2],
Iakovos S. Venieris[1], and Dimitra-Theodora I. Kaklamani[1]

[1] School of Electrical and Computer Engineering, National Technical University of Athens,
Athens, Greece
marelpap@icbnet.ece.ntua.gr, venieris@cs.ntua.gr,
dkaklam@mail.ntua.gr
[2] Department of Electronics Engineering, Technological Education Institute of Piraeus,
Aegaleo, Greece
bpatr@teipir.gr

Abstract. SPAGOS project brings about a framework that, unlike current approaches, fosters a holistic solution for security and privacy-awareness in the provision of eGovernment services. In that respect, it proposes a distributed platform spanning across all the entities participating at the eGov service provision chain and managing the communication, storage and processing of information in a secure and privacy-aware manner. The core principles leveraged towards the creation of secure transactions are the use of advanced security and privacy mechanisms that have never been used within eGov and an advanced role of the eIDs, notably not only as passive identification tokens, but as essential functional components undertaking critical processing tasks.

Keywords: eGovernment · eID · Privacy · Security

1 The Need for Security and Privacy in eGovernment

Going beyond the recognition of the potential that Information and Communication Technologies (ICT) can offer to the public administration and governance procedures, technology trends (mobile computing, social media) have introduced new challenges in eGovernment service design and implementation. The result is a shift from presentation and transaction services towards the seamless integration of online and offline features, interoperation between organisations, and one-stop service provision [1]. The expected benefits are in the improvement of quality of provided services, simplification, increased accessibility, and savings in time and money.

On the other hand, the road towards integration, transparency and interoperability in eGov services introduces challenges with respect to information security and privacy. Taking into account the importance and criticality of systems involved in a comprehensive eGov services framework (i.e., health systems, tax services, voting), the impact of a security breach is enormous and grows exponentially with the amount of personal information collected. Moreover, privacy implications related to the use of personal information and the corresponding legal issues need also to be

© Springer International Publishing Switzerland 2015
S.K. Katsikas and A.B. Sideridis (Eds.): E-Democracy 2015, CCIS 570, pp. 223–227, 2015.
DOI: 10.1007/978-3-319-27164-4_20

taken under consideration [2]. As a result, the need for conforming both to the needs of customization and quality improvement of the offered services and the compliance to the regulatory framework call for solutions that incorporate personal data management schemes that can protect the sensitive and identifiable personal data used in eGov. In this context, the eGov Action Plan 2011–15 [3] that complements the targets of the Digital Agenda for Europe is based on the provision of increased access to public information, the participation of multiple stakeholders in the policy process and the support of seamless eGov services in the European Union. These policy priorities cannot be implemented without the support of technical solutions ensuring security and privacy, without compromising interoperability.

The architecture and mechanisms of the SPAGOS project [4] aim at offering a platform enabling the provision of secure and privacy-aware eGov services. The architecture design has been based on the adoption of a distributed model hosting the processing components of each organisation participating at the eGov service provision chain. The SPAGOS platform is mainly in charge of all security and privacy provisions enforcement, including storage and communication of data, interoperation with peer platform instances, authentication, authorisation, access control, as well as task delegation to eIDs.

2   Description of the SPAGOS Architecture

The architecture of the SPAGOS ecosystem with the enabling technologies and the tools included can be used for the design, definition and provision of eGovernment services in terms of procedures, integration of supporting technologies for privacy protection and detection of possible failure points. It follows the Service-Oriented Architecture (SOA) model, which treats software as a set of services and offers the ability to combine existing services in order to create not only more complex services but also entire business processes. As shown in Fig. 1, the SPAGOS ecosystem consists of the following main entities: (a) Users with electronic IDentity (eID) cards, (b) a Trust Management platform – the Central eGov Portal, (c) the SPAGOS platform, and (d) Service Providers. What is more, this ecosystem is consisted of agents acting on behalf of the Service Providers and the Consumers (Users). Multi-Agent Systems (MAS) can offer sophisticated (combined with the technologies of the Semantic Web) services, dynamic service binding and service choreographies.

According to the SPAGOS ecosystem specifications, each citizen-user of the system holds his/her eID card, which constitutes the means of getting access to services as it is used for the authentication and authorisation of the user in the eGov service provision chain. As the eID contains user's data, attributes, as well as privacy preferences required for access control and it is also considered as a secure execution environment for data encryption/decryption, Java Card Connected Edition 3.0 was our choice for implementing the eID as: (a) it is able to communicate with the rest of the SPAGOS platform components via the Java Card^{TM} application programming interface (API) implemented in Java, (b) it provides all the technological capabilities to support the special eID requirements, and (c) it supports web services for communication with the Central Portal of the eGov services.

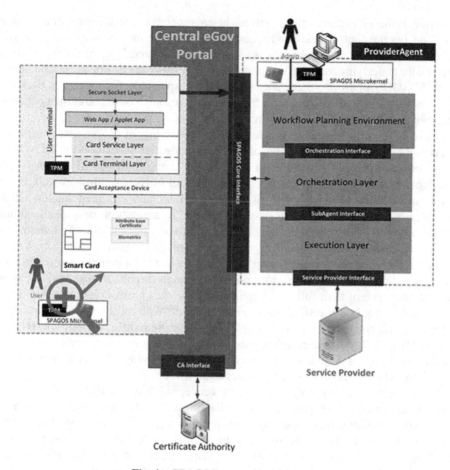

Fig. 1. SPAGOS system architecture

As eGovernment services deal with sensitive data and a variety of organisations coming from both the public and the private sectors have to interact for their provision with a variety of roles and responsibilities applying to people involved in this value chain, recent advances in cryptography are leveraged, especially Identity- and Attribute-Based Encryption [5], putting in place an integrated crypto scheme for data protection, ensuring the security of eGov transactions. This way, data, involved in these transactions, incorporate access policies inside them, thus reducing the need for trustworthy storage systems and complex schemes for maintaining access policies across the eGov distributed services, enabling also information confidentiality when traversing complex service chains.

To meet the needs for enhanced protection of personal data in a multiple stakeholders' environment, recent advances in access control are also leveraged. In particular, to control unauthorised access to data, violations of privacy, protection of confidentiality and integrity and use of services provided within the eGovernment, an Attribute-Based Access Control (ABAC) model is used [6], taking into account the high degree of data sensitivity involved in transactions between heterogeneous organisations during service provision. For the control of access requests, policies are defined, which determine how the access is given to data and services as well as how citizens' personal data are used based on the underlying purpose, and implemented by using access control mechanisms. In the SPAGOS platform, there are components responsible for managing policies, processing and evaluating the request for access to a resource based on certain policies, obtaining authority decision and enforcing it.

An issue directly related to the secure interoperability of eGovernment services concerns the modelling and designing of processes using high-level tools that allow high degree of abstraction. State-of-the-art tools do not settle the issue of personal data protection, as they don't take into account the control of the data flow as well as the operations between the components of software architectures designed and modelled. Moreover, many approaches focus on the annotation of abstract process specifications with security and privacy features, without taking into account the special requirements of each service which may need different mechanisms to be used so as to achieve the desired level of data protection. Trying to address the needs for combining the easiness of implementing (direct from design) service components through the use of visual tools with the guarantee of their full compatibility with the data protection requirements via their possibly required transformation and enrichment with all the necessary security and privacy mechanisms, we have implemented the **Semantic WORkflow Design (SWORD) tool** for defining, testing and validating secure eGov service provision procedures through a graphical user interface (GUI) deploying a Visual Editor using a drag, drop and connect service components approach.

Additionally, due to the interoperability between different stakeholders required, semantic technologies are applied as a mechanism for resolving semantic differences between organisations, otherwise electronic processes may fail. A **specified semantic information** model constitutes the basis upon which logical inference regarding the operation of the underlying systems occurs. Semantic classification of different data types and services, processes and procedures constitutes the fundamental basis of the model and reflects the key components participating in eGov service provision, thus exploiting their full "knowledge capacity". Furthermore, taking into account the principles of access control models based on roles, the roles of the entities involved in the service provision chain is a major parameter and therefore, semantic classification and their incorporation into the model become necessary. In this context, operational and access policies is built atop semantic knowledge, providing a great potential or reasoning towards patterns for feeding the crypto policies. The development of the aforementioned model allows the specification of eGov procedures and access control rules for high-expressiveness.

Acknowledgement. The work presented here has been performed in the context of the SPAGOS project, funded by the EU and the Greek General Secretariat for Research and Technology, under the Action Cooperation II (2011) framework.

References

1. Layne, K., Lee, J.: Developing fully functional e-government: a four stage model. Gov. Inf. Q. **18**(2), 122–136 (2001)
2. Igglezakis, I.: Privacy protection and eGov. In: Lambrinoudakis, C., Mitrou, L., Gritzalis, S., Katsikas, S.K. (eds.) Privacy and Information and Communication Technologies: Technical and Legal Issues. Papasotiriou Pubs, Athens (2010). ISBN: 978-960-7182-70-8
3. The European eGov Action Plan 2011–2015. http://ec.europa.eu/information_society/activities/eGov/action_plan_2011_2015/docs/action_plan_en_act_part1_v2.pdf
4. Secure & Privacy-Aware eGOvernment Services – SPAGOS project. http://research.icbnet.ntua.gr/spagos. Accessed 25 September 2015
5. Bethencourt, J., Sahai, A., Waters, B.: Ciphertext-policy attribute-based encryption. In: Proceedings of the 2007 IEEE Symposium on Security and Privacy (S&P 2007), Oakland, USA, 20–23 May 2007 (2007)
6. Yuan, E., Tong, J.: Attributed based access control (ABAC) for web services. In: ICWS 2005: Proceedings of the IEEE International Conference on Web Services (2005)

TRILLION: Trusted, Citizen - LEA Collaboration Over Social Networks

Charalampos Patrikakis[✉] and Aristidis Konstantas

Department of Electronics, Technological Education Institute of Piraeus,
250 Thivon str., 12244 Athens, Greece
bpatr@teip.gr

Abstract. TRILLION proposes an open, flexible, secure and resilient socio-technical platform to foster effective collaboration of citizens and law enforcement officers. Using the TRILLION platform, citizens will be able to report crimes, suspicious behaviour and incidents, identify hazards and assist law enforcement agents through active participation for achieving better urban security management. On the other hand, Law Enforcement Agencies (LEAs) will be able to detect incidents in a more efficient, content and context aware manner, locate on-site citizens, other LEA representatives and first responders communicate with them, request more information and assign them specific actions to address on-going incidents.

1 Concept

Social networks are increasingly used in relation to public safety and emergency response, but typically in an ad hoc manner and not to their full potential.

For example, police departments often communicate critical information during emergencies to their followers, and Twitter users on the ground often broadcast first-hand information that can be useful to first responders and the public. Citizen and volunteer oriented approaches are also used, such as for instance the Ushahidi [1] approach, the FloodVolunteers [2] online web site etc.

However, these approaches do not yet exploit the full potential of social networks, with limitations linked to implementations based on specific local LEA departments, limited to one-directional reporting, or focused mainly on the technological challenges of real-time communication without a full integration of all communication needs.

TRILLION, a 36 month project funded by European Commission - Horizon 2020 and consisted of a 12 partner's team, from 8 countries (Italy, Greece, Spain, Portugal, Sweden, UK, Slovenia and Netherlands), instead follows a fundamentally multidisciplinary approach, where social scientists, technologists and law enforcement agencies from across Europe and beyond work together to establish the ethical, legal, privacy and security considerations, and jointly develop the necessary socio-technical infrastructure for the cooperation of citizens and LEAs.

Based on the forecast that use of social networks, smartphones and related devices will continue to increase, **TRILLION** [3] **delivers an innovative platform** focusing on the following key pillars:

© Springer International Publishing Switzerland 2015
S.K. Katsikas and A.B. Sideridis (Eds.): E-Democracy 2015, CCIS 570, pp. 228–232, 2015.
DOI: 10.1007/978-3-319-27164-4_21

- *bi-directional interaction* between all users (LEAs and citizens),
- *trusted* communication between users (both citizens and LEAs),
- establishment of a trustworthy and privacy preserving framework to which citizens will *instinctively* turn to in order to to report a risk or to find information about a situation,
- *fast, efficient and secure* communication methods for incident reporting.

TRILLION proposes an open, flexible, secure and resilient socio-technical platform to foster effective collaboration of citizens and law enforcement officers. Using the TRILLION platform, citizens will be able to report crimes, suspicious behaviour and incidents, identify hazards and assist law enforcement agents through active participation for achieving better urban security management. On the other hand, Law Enforcement Agencies (LEAs) will be able to detect incidents in a more efficient, content and context aware manner, locate on-site citizens, other LEA representatives and first responders communicate with them, request more information and assign them specific actions to address on-going incidents. TRILLION builds on the following steps:

- A trust-building platform: TRILLION aims to create full collaboration between citizens and LEAs through trust relationships, in their common goal of a secure society. Moving far beyond one-way information, the TRILLION platform aims to create added value to all stakeholders, providing personalized information to the citizens and up to date situational awareness to the LEAs in a fast and efficient way, through informative, yet, intuitive data analytics.
- An intuitive platform: TRILLION aims to be "the place to turn to" by default. To ease not only adoption but also to make the platform attractive, TRILLION develops two types of serious games used for training and dissemination purposes. The serious game approach is used on the one hand to train LEAs, and on the other hand to attract citizens (tasks 5.5, 7.1). In both cases, TRILLION builds on approaches previously used by partners.
- An innovative platform: TRILLION will integrate state of the art technologies into a comprehensive toolset that will allow near real-time information extraction from streams of data collected from both social networks and the dedicated TRILLION applications. The plethora of data collected will be filtered, indexed and transformed into rich, context-aware information that will be further enhanced, where necessary, using standard information schemes (e.g. dublincore). A Service-Oriented Architecture will integrate all TRILLION tools for Data Discovery and Extraction, Information fusion and Collaboration, to be represented and managed as services. The related research work for designing and implementing the above technological framework is expected to build upon and advance state of the art techniques on context and situational awareness and data reasoning and representation
- A secure and resilient platform: TRILLION's role as a significant tool in support of community policing is naturally expected to make it an attractive target for malicious cyber attackers. Breaching the confidentiality of its communications would not only affect the privacy of citizens, but could also compromise the security of ongoing policing operations. Breaching its data integrity would mean that LEAs would take decisions that are based on false information. For example, by generating false reports

of a riot taking place in one part of a city, criminals could direct police resources away from their real target. Breaching TRILLION's data availability with denial-of-service or other cyber attacks would, in the short term, reduce its usefulness to its users and, in the long term, reduce its users' confidence that they can rely on it. Therefore, TRILLION introduces an information and communication security framework starting with a secure by design approach but also taking care of the dynamics required in handling the evolution of cyber-security attacks.

- A privacy-aware platform: the sharing of information (including personal data) between citizens and LEAs - a fundamental aspect of TRILLION - creates an overarching requirement for the protection of privacy that must satisfy the related legislation, directives and codes of practice. TRILLION, taking into account on one hand this enhanced need for protection of information during access and use of personal data (especially when social networks are involved), and on the other the need for credible information reporting regarding criminal or suspicious activities, will adopt a "Privacy by design" approach.

An overview of the TRILLION concept, highlighting the multi-disciplinary approach, the variety of users, the multiplicity of communication mechanisms and channels and the advanced data fusion and integration levels, is presented in the Fig. 1.

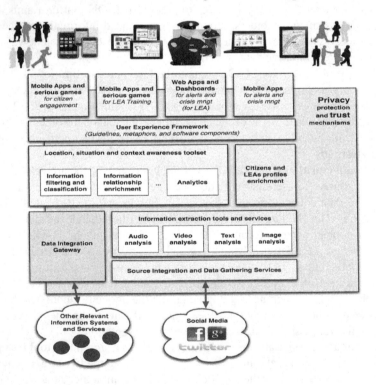

Fig. 1. Overview of the TRILLION platform architecture.

2 Research Challenges and Approach

TRILLION will address the following challenges:

- **Facilitate collaboration between citizens and LEAs**, it provides multiple channels for incident discovery, prediction, reporting and interaction. Users will have the choice of using existing social networks or directly report incidents via native mobile applications. Information collected will be used to detect in real-time situations that are or may become critical in the short to medium term.
- **Optimise the acquisition and completeness of the information while respecting privacy and regulations at EU and national levels**, it delivers a complete platform, building on the complementary expertise of its consortium and experience of its user base. Advanced data mining and classification techniques will provide the context and relevance of information exchanged in a user-friendly manner, while a security framework will ensure the privacy and integrity of user data, as well as resilience of the system.
- **Increase awareness and foster uptake of the solution**, it complements the platform by two Serious Game applications – one to ease the training of LEAs, the other to create increased awareness and understanding by the citizens of how they can contribute to improve urban security and gain a higher sense of security about their habitat. A careful selection of end users across different contexts and Member States, actively involved in the project either as full partners or as affiliate to project partners, ensures that requirements and assessment of the projects solutions incorporate a pan-European perspective on the issue.
- **Ensure full alignment to the needs of users**, it tests this environment by building on its prior experience in working with citizens and public authorities and on the expertise of its law enforcement partners. Different piloting and early validation phases will be held across different locations and different contexts, in The Netherlands, Italy, Portugal, the United Kingdom, Sweden and the USA.

TRILLION's open, flexible, secure and resilient socio-technical platform for the collaboration of citizens and law enforcement officers will integrate new knowledge and new technologies developed within the project, especially in the areas of personal device applications, situational awareness toolsets, social media data analysis, security and privacy, and game based training tools. It will benefit technology exploitation and transfer between research institutions and Information Technology providers, thus promoting new knowledge integration and innovation and enhancing the growth of mobile communications, information technology and social networking companies in Europe. The novel technologies developed within the project will empower LEAs to integrate new knowledge (both in social sciences and in technology) related to incident detection, personnel communication and information exchange. Along with their operational efficiency, this will also greatly improve their capacity for innovation.

The final results will be evaluated through a four stage approach in which the partners of the project representing end users will be actively involved in:

- training sessions: serious gaming tools tested by citizens and LEAs
- mock-ups: create early interaction on specific features with the citizens and the LEAs, and
- two pilots, namely:
  - pilot α: scenario based testing of the first prototype with operational users, and
  - pilot β: scenario based testing of the fully integrated TRILLION platform users' environments.

The high level of involvement of end user representatives in TRILLION ensuring a thorough assessment of project's results is depicted in Fig. 2.

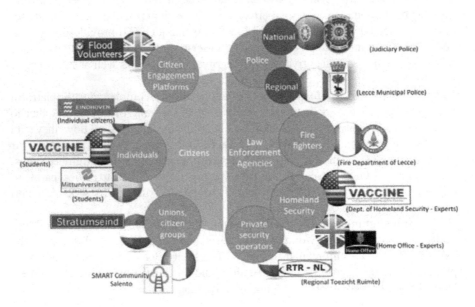

Fig. 2. Participation of end user representatives in TRILLION.

Acknowledgment. The project has received funding from European Commission as part of the Horizon 2020 – the Framework Programme for Research and Innovation (2014–2020) under the call H2020-FCT-2014, REA grant agreement n° [653256].

References

1. Ushahidi home page. http://www.ushahidi.com
2. Flood Volunteers home page. http://floodvolunteers.co.uk/
3. TRILLION: TRusted, CItizen - LEA colLaboratIon over sOcial Networks (2015). http://trillion-project.eng.it

Author Index

Printed in the United States
By Bookmasters